Culture, Transformation and Identity

Culture, Transformation and Identity

Travel, Fiction, Autobiography

Edited by
Urmil Talwar
Bandana Chakrabarty

Institute for Research in Interdisciplinary Studies, Jaipur

RAWAT PUBLICATIONS

Jaipur • New Delhi • Bangalore • Hyderabad • Guwahati • Kolkata

ISBN 978-81-316-0674-2

Published by
Prem Rawat for **Rawat Publications**
Satyam Apts, Sector 3, Jawahar Nagar, Jaipur 302 004 (India)
Phone: 0141 265 1748 / 7006 Fax: 0141 265 1748
E-mail: info@rawatbooks.com
Website: www.rawatbooks.com

New Delhi Office
4858/24, Ansari Road, Daryaganj, New Delhi 110 002
Phone: 011 2326 3290

Also at *Bangalore, Hyderabad, Guwahati* and *Kolkata*

Typeset by Rawat Computers, Jaipur

Printed at Nice Printing Press, New Delhi

Contents

Introduction

This collection of essays titled *Culture, Transformation and Identity: Travel, Fiction, Autobiography*, in itself has been a voyage of explorations and understanding. Ideas are innocent at their birth, but as they grow, they expand and spread themselves and generate their own complexities. This book brings together different geographical, historical and psychological journeys that cannot be summed up by the word 'travelogue'. History provides enough evidence of the myriad ways and the innumerable reasons why we travel or relate to a culture in preference to another. The causes may be many – quest for knowledge or spiritual peace, escape from oneself and one's past, a new beginning, a search for roots, identity and in many cases adventure and conquest, business or trade. Our ancestors have travelled far and wide marking out silk routes, spreading religious faiths, conveying ideas and knowledge to other regions interacting with other cultures. Another direction of travel has been escape: exiles, crossing borders through difficult terrains in constant fear of political or religious prosecution. But at heart travel is a dialogic process.

The first step in this journey was a seminar on 'Geoscapes of the Mind: Travel, Transformation and Belonging', organised by IRIS in June 2012. Geoscapes is a concept which travelled much beyond the physical act of travel and sought to include within its acts of imagination and adoption – experiences which transform the cartography present in the mind, affecting at once one's affiliation and notion of identity and claiming for oneself a transformed sense of tradition and history. The seminar opened itself out in multiple directions – imagination, history, geography and religion – and generated cross-cultural dialogues which emphasised constructs of identity and nation, community and belonging and opened confined spaces.

Geoscapes in itself is an encompassing concept as it embraces the relationship of both the emotional and intellectual self to the other – the other person, tradition or culture. It further is an act of self-reflection, an absorbing into the self of an exterior phenomenon and fulfills the psychological need for belonging. If projected through this framework it embodies an internal replication of the Lacanian mirror image. As an act of representation it is a mimetic act in the Aristotelian sense, to which one could easily bring Paul Ricoeur's three stage progress of the act in *Time and Narrative* (three volumes published respectively in 1984, 1985, 1988) as mimesis$_1$, mimesis$_2$ mimesis$_3$. Ricoeur emphasises the role of mimesis$_2$, which is the process of mediation between the perceived reality and the final narrative representation. Geoscapes can find a place in travel writing, creative writing, diaries and even letters. Embedded in different forms they impact our thinking as well as our imagined worlds. It is hard to think of human existence without 'imagined' realities. Story telling is one such act which evokes visual images perhaps very distant from our lives and realities. How does the written and the heard connect? What links them and informs our ideas? It is perhaps the human ability to imagine.

The act of writing is like a conveyor belt, carrying the outside to the internal reception centres and then again working towards the outside to spread its wings in several directions. Eunice de Souza, a renowned Indian poet, in her 'Keynote Address' opened out this scenario for us. She works across borders of language and culture, form and symbolism and traces the journey of poetry, not in a literal sense, but that which constitutes cross-borders of language and culture, form and symbolism. The general trend is to prioritise 'impersonal' poetry written by men over 'confessional' poetry written by women. She suggests women poets to avoid the personal, the 'self' and write about 'myth' and 'history'. de Souza advocates that women writers should write about their myths and their histories, a way of rising above the personal. Myth distances as well as expresses.

Another creative writer, Karen Swenson is also an acclaimed poet and novelist, from America who has travelled extensively over the past four decades, has written widely on her travels to countries such as Malaysia and Thailand, and also on her trips to the provinces of childhood memory. She believes that the value of travel has more to do with the self which is the writer as writer brings to a place an impression he or she takes from the landscape or the people there. We met her in Jaipur in December 2013 at one of her poetry reading sessions and this piece 'Passing on Travel Lessons', especially written for this book, allows the reader an entry into the space of her memories and mind.

We have two essays which explore the past as they engage with Vedic and Buddhist texts and the relationship of travel to history and knowledge constructs. Divya Joshi in her article 'Time and Space Travel in Ancient Vedic Texts' elucidates the parallels between *Advaita Vedanta* and modern physics especially in relation to concepts like *akasa* in *Advaita Vedanta* and vacuum in quantum physics. She concludes that relativity has shown that time and space are inextricably linked and any change in one immediately and unmitigatedly causes change in the other. In her essay 'The Pilgrimage of Buddhist Epistemology in the Asian Space' Ranjana Jaitly depicts the transformation brought about in the society by the advent and spread of Buddhism in the Asian countries. She also describes the impact of Buddhism on cultures and cultural relationships in these countries.

As we move further into the volume the essay on the Canadian literary critic and literary theorist, Northrop Frye becomes the focus of Pooja Joshi's essay. She discusses the four basic narrative patterns or genres from *The Anatomy of Criticism* – romance, comedy, tragedy and irony or satire – and takes further this comparison with the seasonal cycle – spring, summer, autumn and winter – in her article 'Northrop Frye: A Poetics of Seasons'. This reminds us of the Indian poetic tradition, of the *barah masa* and Kalidasa's *Ritusamhar*.

Similarly, Santosh Gupta's article 'Reviewing the Orient: Portrayals of China in the Novels of Kazuo Ishiguro and Kunal Basu' juxtaposes the precolonial and postcolonial point of view of representation of China through the works of Ishiguro and Basu in light of Said's *Orientalism* and *Culture and Imperialism*. She analyses the colonial impact on the native or the indigenous peoples calling for a reworking of Oriental frames. Working backwards into the nineteenth century Bandana Chakrabarty explores the lives of *memsahibs* who travelled to India and faced the challenges of a new and alien environment and how they gradually contributed to empire building in her article 'The *Memsahibs*: Transcending Boundaries'. For the British women who travelled to India, their role was both a challenge and inspiration. One would like to guess as to how much these experiences contributed to gender independence and empowerment.

In 'Gandhi's Journey: Transformative Experiences' S. Asha takes up a thorough study of Gandhi's biography, portrayal of Gandhi in literary writings and various films to explore how journeys bring about a change in the thought, deed and belief of an individual with change in locations. Gandhi's travel was multidimensional and while the physical location offered its own challenge, the political situation transformed him completely from a western-dressed young lawyer to the man who was to become a Mahatma. The sartorial changes he brought about in his own personal life correspond to the intellectual shifts. Another major thinker and contemporary of Gandhi, Mohammad Iqbal is the subject of Samina Khan's essay 'Dynamics of Evolutionary Reflections: A Study of Iqbal's Select Urdu Poems'. She asserts that Iqbal was a man whose ideas were ahead of his times as he revived the classical spirit of Islam but at the same time he wanted to reform the Muslim society by getting rid of its backwardness and accepting the challenges of the new world. Bringing together Iqbal's revolutionary spirit with his religious interpretations Khan also throws light on the power of the word. Prerna Vanjani proceeds to problematise space as reflected in the autobiographical works of a veteran Indian author R.K. Narayan in her paper 'Microcosms in R.K. Narayan's *My Days* and *My Dateless Diary.* She investigates the construction of the geoscapes of Malgudi and America and also explores the inner spaces of the mind through his imagination.

Jasbir Jain's essay explores Naipaul's dilemma of 'not belonging' and constantly weighing in his mind the choice available to him between his home, his place of education and the place of ancestral origins. In his novel, *The Enigma of Arrival,* he experiments with the various dimensions of belonging. How does one belong?

By knowing the history, the landscape, the environment or the world of Art? Jasbir Jain examines an outsider's way of belonging to a culture with geographical images mingling with histories, reaching back in time and overladen with multiple experiences of concretising the writer's perceptions in her paper titled 'Geoscapes of the Mind: Unravelling Naipaul's *The Enigma of Arrival*'. Sangeeta Handa's analysis of Vassanji's *A Place Within* traces the history of contemporary travel writing and explores the writer's double journey with an agenda to rediscover the land of his ancestors in her article 'Global Politics of Contemporary Travel Writing in M.G. Vassanji's *A Place Within*'. No journey perhaps is undertaken with a purpose but all of them inevitably transcend their singleness of focus as the writer's self constantly keeps on responding at multi-levels, playing with memory and the visible. In 'The Essence of Spain in Hemingway's Work' Shahla Ghauri depicts how bullfighting, a popular sport of Spain, becomes a tragedy in the realm of art which makes the artist conscious of the brevity of life in the face of death. Human beings also have more than one emotional encroachings. In 'Journeys to her Homeland: Lessing's *African Laughter* and *Under My Skin*' Preeti Bhatt and Manju Nemad contrast both these works and attempt to examine the writer's views about home, memory and identity which acquire a multilayered significance, due to her peculiar position of being both an insider and outsider in Southern Rhodesia. Urmil Talwar examines the disparate forms and intentions of travel and mobility that the characters experience and reconstruct, and discusses reterritorialising of space in *The Glass Palace*. The paper 'Travelling Subjectivities and Bridging Discourses in Ghosh's *The Glass Palace*' also explores the avenues that establish compatibility and cross-cultural understanding which creates respect for individuals. Moving to poetry like Samina Khan, Rimika Singhvi discusses the poems of Imtiaz Dharker whose cultural experiences of Pakistan, England and India have helped her in understanding religion and culture, identity and belonging as components of the self in her paper 'From Behind the Veil and Beyond: The Self in Transit in the Poetical Works of Imtiaz Dharker'.

Rama Hirawat in 'Sojourns in the Geoscapes of the Mind: Interrogating Select Works of Diana Abu Jaber' explores the mapping of memories and dreams through architectural spaces like the room and the kitchen to delineate the diasporic experiences of

Abu Jaber. In 'The Self in Transit: Tamim Ansary's *West of Kabul, East of New York'* Namita Singh examines the author's negotiation of the sense of belonging and non-belonging to his homeland and the merging of the dual identity to form a new identity. Akansha Kaushik in 'Travel and Transformation of the Self: Gilbert's *Eat Pray Love*' explores how Gilbert reconciles to her personal tragedy imbibing in her life the precepts from three different cultures – Italian, Indian and Indonesian – that give meaning to her life.

Putting together of this volume has been a journey both of learning and pleasure as we have explored the lesser known areas of Vedic and Buddhist texts, Iqbal's Urdu poetry, Northrop Frye's criticism and honed our skills and sharpened our critical faculties while we found our way in this maze of scholarship. The essays included in this volume traverse a whole range from the religious to the political, from the personal to the national and from the different markers of culture such as cuisine to the different markers of power such as trade and empathy. They express the immense possibilities of the human mind as they go to work with interpersonal strategies. We thank all our contributors, senior mentors, young friends and co-scholars from different states of India who have enabled us to meet the deadline. We are grateful to Eunice de Souza for allowing us to include her Keynote address; Karen whom we met at an IRIS meeting was gracious enough to accede to our request and sent us her travel piece. Our sincere thanks are to Jasbir Jain Director IRIS who has always enlightened our intellectual journey with her erudite suggestions. She encourages young scholars to make presentations and provides useful suggestions for strengthening their scholarly pursuits. The seminar organised by her gave us a critical thinking space for the issues discussed in this book. We are extremely grateful to her for having faith in us and allowing us this opportunity to bring out this volume.

1 Transformations

Eunice de Souza

Many years ago, I was looking through an anthology of world poetry when I came across an extract from *The Egyptian Book of the Dead*. It reads:

He holdeth fast to the Memory of his identity
In the Great House, and in the House of Fire,
On the dark night of counting all the years,
On the dark nights when months and years are numbered,
O let my name be given back to me!
When the Divine One on the Eastern Stairs
Shall cause me to sit down with him in peace,
And every God proclaims his name before me,
Let me remember the name I bore! (Doren, 200)

The book is dated 3500 BC. I find it moving to be able to make a connection with people who lived so long ago. It speaks so directly to our need to be identifiable and coherent, to believe in an after-life in which we continue to be so. I am who I am. Perhaps it is something to do with age, with time passing, with the loss of friends, but it seems to me that the self, however fractured, is all we have. And, for some of us, the poetic self.

Poets may or may not travel in literal terms but they talk to each other across centuries, across cultures. An Australian poet may write a ghazal, an Indian poet, a sonnet, a Mexican poet about Delhi, an Indian poet about Chinese poets. In our own culture men have talked in the voices of women, religious and secular are sometimes indistinguishable. Poets travel as well, constantly crossing boundaries of language, form, symbolism. Some writers create in more than one language. Others are driven into exile, start again in demanding circumstances. Forms travel: the sonnet from France to Italy to England to India. And to refer to other arts for a moment, Kathak has evolved into Flamenco, there are Hindi words in Romany. Shakespeare's *Macbeth* turns into a Japanese classic. It's a busy and adventurous world out there. The original global village. We read them, as Harold Bloom remarks, (he was talking about literature) 'to strengthen the self, and to learn its authentic interests' (22). Certainly, poets write for the same reason.

But the self in general and the poetic self in particular are always under attack from those who discriminate on the grounds of gender, caste, or language. In this connection, what I would like to examine in this paper is certain frequently used labels, used to diminish what we call the self in poetry: privileging the term 'impersonal' over 'confessional,' for instance, for reasons that are pseudo-philosophical, or part of current cultural practice. As I hope we shall see, they are misleading, and lead us into unrewarding territory.

Classical Tamil poetry is divided into poems of the inner world and those of the outer, and there are at least a few poems that attempt to blend the two. Classical Sanskrit poetry is also considered impersonal. But critical discussion of these poems in Sanskrit and Tamil does not seem to me to carry the same kind of baggage that the Anglophone terms, used in Indian criticism, 'impersonal' and 'confessional' poems do. Both as a reader and as a practitioner of poetry, I feel the terminology misleading. When writing, a poet has to be both inside and outside the poem, express himself or herself, and then stand outside what is written to judge whether each word carries the weight it should, whether emotions are overstated or understated. So every poem, regardless of the form it takes is both personal and impersonal at the same time. It cannot be otherwise. Strangest of all is the fact that when one looks at the completed poem, one wonders from where it came, and whether one could indeed have written it. The entire process remains a mystery, and no amount of theory attempting to demystify literature can change that.

T.S. Eliot is regarded as the high priest of 'impersonality' and this term is applied as the norm, regardless of the fact that his statements were made in relation to another time and place, and his own need to distance himself from his predecessors. In addition, Eliot was talking about the poet's relationship to tradition, and it is in this context that he talks of the emptying out of the poet's personality, not an emptying out per se. But Eliot, in this misunderstood form is used against poets such as, most obviously, Sylvia Plath, Anne Sexton, Kamala Das and others fall into the category of poetry of which a certain kind of critic cannot approve. Here are some sample statements: Talking about a specific Dom Moraes poem a critic writes, 'In spite of its rich imagery, the whirlpool of the self leads ultimately to the void' (Sarang 19). Kamala Das writes, 'The failure to find love leaves the poet in the claustrophobic world of the self (Sarang 27). Eunice de Souza, allegedly following in the footsteps of Sylvia Plath and Anne Sexton, 'may be aware of the danger inherent in the mode – an ever – narrowing poetic world, ending up in the void' (Sarang 28). The reference to Tukaram indicates that she is 'reaching out of the circular well of the self' (Sarang 28). The 'confessional' is by and large associated with women, self-indulgent ones. And as a sub-set we are treated to the term 'feminine sensibility,' a term with little or no meaning, which trivialises women and their concerns.

Critics such as the one just quoted tend to forget about or ignore the question of a persona. Person to persona is already the crucial step out of 'the well of self'. In one of my poems in *A Necklace of Skulls* I say:

> Don't look for my life in these poems
> Poems can have order, sanity, aesthetic distance from debris. (70)

And Yeats says somewhere, 'A poet is never the bundle of accident and incoherence that sits down to breakfast; he has been reborn as an idea, something intended, complete' (qtd Gordon 2). Given the weight Eliot's theories command, in their misunderstood form, I was interested, when reading Lyndall Gordon's biography of Eliot, to find her say, 'As more is gradually known of Eliot's life, the clearer it seems that the 'impersonal' façade of his poetry ... masks an often quite literal reworking of personal experience'. Eliot wrote that there is a 'transfusion of the personality or, in a deeper sense, the life of the author into the character' (2). She sees the major poems as a pilgrimage, a search for spirituality, a confession of failure. This confessional urge, this notion of 'pilgrimage from imperfection to perfection was deeply rooted in Eliot's family and their Puritan past ... It is not possible to understand Eliot's visions and the associated confessional impulse outside the context of a native tradition ... Many New Englanders kept private records of their religious adventures, noting also their soul's health and their progress towards grace' (90).

Confession as a concept is central to Christianity – public in Protestant and fundamentalist sects, private in Catholicism. It acknowledges the culpability of the person confessing, his willingness to atone, to accept the penance given to him/her. *Mea culpa, mea culpa, mea maxima culpa.* (Through my fault, through my fault, through my most grievous fault). But obviously, confession used in literature has to have form. It cannot be a maudlin outpouring.

Interestingly, David Morse, in his *Perspectives on Romanticism: A Transformational Analysis*, relates this tradition of confession in Protestant practice to Romanticism in literary practice. Protestantism and Romanticism are not synonymous terms. 'Nevertheless,' he says, 'a study in the field of aesthetic theory can give their relation a distinctive focus ... (The creation of) a set of values and assumptions which we commonly identify as Romantic was brought about by critics and writers for whom the Bible, *Paradise Lost, A Pilgrim's Progress* and the sermon were more crucial reference points than Horace or Cicero ...' (103). Summarising various views, Morse concludes that 'the assertion of Protestant values in literature produces all the main components of Romantic aesthetics: the expression of a personal vision; the concern with subjectivity; the belief in a deep self; art as an inward rather than external mirroring; the rejection of rules as a restriction on the freedom of the autonomous self ...' (156).

Eliot spoke through the three Magi, through Tiresias, and through Prufrock. Plath used a small child who expresses both anger and anguish at the way her father betrayed her by dying. We have to remember that if we feel her use of the term 'Nazi' is intemperate, or out of proportion to a personal tragedy, 'Lady Lazarus' examines suicide quite dispassionately.

What of poets such as the Elizabethans who worked within a pattern of imagery inherited from Europe, and, possibly further back, from the Moors? The woman who is inaccessible, cold, beautiful, with hair like gold, teeth like pearls and, etc. is the subject of many of these sonnets. Many of these sonnets were routine, merely a demonstration of the skills a gentleman had to acquire. But when we look at some of Shakespeare's sonnets we recognise that he knows the tradition well enough but decides to subvert it in poems that are deeply personal and at the same time acknowledge the inherited tradition. Think of 'My mistress' eyes are nothing like the sun' (Sonnet cxxx). And of the one of the most extraordinary confessional sonnets: 'When my mistress swears she is made of truth/I do believe her though I know she lies' (Sonnet cxxxv; iii).

Classical Indian poetry, both Sanskrit and Tamil tends to be called 'impersonal' because the protagonist in the poem does not have an individual name. There are rules about whether a man can express jealousy, for instance. And the poets work within a traditional pattern of imagery. At the same time it is worth looking at a particular poem, no. 143 in the John Brough anthology, written by Amaru:

> She neither turned away, nor yet began
> To speak harsh words, nor did she bar the door;
> But looked at him who was her love before
> As if he were an ordinary man. (89)

The woman may not have a name, but her piercing sense of disillusionment is unforgettable. Indian women have been writing about the self from the time of the Vedas, on secular and religious themes. Among the hymns in the Vedas, attributed to women, for instance, is one by Apala who was rejected by her husband because she had a disfiguring skin disease. She prays to Indra in astonishingly intimate terms: 'Make these three places sprout, O Indra; my daddy's head and field, and this part of me below my waist' (O'Flaherty 256–57). Buddhist nuns have rejoiced at getting rid of brutish husbands (Macnicol 44). Bhakti poets, both male and female introduce their names into the hymn, or song, or prayer. For women the building of a confident self, unrelated to the roles of daughter, wife, or daughter-in-law is essential. Far from descending into the void, they, through their writing are emerging out of the void in which they are expected to feel they have no life of their own. We have been told to avoid the self, and talk about myth and history. Well, we are writing about myth and history. Our myths, our history.

References

Bloom, Harold. *How to Read and Why.* London: Fourth Estate, 2000.

Brough, John. trans. *Poems from the Sanskrit.* London: Penguin Books, 1968.

David. *Perspectives on Romanticism: A Transformational Analysis.* London: Macmillan, 1981.

DeSouza, Eunice. *A Necklace of Skulls.* New Delhi: Penguin Books, 2000. p. 70

Doren, Mark Van. ed. 1928. *An Anthology of World Literature.* NY: A&C Boni. Rpt. 1939. London: Cassell and Co. Ltd.

Eliot, T.S., 'Tradition and the Individual Talent' in *The Sacred Wood.* New York: Alfred A. Knopf, 1921.

Lyndall, Gordon. *Eliot's Early Years.* Oxford: OUP, 1977. p. 2.

Macnicol, Margaret ed. *Poems by Indian Women.* Calcutta: Association Press, 1923.

O'Flaherty, Wendy. Trans. and annotated. *The Rig Veda.* Harmondsworth: Penguin Books, 1981.

Sarang, Vilas. ed. *Indian English Poetry.* Disha Books. Bombay: Orient Longman Ltd. 1989.

2 Passing on Travel Lessons

Karen Swenson

She was, Dutch, in her sixties, not very tall but slender and obviously physically tough as rawhide, her white hair cut short in crisp curls around her head. Talking to her over dinner in the Tashi, one restaurant in Lhasa, I learned that she had hitch hiked in from Kashgar to Lhasa and was about to hitch hike on to Chengdu where she would take a plane to Hong Kong to meet a friend. I was very impressed.

However, I was even more impressed, indeed in awe, when she showed up three days later back in Lhasa. She had been able to ride on trucks to Amdo, in eastern Tibet, but shortly after that she had been stopped by a Chinese policeman who had ordered her out of the cab of her truck and asked her what she was doing.

She explained that she was on her way to Chengdu to fly to Hong Kong. He was horrified.

'You are not permitted to hitch hike. You are not permitted on this road to Chengdu. I should fine you. Big fine. But you are same age as my mother so no fine. But my mother never, never do what you doing'.

When she told me this we both laughed. No, a Chinese woman in her sixties would spend her time sitting with her grandchildren and bossing her daughters-in-law, not jouncing across China in the dusty cab of a truck. But those Chinese attitudes also had had their counterparts in Holland when she had begun her travelling career forty years before. She told me that when she started travelling with a backpack, working to fund her travel desires, not a house, not a car, not a marriage with children, many in her family stopped knowing her. She was too peculiar for them. She was outside their idea of what was 'acceptable' or perhaps even, 'respectable'.

The happy ending to this story was that the children of those relatives who had refused to know her when she became a traveller, now wanted to spend time with her, hear her stories. They wanted to learn from her how to travel and, by extension, they were asking her to teach them how to see the world. They were rejecting their parents' closed view for her much more open sense of the world. To have the young turn to you to learn about experiencing the world from a different perspective is an honour.

She, indeed, flew on to Hong Kong to meet her friend, I never saw her again, but she served as inspiration for me, as a lesson. I was headed with nine other people to Kailash to do the pilgrimage in which you circumambulate the mountain. At the end of our circumambulation my companions were going to cross over into Nepal and go to Kathmandu. I wanted to return to Lhasa but until I talked to her I wasn't sure how to do this. Now I knew. I would hitch hike.

Therefore, some weeks later when we reached Lang La, a mountain pass on the way to Nyalam and the border, I jumped down from the back of the baby blue truck I had been travelling in for weeks with my companions, dragged our guide over to two trucks whose noses were pointed northeast and told him to find out how much they would charge to take me to Lhasa. They were only going as far as Shigatze, they told him but I could get a bus from Shigatze to Lhasa with no problem. The driver wanted 200 yuan to take me. He was not interested in bargaining. I hauled my pack off of one baby blue truck and but it in my new baby blue truck, embraced my companions and climbed into the cab of my new truck. The driver was immensely disappointed when he realised I spoke no Tibetan.

We spent the afternoon driving back through the landscape I had seen in the morning, the boney, ascetic earth of southwestern Tibet. There was brittle looking, grey-green scrub, small violently pink wild flowers that clutched the earth against the constant pull of the wind, and rock glowing in all kinds of colours. There were mountains with red sides, or dappled with green slabs of stone, the shade of oxidised copper or streaked with sulfurous yellow as though an abstract painter had been let loose with a broad brush. As evening fell I watched herds of antelope on slender legs galloping along side the road. I was touched by how careful the driver was not to run over the big jackrabbits that made Nureyev leaps across the road in panic, seemingly intent on suicide beneath our wheels. Before dark we pulled into a truck stop where there were rooms around an open rectangle within which trucks were parked. Over a dinner of ramen noodles my Tibetan phrase book was passed around as everyone laughed at the phrase 'Pö-la yak yawray,' 'There are yaks in Tibet,' which did not advance conversation much. However, I was able to get across that I came from the US. I went to my room, which had a sort of bench for a bed, covered with a rug as well as a duvet heavy as a layer of cement. I wound a piece of wire around a nail to keep the door closed and crawled into my sleeping bag pulling the leaden duvet over it.

At 5 am, when the truckers started revving their motors, I awoke to find that not knowing where I was, combined with the inability to communicate with the people around me, gave me a surreal, floating sensation.

We started off at eight and soon arrived in Old Dingeri, a Tibetan town built on ridges of terraces along the side of a mountain. The area around the base of the hill was a mix of Tibetan houses and dusty nomad tents. The three drivers in my two-truck caravan were intent on buying dried meat. Outside the nomad tents were clotheslines with slices of meat hung over them. It was a monochrome scene, the colour of whole-wheat flour – pale tents, pale houses, and pale smoke rising from them all. Overhead hundreds of ravens lifted and settled among the black dogs, donkey and horses, hoping for a chance to steal some of the meat off a clothesline.

We drove out of town crunching through the frozen meanders of the Phung Chu River, which was at that season just a shrunken stream since in the fall there is little melt from the glaciers. The drivers were trying to locate a road, a short cut, but were unsuccessful. Passing us were Land Cruisers full of people going to Everest Base Camp. I thought I saw Everest, but years later on another trip to Dingeri found it was a neighbouring mountain. As we drove out of town we passed Chinese soldiers in green uniforms looking dusty and tired. They did not seem pleased to see my

Western face up in the truck's cab. I couldn't blame them since it must be the worst possible duty to end up in this cold parched landscape suitable for saints and other ascetics.

Following the road through mountains that appeared to be totally devoid of vegetation we arrived a dreary checkpoint surrounded by a glinting field of broken beer bottles and discarded white plastic noodle bowls that will remain undecayed for posterity's posterity. It was, I believe, called Baila and had a store and a restaurant with a billiard table in front. The Chinese owner charged me four times what he charged my driver for the same lunch. The Tibetan inhabitants, of this oasis of civilisation, were a desperate family who begged before the restaurant door. The father played an instrument like a mandolin while the children put out their palms. I heaped up on the dusty billiard table handfuls of raisins for them.

At this checkpoint my driver realised I had no travel permit for Lhasa. His worry sprouted paranoia in me, which grew leaves when I talked to a very tall, young, bearded American who was headed to the border in one of the trucks. He had been travelling to Lhasa but at the Lhatze checkpoint had been turned back because he had no permit. He hadn't thought to smile innocently and ask if he could buy a permit or to put a twenty-dollar bill in his passport. I promptly did this. We weren't going to Lhatze my driver told me so I didn't have to worry about that.

The land we travelled though after the checkpoint was either wildly jagged or flat. The level parts were covered with farms where people were winnowing, threshing and shooing cows and donkeys away from harvested grain. It looked like a good harvest but when I got to Lhasa I was told that the Chinese had forced the Tibetans to sell so much of the harvest and at such low prices that people were afraid there might be famine that winter.

Late in the afternoon we stopped at a farm. I knew this was a scheduled stop because the farmer's wife, seeing us, bustled into the house and returned with a kettle of *chang*. This is a weak homemade beer. The drivers took a wicker box wrapped neatly in a woman's handkerchief from one of their packs. It contained the dried meat they had bought in Dingeri. This is called 'old meat,' an accurate if not appetizing description, and is not cured or smoked. It is just air-dried.

We perched on tussocks of grass. I was given a few ribs to try. I found the meat delicious but very difficult to wrench off the bone. While I was getting my teeth into the meat, the children of the household, their noses snotty, their hands black from handling pots from the fire, began to circle us. The eldest boy was the first to come near me. His goal was my daypack, not for what was inside but to play with and learn how to manipulate the buckles that fastened it around my waist. I fed him, his brothers and sisters dried dates, raisins and apricots. He moved on from the daypack to my Reeboks, which had fascinating Velcro fasteners. His brothers and sisters watched him gravely.

My drivers bantered with the farm wife, urging her to take some of the 'old meat' which she did just as we were leaving. I was delighted when, climbing back into the truck cab, I saw the little boy wave, smile and even stick out his tongue at me, a Tibetan way of showing respect.

Night was falling and the driver was weaving around leaping rabbits on the road, avoiding the sheep, which were hysterically trying to run in three different directions at once and the unmoving cows. We drove up to a monastery. I thought we would spend the night but it turned out that we were doing a delivery. The driver had a package for one of the monks. While the men talked I was given yak butter tea, yak cheese and candies to munch on. The driver took another package from the lama and we started out again.

About ten minutes later the truck began to make a chick-i-chung noise. I could smell burning rubber. The driver stopped and borrowed my flashlight to look under the truck but he found nothing. We continued in the dark. Suddenly in a town he stopped in front of a tatty hotel opposite a disco. It took ten minutes and a lot of work with my phrase book before the driver, giving me a bemused look, pointed firmly at the ground before his feet said, 'Shigatze, Shigatze'. 'Oh,' I said, finally understanding. He then pointed his finger back and forth along the street saying, 'Bus Lhasa'.

I paid him his 200 – yuan and hefted my bags upstairs to my room, which had a view of the disco's flashing lights. I could hear the base line of the song that was being played very clearly. I got the man downstairs to replace the bulb that was out in the tiny hall before my door that locked with a twist of wire over a nail. At 7 am I dragged my pack down the stairs, gave the doorkeeper who stank of *chang* and obviously had a hangover some of my dried fruit and took my place at the curb to wait for the Lhasa bus.

I will always thank my Dutch teacher for her lesson. I would never have thought of hitch hiking without her example. Without her as a role model I would not have had one of my most precious memories of Tibet. She passed on to me her courage and experience. I hope to pass it on to others.

3 Time and Space Travel in Ancient Vedic Texts

Divya Joshi

Towards the end of the 19th century, the Hindu monk and reformer Swami Vivekananda claimed that modern science was inevitably converging towards *Advaita Vedanta*, an important philosophico-religious system in Hinduism. In the decades that followed, in the midst of the revolution occasioned by the emergence of Einstein's relativity and quantum physics, a growing number of authors claimed to discover striking 'parallels' between *Advaita Vedanta* and modern physics. Such claims of convergence have continued to the present day, especially in relation to two concepts, *akasa* in *Advaita Vedanta* and vacuum in quantum physics. Both concepts would refer to the same reality – an enduring, subtle and all – pervading physical substratum out of which the constituents of the world come into existence and to which they ultimately return.

Analytic philosophy too concerned with the issues surrounding ontology, epistemology, and character of space and time focuses on a number of basic issues whether time and space exist independently of the mind, whether they exist independently of one another, what accounts for time's apparently unidirectional flow, whether times other than the present moment exist, and also questions about the nature of identity (particularly the nature of identity over time).

Indian spiritual traditions have given Indian culture a composite rhythm – a rhythm which is unique and distinctive in itself. Time has acquired significance partly because of its all comprehensive nature, and partly because of its insistence on the possibilities of binaries. According to Arjun Sinh K. Parmar, 'the concepts of time gather importance and meaning in the context of autonomous construction of binaries, such as Time/time, eternal/temporal, timeless/time, construction/deconstruction, good/evil, spiritual/physical, and material' (43–44). It has been variously viewed as a substance, single, omnipresent, permanent, the measure or dimension of things possessing movement. It is the very self (*atman*) or essence of everything and the manifestation of an activity that makes the universe assume a sequence.

Time is often perceived as having a dynamic quality, where absolute time equates to duration, and relative time is a measure of duration, and hence of absolute time. In astronomy, absolute time is distinguished from relative time by the equation of common time because natural days, which are commonly considered equal for the purpose of measuring time, are actually unequal. Astronomers correct this inequality in order to measure celestial motions on the basis of a truer time.

Similarly the absolute and relational views of space largely mirror their temporal counterparts. Absolute space, of its own nature without reference to anything external, always remains homogeneous and immovable, says Van Fraassen (131). Relative space is any movable measure or dimension of this absolute space. When Albert Einstein devised the Theory of General Relativity, he envisioned space and time not as rigid yardsticks for reality, but as one combined entity, space – time that could be deformed and even penetrated. Einstein's general relativity solutions provide three different types of universe: (1) an N-dimensional sphere, (2) an N-dimensional pseudo sphere and (3) a flat universe. Area consisting of lower part of upper *loka* and upper part of lower *loka* resemble N-dimensional pseudosphere and the *Brahma loka* zone of upper *loka* is a good approximation to N-dimensional sphere. The lower end of *loka* is closed and this represents a finite flat shape. Theologians have speculated that the afterlife, heaven, hell, angels, and our souls could reside in a fourth dimension – that God and Satan could literally be lumps of hyper matter in a four-dimensional space inches away from our ordinary three-dimensional world.

According to Rea, 'The theory of special and general relativity suggests that suitable geometries of space-time or specific types of motion in space, might allow time travel into the past and future if these geometries or motions are possible' (33–34). In technical papers, physicists generally avoid the common place language of 'moving' or 'travelling' through time because movement normally refers only to a change in spatial position as the time coordinate is varied, and instead discuss the possibility of closed time like curves, which are worldliness that form closed loops in space-time, allowing objects to return to their own past.

For years the literary world has enthralled us with tales of time travellers and their adventures, and in modern times science has piqued our interest with the idea that time and space travel might just become a reality some day. According to Flynn and Nova two categories of time travel exist in the literary world. The first category is time travel by means that science has overwhelmingly decided as not feasible. Magic, temporal portals and classic time machine are few examples of literary time devices that have little promise of becoming reality. The second category is those devices which hold at least some potential to become a reality. Quantum time travel and worm holes are examples of this type.

The concept of time travel has been around for nearly 3000 years. The idea of travelling through time to the past, present and future has been used in ancient folklore and modern fiction for centuries, finest examples being the Japanese tale of *Urashima Taro* and Irving's *Rip Van Winkle*. The concept of 'time-travel' and 'parallel worlds' is not confined to the science fiction genre, says Leslie Adelson, and they can be used more as a stylistic tool for social spiritual commentary than for thrilling narrative entertainment (98–99). Vedic literature demonstrated realities not only in physical or cultural space but also parallel realities in time. Playful references to alternate dimensions and extraterrestrial beings are tools to get readers 'to practice perceiving invisible dimensions of reality,' like the past and future. No one ever sees or describes extraterrestrials in Vedic texts; they are simply known to exist, as invisible but real phenomena, much like the past and future in people's minds.

Time travel is the concept of moving between different points in time in a manner analogous to moving between different points in space. Time travel could hypothetically involve moving backward in time to a moment earlier than the starting point, or forward to the future of that point without the need for the traveller to experience the intervening period. Although time travel has been a common plot device in science fiction and theories of general relativity allow methods for forms of one-way travel into the future via time dilation. Modern physics allows for remarkable transformations of space and time and apparently, similar ideas are found in Vedic literature.

The ancient vedic seers knew about the phenomenon of relativity, the *Mahabharata* mentions the story a king named Kakudmi, who was able to travel to the world of Brahma and experience Brahma's scale of time. Taking his own daughter, Revati, Kakudmi went to Lord Brahma in *Brahmaloka,* which is transcendental to the three modes of material nature, and inquired about a husband for her. When Kakudmi arrived there, Lord Brahma was engaged in hearing musical performances by the *Gandharvas* and had not a moment to talk with him. Therefore Kakudmi waited, and at the end of the musical performances he offered his obeisance to Lord Brahma and thus submitted his long-standing desire:

> After hearing his words, Lord Brahma, said to Kakudmi, 'O King, all those whom you may have decided within the core of your heart to accept as your son-in-law have passed away in the course of time. Twenty-seven *catur-yugas* have already passed. Those upon whom you may have decided are now gone, and so are their sons, grandsons, and other descendants. You cannot even hear about their names. (*Srimad Bhagavatam* 9.3.28–32)

One *catur-yuga* lasts 4,320,000 years. With this information, we can estimate the rate of time dilation on *Brahmaloka*. If the concert given by the *Gandharvas* took about one hour in Brahma's time scale, then that hour must correspond to 27 times 4,320,000 earth years. It is interesting that this estimate closely matches one for time dilation in another story involving Brahma. Although the time dilation involved in visits to '*Brahmaloka*' is extreme, such large time dilations do arise in the theories of modern physics. It is curious that according to the *Srimad Bhagavatam* the physical universe is surrounded by a shell, and '*Brahmaloka*' is located very close to that shell. The *Bhagavatam* gives the diameter of this shell as 500 million *yojanas*, which, using the standard figure of 8 miles per *yojana,* comes out to 4 billion miles. According to Einstein's theory a man will find he has not aged as much as his identical twin brother who stayed home. Time will have passed more slowly in the space than on earth. This disparity known as time dilation allow for remarkable transformations of space and time. Another story is of the *brahma-vimohana lila*, or the bewilderment of Brahma by Krishna. Krishna descended to the earth as on *avatara* and was playing as a young cowherd boy, tending cows. Though Brahma was absent for one earth year, on his time scale only a moment a *truti* had passed. Similarly description and location of the *Brahmaloka* seems consistent with the idea that space in *Brahmaloka* may undergo transformations incomprehensible from our earthly standpoint.

What makes this ancient Hindu tale so interesting is that this is exactly what happens to a space traveller who journeys far out into space travelling far away from the Earth, we encounter the phenomenon called time dilation. As one accelerates to this great velocity, special relativity theory kicks in and the astronaut on this journey in space ages very slowly. The theory of special relativity generalised Galileo's principle of relativity that all uniform motion is relative and there is no absolute and well defined state of rest. It incorporates the principle that the speed of light is the same for all inertial observers regardless of the state of motion of the source. It introduces space time interval which is invariant.

Sadaputa Das is of the view that like in any other civilisation astronomical concepts were found in ancient Indian texts. The Vedic texts are repositories of several mythologies developed around stellar constellations (64–69). References to planets, *nakshatras*, motion of sun and moon are found in Rig Veda. The details of *darsapurnamasa,* i.e. the new – and full moon sacrifices, the *caturmasa* or four monthly sacrifices, seasons, and month names are stated specifically in *Yajurveda*. The importance of the winter solstice is emphasised through the *mahavrata* rites which are also dealt with at length in the Brahmanas of *Samaveda*. The *Atharvaveda* also contain stray passages of astronomical consequence, such as the solar eclipse, the mention of Rahu for the first time, intercalation with a thirteenth month and a list of 28 *naksatras* including *Abhijit*. India's cosmology is very similar in some respect to modern Western astronomy. *Narayana* (the supreme divine being) is beyond the *Avyakta* (undifferentiated nature) and has no corresponding concept but the next stage *avyakta* can find its equivalent as the state of singularity. Nature, Vedanta says has two dimensions, the differentiated (manifested universe) and the undifferentiated. From the *avyakta* comes the *vyakta*, the manifested what the verse calls the *Brahmanda*, the cosmic egg containing millions of universe. This is how the vision of the infinite time and space is described in The Bhagvad Gita:

Sahasra yuga paryantam aharyad brahmano viduh:
Ratrim yuga sahasrantam te horatravido janah (8, 17)

They who know the true measure of day and night know the Brahma, which ends in a thousand *yugas*. The whole of Reality includes time and eternity, eternity which is the *aksara Brahman*, the imperishable Reality. Time is where evolution and activity goes on, beyond which is the one absolutely imperishable changeless Reality. So we have got both time and eternity as Reality; where time and timelessness are its two aspects, *'Aham eva aksayah kalo'* (I alone am inexhaustible Time). Einstein combined space and time into space-time continuum. A united space-time is the reality today and everything in that space-time is an event not a thing or an entity. Time movement converts all entities into events. Time combined with the three dimensions of space is the reality of the world, the four dimensional continuum according to Einstein's relativity theory. Similarly space or *akasa* is all pervading from the point of view of nuclear physics because within the atom and between atoms there is space.

In the Vedic texts, the universe was conceived as of three distinct parts – the earth, the firmament and the heavens. Going beyond *Brahmaloka*, one comes to the shell of the universe, d[illegible]ribed in vedic literature as a region of transition from the [illegible]l world to the spiritual world. Since the *Bhagvatam* regards [illegible]e know it as a physical element (called *akasha* or ether), [illegible]ks the end of distance measurements as we know them. [illegible]e universe also marks the end of time. According to vedic literature, a liberated soul is able to cross the shell of the universe and enter the transcendental region of *Vaikuntha*, where material time does not exist.

Ancient India was an open Galactic society with a great diversity of beings originating from different worlds or '*lokas*' interacting in the development of human civilisation. Insofar as these beings required advanced technologies to move themselves through time and space, they can be regarded as extraterrestrials. In cases where these beings could move between worlds without technology, they can be regarded as celestials. The *Puranas* give numerous accounts of how the celestials would intervene in a time of cultural degeneracy to restore of the *Sanatana Dharma* and help the *Devas* in their perennial conflict with the *Asuras*.

The Vedas and later Indian literature also describe *vimanas* of various shapes and sizes.: (a) Aerial Chariots intended for individuals or smaller groups, mainly for pleasure travel. (Aerial chariots were referred to as 'Ratha' in the time of the Rig Veda and later the terminology changed to *vimana*. The *Pushpaka vimana* is one of the most important examples of this kind of *vimana* technology.), (b) Flying Palaces and Flying cities, which were obviously much larger in scale and operation, (c) *vimanas* intended for interstellar travel (Such *vimanas* were called *Nakshatramandalas* (nakshatra meaning star) and possibly there existed aircrafts capable of flying across galaxies. Apparently, these interstellar aircrafts were powered by *laghima*, the power of the ego, which is responsible for the levitation exhibited by Hindu yogis.

The *Samarangana Sutradhara*, an important Vedic text containing details of *vimana* technology states clearly that the planes were designed so as to imitate palaces on ground. An ancient Vedic epic –*Arthashaastra* – by Sage Kautilya refers to a flying city called *Saubha*, which belonged to King Harishchandra. In fact there is reference to *Saubhikas* amongst the various tradespeople of the time, pointing towards people who were trained to operate the *Saubha*. In the Vedas the Sun and the Indra and several other Vedic deities are transported by flying wheeled chariots pulled by animals, usually horses (but the Vedic god Pusan's chariot is pulled by goats). In the Ramayana, the demon-lord Ravana's flying vehicle was called *Pushpaka*. *Pushpaka* was originally made by Maya for

Kubera, the God of wealth, but was later stolen, along with Lanka, by his half-brother, the demon king Ravana.

Sanskrit texts are filled with references to gods who fought battles in the sky using *vimanas* equipped with weapons as deadly as any we can deploy in these more enlightened times. The core epic of the *Mahabharata* mentions no *vimanas*, but *vimanas* often occur in the large amount of matter which was added to the Mahabharata corpus later. One example is that the *Asura Maya* had a *vimana* measuring twelve cubits in circumference, with four strong wheels. In one exchange, the hero, Krishna, is pursuing his enemy, Asura Salva, in the sky, when Salva's *vimana*, the *Saubhapura,* is made invisible in some way.

The mention of airplanes is found many times throughout Vedic literature, including the following verse from the *Yajur Veda* describes the movement of such machines:

> O royal skilled engineer, construct sea-boats, propelled on water by our experts, and airplanes, moving and flying upward, after the clouds that reside in the mid-region, that fly as the boats move on the sea, that fly high over and below the watery clouds. Be thou, thereby, prosperous in this world created by the Omnipresent God, and flier in both air and lightening. *(Yajur Veda 10.19)*

The *Rig Veda,* the oldest document of the human race includes references to various modes of transportation, the *Jalayan* – a vehicle designed to operate in air and water. (*Rig Veda 6.58.3*), *Kaara* – a vehicle that operates on ground and in water. (*Rig Veda 9.14.1*), *Tritala* – a vehicle consisting of three stories. (*Rig Veda 3.14.1*), *Trichakra Ratha* – a three-wheeled vehicle designed to operate in the air. (*Rig Veda 4.36.1*), *Vaayu Ratha* – a gas or wind-powered chariot. (*Rig Veda 5.41.6*), *Vidyut Ratha* – a vehicle that operates on power. (*Rig Veda 3.14.1*). *Kathasaritsagara* refers to highly talented woodworkers called *Rajyadhara* and *Pranadhara.* The former was so skilled in mechanical contrivances that he could make ocean crossing chariots. And the latter manufactured a flying chariot to carry a thousand passengers in the air. These chariots were stated to be as fast as thought itself.

Thus we see that there are many ways that 'time' and 'space' can be shown to have a relationship. A simple example is found in the game of chess. Chess strategy involves interplay between space (how many of the 64 squares of the board you control), and time (how many moves that you are ahead or behind your opponent). Experienced players often 'trade' space for time, having to use their intuition as to whether they are getting the 'better end of the deal'. Only after a beginner understands this 'dimension,' of the game, can he move forward to becoming an advanced player. In mathematics, there are complex equations that cannot be solved without introducing a '4th dimension' (something beyond the X, Y and Z coordinates in 3-dimensional space). Again, without 'expanding' beyond the elementary and obvious, one cannot advance to the next level of understanding. Physics has shown that there are relationships between things like energy and mass, as well as time and space, Einstein's famous equation, $E=mc^2$ (Energy equals mass times the constant of the speed of light, squared) was one of the first to link two such elements. Experiments have been done sending atomic clocks through the atmosphere in different directions, arriving at the same destination at the same moment – however when the clocks were checked, the times were different, thus showing that speed through space affected time.

The Vedic texts not only explain and explore the philosophy of three-dimensional existence vis-à-vis the fourth dimension and parallel universes as a concept of another time and space but also explain the inner process by which we can access knowledge of the past and future in the present, and also whether this form of time travel is acquired by transcending the five Earthly anchors of the ego mind which otherwise leave us locked into the illusory self?

To conclude we find that relativity has shown that time and space are inextricably linked and according to Bell's theorem involving non-local features of the universe; objects once in contact, though separated spatially, even if placed at distant ends of the universe, are somehow in inseparable contact. Since any change in one immediately and unmitigatedly causes change in the other, this is a nonlocal occurrence, meaning that any information passing between the two objects would have to travel faster than the speed of light to cause such instantaneous change. Since it is impossible for the speed of light to be exceeded, according to the special theory of relativity, this event is said to be non-causal, i.e. not caused by the transfer of any conceivable kind of energy passing between the distant objects. Mihir Joshi in his article, 'The *Mahabharata* and the Science' says that Sir Isaac Newton attempted to explain time as;

> Absolute, true, and mathematical time, of itself, and from its own nature, flows equally without relation to anything external, and by another name is called duration, relative, apparent, and common time is some sensible and external measure of duration by means of motion, which is commonly used instead of true time, such as an hour, a day, a month, a year (73).

In a broad sense, time is associated with any physical thing from its beginning to end; this can be applied to the universe also. The spaces constructed in ancient Indian texts along with the time travel motif not only locate the action in a socio-cultural or psychological context, but also serves as a parallel or alternate reality. It also has an ideological function because it literally provides the necessary distancing effect that science fiction needs to be able to metaphorically address the most pressing issues and themes that concern people in the present. We all have roots in the universe. Conscious mental activity exerts measurable effects on the physical world. As is said in the *Bhagavad Gita*: 'Without and within all beings the unmoving and also the moving, because of its subtlety, unknowable; and near and far away is that (God)'(*Bhagavad Gita* 13, 15).

References

Brown, C.L. *'What is Space?' A largely Wittgensteinian Approach Towards a Dissolution of the Question: 'What is Space?'* London: OUP, 2006.

Das, Sadaputa. (Richard L. Thompson) *Vedic Cosmography and Astronomy.* Los Angeles: Bhaktivedanta Book Trust, 1989.

Flynn, John L. 'Time Travel Literature'. Web Source http://www.towsonedu/-flynn/timetv.html, viewed on 13 April 2003.

Gal-Or, Benjamin. 'Cosmology, Physics and Philosophy'. New York: Springer-Verlag, 1987.

Joshi, Mihir J. 'The Mahabharata and Science'. Ed. Arjun Sinh K. Parmar. *Critical Perspective on the Mahabharata*. New Delhi: Sarup & Sons, 2002.

Kluge, Alexander and Yoko Tawada. 'The Future of Futurity: Time Travel, Parallel Worlds'. Web Source. http://www.exactspent.com/philosophyofspaceandtime.htm. viewed on 25.7. 2011.

Kuppuram, G. *India Through the Ages: History, Art Culture and Religion.* New Delhi: Sarup and Sons, 1996

Nova, 'Time Travel', Web Source http://wwwpbs.org/wgbh/nova/time/, viewed on 13.04.03.

Parmar, Arjun Sinh K. Ed. *Critical Perspectives on the Mahabharata.* New Delhi: Swarop & Sons. 2002.

Pattnaik, Devdutta. *Jaya, An Illustrated Retelling of the Mahabharata.* New Delhi: Penguin, 2010.

Rea, M.C., 'Four Dimensionalism' in *The Oxford Handbook for Metaphysics*. London: Oxford Univ. Press, 2003.

Shrimad Bhagavatam. Gorakhpur: Gita Press.

Swami Ranganathananda. *Universal Message of the Bhagvadgita*. Kolkata: Advaita Ashram, 2006.

Van Fraassen, Bas. *An Introduction to the Philosophy of Space and Time*. India: Random House, 1970.

4 The Pilgrimage of Buddhist Epistemology in the Asian Space

Ranjana Jaitly

The evolution of the human being is a history of migrations and admixture. Cultures are born on the banks of rivers and carried forth along the tributaries. Man carted ideas with their merchandise as they traversed the boundless terrain of prehistory. Apart from the movement of *homo sapiens*, the topography of the earth's surface changed due to historical earthquakes forming tectonics reconstructions, changing weather patterns, shifting shore lines. These geological processes affected the travelling races and culture. 'Eventually all things merge into one, and the river runs through it. The river was cut by the world's great flood and runs over rocks from the basement of time. On some of the rocks are timeless raindrops, under the rocks are the world's words, and some of the words are theirs. I am haunted by the waters.[1]

Many races entered the 'Indian Sub-continent as it has been described by global cartographers, through land and see routes. Hypothetically, the races that entered this space were the Neanderthal,[2] Proto-Austroloid,[3] Mediterranean,[4] Negroid[5] and Mongoloids.[6] Anthropologically races are categorised on the basis of morphology, cranial index, skeletal remains, carbon dating of tools and human remains (DNA), potsherds, burial ritual, et al. The Mongoloids and culturally akin races spread from the Himalayas to the Brahmaputra plains lying on the north-eastern tip of India, surrounded by Tibet in the North and north-east; Bhutan in the west and Assam and Nagaland in the south. The majority of the people of the Himalayan range and of the foothills are native to Tibet and Burma. Many of these republican tribes[7] living at the foothills of Nepal, which was part of Uttar Pradesh, are now in Arunachal Pradesh. Arunachal so called for it is the 'land of the rising sun',[8] land of dawn; literally 'mountains' was where these plutocratic[9] autonomous, republican states and small monarchical states existed. Thus parallel cultural and religious traits can be seen.

Sakyamuni Gautam belonged to such an aristocratic Sakya clan of Kapilvastu, Mahavir, the twenty fourth Tirthankara, belonged to the Gyantric clan of Kundapura, a suburb of Vaishali. These small confederacies were within the Nepal border.[10] Therefore through cultural mobility, the Asian cultures vis-à-vis their cosmogony, cosmology and epistemology, worked through commonalities and differences. Buddhist epistemology arose from Buddha's experience. He observed the transience of life and searched for the Truth. Not only did he acquire but sought the verification of that knowledge through sacrifice, endurance and penance. Much before the Gettier[11] problem arose he repudiated a definition of knowledge as 'justified true belief'.

The Vedic and non-vedic cultures had developed by the sixth century BCE on parallel lines, sometimes meeting at cross-roads as the need arose. The Vedic was thought to be the *pravritti mārga*, the non-vedic the *nivritti mārga*.[12] *Pravritti* or path of outward life is one of worldly activity, karma yoga culminating into devotion, bhakti-yoga. *Nivritti mārga* is the inward path through contemplation, introspection and meditation. The latter probably is prevedic, generally followed by shramans (the mendicants), ascetics, munis (silent ones) and sadhus. The former is essentially the ideal of the Vedic Brahmanical society. The Vedas are revealed, intuitive, supra-normal truths of the rishis (seers), the synthesis and resolution of which is to be seen in the *Upanishads*,[13] and the *Bhagavada Gita*[14] bestowing upon Hinduism a more intelligible and broader framework.

Buddha's observations and query led him to believe in the intransience and flux of worldly phenomena, arising in a mutually interdependent web of cause and effect.[15] Buddha's *Dharma*

Chakra pravartana[16] kick starts with the *'Chaar-Arya-Satya'* or four fold Noble Truths. His first tenet is that the world is full of suffering; there is a cause for this suffering and *Trishnā* or desire is the cause; but there is a way out of this *dukkha* or suffering through discipline and meditation. The *Ashtnga mārga* (Eightfold path) of discipline and meditation, in Buddhist ethics, is called *Nirodha*, the cessation of suffering attainable by *Samyak Drishti* (Right belief) *Samayak Smriti* (Right thought); *Samyak Vāk* (Speech); *Samyak Karma* (Action); *Samyak ājiva* (Livelihood) *Samyak Vigyān* (Effort); *Samyak Sankalpa* (Resolve); *Samyak Samādhi* (Meditation).[17] The five fundamental precepts *Panchshīla, Ahinsā* (Non violence), (Abstinence from stealing, illicit sexual conduct, intoxicating drinks) and *Satya* (truthfulness), then right exertion, right mindedness, right meditation endows mental control (*Chitta*) and lastly, right resolution and right point of view causes intellectual development (*pragyā*). Right speech, right action and right means of livelihood lead to physical control (*sīla*).[18]

Buddha seems negative in his philosophy marking an intense pessimistic attitude,[19] yet he overturns negativity in the positive direction always stressing on the middle path; maintaining a balance (*samyak*). It was after six years of this struggle that he was convinced that the truth could be attained not by extreme ascetism but by leading an ordinary course of life. This is the aesthetics of Buddhism.[20] Buddha's repeated pursuance of practical methods to overcome ignorance, thirst, attachment, etc. in contravention to academic speculation about the Beyond, the Ultimate, formulates a metaphysical approach viewed in the instructions to his followers.[21] The real world being transient is evanescent, virtual, an illusion. 'The phenomenal world has no real existence to the unenlightened. Certain causes and conditions (*hetupragtyaya*) make a thing appear to exist, like waves on the sea'.[22] Drawing heavily from the *Upanishads*, Shankaracharya the Advait Vedantist also believes in '*Maya*', an illusion thus proving the parallel lines of the vedic and non-vedic thought. The Buddhist ethical precepts are hinged to the twelve links or *nidānas,* which are the aggregate of a person's 'present' character, the result of the effects of these previous actions. The *nidānas* show the causal relations between death and birth called *Pratītyasamutpāda,* dependent origination.[23] This is the psychological phenomenon that sustains *dukkha* and the possibility to reverse this chain, leading to *nibbāna* (nirvāna). The first is *Avidya* (ignorance); then, *Sanskāra* (mental formation); *Vigyāna* (consciousness); *Nāmrupa* (mind and matter); *Sadyātana* (the sense arise); *Sparsha* (contact); *Vedāna* (feeling); *Trishnā* (craving); *Upādāna* (clinging); *Bhava* (becoming); *Jāti* (birth); *jarāmarna* (ageing and dying).

Buddhism developed from an investigating analytical questioning to an unquestioning acceptance of the *Tripitaka*[24] alleged to be the authority of the Buddha. Rhys Davids states that the teachings of Buddha as collected in the *Sutta Pitaka* are not only his spoken words but also of his disciples. About the third century BCE Buddhism developed as a powerful factor in the culture of India and also a large part of Asia. It is at this time that Buddhism pronged into the two groups of monks described as easterners and westerners, the former living mostly at Vaishāli and Pātliputra and the latter at Kaushāmbi, Patheyya and Avanti.[25] The differences arose because of doctrinal and disciplinary rules. The easterners were known as the *Mahāsanghikas* while the westerners as *Therevāda*. The oldest sect according to Tibetan tradition adopted Pali as the language of the *Pitakas* where as the most important sect of the *Theravāda*, the *Sarvastivāda*, preferred Sanskrit.

The rise of Magadhanra imperialism[26] coincides with the life of Buddha and spread of Buddhism. Much of the history of the preceding years is recorded in the Buddhist literature. An approximate genealogical description reflects a sense of history as much as the political patronage derived from the rules. The first Buddhist council, soon after Buddha's death is said to have been held under the auspices of King Ajātashatru, the second king of Magadha. It is not possible to determine how much of the Buddhist religio-philosophy and monastic organisation developed before this council. The *Theravāda* was propagated in Sri Lanka (Ceylon) by Ashoka's son Mahendra who carried the Pali Pitaka to that country.[27] Mahendra's sister Sanghmitra accompanied him. She is supposed to have taken a stem of the Bodhi tree and established the nun's monastery. The missionary activities of Ashoka carried Buddhism far and wide. Amongst these were Kashmir and Gandhāra, the Indo-Greek settlements of the North-west and Ceylon. Buddhism reached the Tamil country at this time.[28] Ceylon had two very large monasteries known as *Mahāvihāra* and *Abhyagirvihāra*, the first was of the *Theravāda* and the second was for the less orthodox sects.

The death of Buddha caused the split in the ranks of the monks fragmenting the base into many divisions. Once the discussions started the Buddhist Sangh multiplied into eleven sects of the *Thervāda* and seven of the *Acharyavāda*. All the eighteen sects were fundamentally *Hinayāna* (lesser vehicle). Later *Acharyavāda* splintered into a few sub-sects and introduced new doctrines which paved the way for *Māhayanis* which entered the *Abhidhama Pitaka*.

Between the fifth and seventh centuries *Māhayāna* reigned supreme. Its history can be traced to a much earlier period,[29] taking a definite shape by the first century CE. By the second century a change in outlook can be perceived because of the more liberal interpretation of the disciplinary rules. The new *Bodhisattva* ideal, which implied that even a householder, apart from the recluse could perform certain meritorious acts (*paramitas*)[30] in order to attain Buddhahood. The laity was allowed to take the *Trisharnā* (the three jewels of the Buddha, *dhamma, sangha*) observe temporarily eight of the ten moral precepts and offer gifts to the Sangha, without any provision for organised worship or ritual. This is the first time when directions for erecting *stupas* and *chaityas* (burial mounds and shrines) are given and the laity asked to worship at the *stupas* with garlands and unguents. Pilgrimages to the four places sanctified by the Buddha's birth, his attainment of Enlightenment (*Boddhi*), his first promulgation of the *Dhamma* (*Dharma Chakra Pravartana*) and his entry into *Nirvana* (*Mahaparinibbāna*). These directions given to the laity were undoubtedly interpretations of a later date which may be assigned to the Ashoka period.[31]

Extensive contacts however started about the second century CE because of the expansion of the Kushāna empire. This was the time in Indian history when hordes of Central Asian Mongol warrior tribes were being displaced from the north western boundaries of China (Chinese Turkestan) to invade through the north western passes of India and also the Tibetan frontiers.[32] The Saka tribes entered first, followed by the Kushāna. The greatest among the Kushānas was Kanishka who ruled over large areas of northern, western and certain southern parts of India. Kanishka became a Buddhist as recorded by Hiuen Tsang and Alberuni. The Fourth

Buddhist Council was convened by him with the purpose of settling certain perplexing opinions of the various creeds exposed by the monks. This synchronises with the emergence of Mahāyānism which contributed to the further development of Buddhism as a popular cult all over India and even far beyond the frontiers. During the fifth and sixth century CE, merchants too played a major role in the spread of religion, particularly Buddhism; they found the ethical and moral teaching of the *Mahāyāna* sect[33] tenable to their existing belief.

In order to understand the cosmogony, cosmology, epistemology of Chinese religion and culture, a brief peep into its history is necessary. As in most ancient traditional cultures, the Chinese revered the natural elements, believing in the spirits of the forest, ancestors, the seasons, etc. Here too, revelation, intuitive knowledge, clairvoyance ruled the cosmos. China's mythical stories, either those created by the primitive people or those written by later scholars are full of human feelings. Fables too are resplendent in which animals and spirits are commonly described as living things with human qualities and human feelings. Chinese mythical stories are intertwined with their history which is based on legends. One interesting story about Creation is that the Dragon Monster conquers Chaos and cuts into pieces which become the Sun, the Moon, etc. Stepping into the Proto-historical phase, we perceive cosmogony evolving into cosmology, when natural elements are anthropomorphised.

The first philosopher of note emerging in the historical period of China is Confucius. It was in the Han dynasty (202 BC–220 CE) that the thoughts of Confucius received official sanction and were further developed into a system known as Confucianism. Confucius (551–479 BCE) was a benevolent agnostic. The central theme of his philosophy is that the world, meaning the 'State' and the 'individual' is the cosmos. He affirms man in society and human nature. In his '*Annal of the State of Lu*' where he was born he does not mention 'god' except 'King'. The word for God is '*Tien*' (never) '*Shang Te*' (abstraction). The king is the son of God and he rules by the grace of God. His efforts were directed towards building an ideal human society. Learning to be human was the goal of Confucianism. In the '*Analects of Confucius*',[34] family relationship is an essential part in the architecture of an ideal society, the doctrine of filial piety is the cornerstone of all ethics.[35] Confucius repeatedly talks on the cultivation of '*ren*' as the quality of having a kind manner. Many of the Asian words do not have exact western equivalents like *'dharma'* is not religion, so also in the *'Analects'* when Confucius is asked to define *'ren'* he generally responds indirectly. According to him, a person with a well-cultivated sense of *'ren'* would speak carefully and modestly, be resolute and firm, be courageous, be free, from worry, unhappiness and insecurity. As known to historians, Confucius grew up at a time when the old order was breaking down, tradition was being questioned. The traditional privileges and rights of the ruling class were being challenged. Confucius was a teacher to the sons of the nobility at a time when formal education was just beginning to take root in China. Therefore, Confucius stressed on morality, good government, believing that rulers and educated men had an obligation to set good examples; to rule by persuasion rather than threat of punishment. Like Buddha, Confucius, to a great extent, was not interested in the world beyond but man-conducting himself to become an example to others. His was entirely a system of morality and not religion.

The history of epistemology is not one of linear, rational progress towards an even more accurate and complete knowledge in the search for truth. Many a times, it is a radical shift of vision in which a multitude of non-rational and non-empirical factors come into play[36] with a thin thread of continuity of tradition. Lao Tse, also known as the 'Old Sage', whom legends and scholars place between the 600–300 BCE, may have been a senior of Confucius, though there are others who say that he was a disciple of the latter. He is attributed with the writing of Tao Te ching, 'Tao' is way of life by men, 'Ching' means text or classic. Taoism searches the meaning of truth, an inward seeking of the spirit of man. The mystery of the universe with its flowing unknowable force attracted him. Like Buddha, he recognised the Unity in the ever changing world. He says 'Be still like a mountain and flow like the river'. 'He who conquers others is strong. He who conquers himself is mighty'.[37] The essence of *Tao* (*Daw*) is in the art of *we wei*, action through emotion. Nature replenishes naturally.

When the Chao dynasty in the third century BCE was drawing to a close, a civil war broke out. Because of this political upheaval and public discontent the worship of Confucius discontinued. It was again revived at the time of the Han dynasty in 195 BCE. Taoism proved an alternative to the Confucius tradition. Tao probably was searching for the cause of socio-political disharmony; a way that would avoid constant feudal warfare and other problems disrupting society. 'Social change is an elusive concept. Can orderly patterns be found in the midst of Chaos?'[38] During this period, the *'I Ching'*, the classic of changes, was reinterpreted as a system of cosmology and philosophy and became intrinsic to Chinese culture. Lao Tse, influenced by this philosophy believes in the dynamic balance of opposites, the *Yin* and the *Yang*. Events evolve in a continuous process, and should be accepted as inevitable. The ideal is simple; to follow what is right for the time. Time is a qualitative moment, a sacred eternity, not just a quantitative movement of the needles in a clock. The two traditions, Confucianism and Taoism co-existed in the country, region and generally within the same individual. In China the analogy is beautifully brought out by the 'Three Golden Eggs' – representing comparison, moderation and humility.

When we view the impact of Buddhist epistemology on Chinese normative and ontological premises, Mahayana Buddhism seems to be a bridge between the two dominant philosophers. The integration of philosophies with social norms and beliefs leads to religious rituals, worship and deification. This curve is seen in almost all religions because the mind grasps the intangible through the tangible. The entrance of Buddhism into China in the third Century CE was bitterly opposed by the Taoists. Buddhists were persecuted indicating a politics of exclusion exemplified by nationalistic fervour and rebellions. Yet the cultural bonds were never broken,[39] working through common factors like the Mauryan emperor Ashoka sending emissaries into Central Asia, Sri Lanka, etc. and later the southern kings of the subcontinent adventuring to the south-east archipelago, thus building a symbiotic, synergetic religio-culture with the two doctrines of Buddhism and Taoism subsisting side by side in peace.

Buddhist monks in China started taking a keen interest in the original texts of Mahāyāna Buddhism and travelled great distances to procure the texts in order to translate them in to Chinese. Fa Hein or Faxian probably was the first and oldest Chinese monk to travel to India.[40] He embarked on his trip in about 399 CE and returned after fourteen years. His passage to India was across the treacherous Taklamakan desert (present day Xinjiang Uyghur, Autonomous region of the Republic of China). He visited the major Buddhist pilgrimage sites in India, also went to Sri Lanka and travelled back by the precarious sea-route to China. Fa Heins 'A Record of Buddhist Kingdoms' tells us that his main concern was the procurement of teachings related to monastic rules (i.e. *Vinaya*). He also underscores the desire for the *Vinaya pitaka* in contemporary China. During the third and fourth century CE Chinese wanted the proper establishment of the Buddhist monastic order since the community of Buddhist in China was increasing. A number of Buddhist texts were translated introducing the *Lotus Sutra*. Here we notice a close relationship of Buddhist epistemology crossing over to the practical and experimental aspects of religious life including art, ritual, meditation and yoga. It becomes clear that Fa Hein in his records wanted to highlight Buddhist practices at the sites he visited. His record includes description of Buddhist monks, their teaching and ritual practices followed by them and the Buddhist legends associated with these sites. Many a times the veneration of Buddha's relics takes centre stage. The demand for Buddhist relics and ritual items in China resulted in the formation of a unique network through which they circulated between south and east Asia. Xuanzang or Yuang Chuang visited India in about 627 CE and promoted Buddhist doctrines in China portraying India as a holy land. His book *Records of the western regions during the Tang dynasty* was meant for the royal patronage as well as an account of a religious pilgrimage to historical foreign states and societies neighbouring Tang China. By the time he came to India monastic institutions and Buddhist doctrines had taken deep root in China. China was becoming an important centre for Buddhist learning outside southern Asia, where Yuan Chuang was venerated[41] in his country even in the Post Tang dynasties and as time passed fantastic Xuanzang stories were told and retold about a legendary figure.

The interaction between the Buddhist world of ideas and symbols became widespread and extensive. From the Central Asian belt it travelled to Korea, Japan and south-east Asia, Burma, Laos and Cambodia. The fascination of Buddhism as it winged its way through the countries is that a *priori* assumption of Buddha for the search of the truth is shrouded over by the beliefs and faiths of the religions already existing in the countries that it entered. The outward manifestations of a mystical philosophy developed as syncretic religions in various countries. Temples and monasteries were built to create an entirely new vocabulary of architecture, sculpture, images and melody. There was a continuous stream of exchange of art and ideas in the Asian sphere. Yet the pristine simplicity of Buddha's teaching got clogged in the mire of ritualism. The Buddhist philosopher Chu Hsia of the twelfth century rightly says 'Buddhism stole the best features of Taoism. Taoism stole the worst features of Buddhism. It is as though one took a jewel from the other, and the loser recouped the loss with a stone'.

These travels of Indian missionaries to China and south-east Asia and those of Chinese travellers to India, have not only transformed men but also religions, faiths and histories and have left a major impact on cultures and cultural relationships.

Notes

1. Maclean, Norman, vide Susan Pater, Kim Me, Reynods, Uhlman, Kristine. '*Geological Processes*', cals. Web Source arizona.edu/ watershed/resourses/doc./
2. Members of a group of the genus Homo, now extinct, known from Pleistocene specimens found in Europe and other parts. Alper, Joe 'Rethinking Neanderthal' *Smithsonian Magazine*, June 2003.
3. Hypothesised group of ancient hunter-gatherer people descended from the first major wave of modern humans to leave the Sub-Saharan. cf *'Prâchîn Bhârat ka Itihâsa'* Chakraverti, D.K. ed. Jha, D.N. and Shrimâti, K.M. Ch. I pp. 1–11, Hindi Mâdhyam Kâryânavya Nideshalaya, Delhi Vishvidyalaya.
4. One of the three races into which the Caucasian race and the people of Europe were divided by anthropologist in the late 18th–19th centuries – dark, swarthy, dark eyes and hair, moderate to short structure and moderate to long skull, sometimes olive in complexion.
5. Term used by forensic and physical anthropologists to refer to individuals and populations that share certain morphological and skeletal traits-brown or black pigmentation and often tightly curled hair.
6. Term used by forensic and physical anthropologists to refer to populations that share phenotypic traits. The word 'mongol' and the suffix 'oid' means resembling. Primarily introduced to describe various Asian, Central Asian, the Americas and Arctic races.
7. Law, B.C. '*Age of Imperial Unity History & Culture of the Indian People*', (HCIP) Ch. 1, pp. 1–17, Bhartiya Vidya Bhavan. Ed. Mazumdar, R.C. Vol. I, 1st edition
8. cf. Japan. The Republic of Kiribati in the Japanese archipelago sees the first rays of the sun; Japan is Nippon, 'The Land of the Rising Sun.'

9. A number of states having Gana Sangha or council as opposed to monarchical governments. Jaiswal, K.P. '*Hindu Polity*', Butterworth, Calcutta, 1924, Manohar Publishers, New Delhi, 1999.
10. cf. Law. B.C. '*North India in the 6th Century BCE Imperial Unity of India*' pp. 6–7
11. Gettier Problems – *Encyclopedia of Philosophy* (Internet) cf. Burns, Mc. Douglas 1st published 1963 www.vgweb.org.
12. Pandey, G.C. '*Vedic Sanskriti*' p. 433, Lokbharti Prakashan, Allahabad.
13. Juan Mascaro – Introduction – '*The Upanishads*' – Translations from Sanskrit, Penguin Books.
14. cf Altekar, A.S. '*State and Government in Ancient India*', ch. II Motilal Banarsidass, 1st Edition Banaras. 1949. Shatpat Brâhmana 13.2.24. Chapter III verse I.
15. Shantiparva Section CCXLI – Suka's conversation with Vyas, his father.
16. '*History and Culture of the Indian People*'. ch. XIX, p. 371. Bhartiya Vidya Bhavan
17. Dasgupta, Surendranath – '*A History of Indian Philosophy*', Vol. I p. 84. Motilal Banarsidas.
18. Digha Nikaya II: *Silam Samadhi panna cha vimmutti cha anuttara/Anubuddha ume dhamma gotamena. yasassina.*
19. '*Vishudal hi magg*' – 'The mind of him who inspires himself with this supreme disgust of all food becomes free from all desires for palatable tastes ....' vide Dasgupta, Surendranath Vol I cf HCIP, pp. 372ff
20. Balm.J. Archie – '*Buddhist Aesthetics*' Web Source www.jstor/org/stablel 427603
21. Dutt, Nalinaksha. '*History and Culture of the Indian People*'. Ch. XIX pp. 370
22. ibid.,
23. Dasgupta, Surendranath – '*A History of Indian Philosophy*'. Vol. I p. 84, Motilal Banarsidas
24. Banerjea, J.N. '*Pali Canon*'. HCIP Vol II p. 396. Formal term for Buddhist scriptures. The complete body of classical Theravadi texts. The most widely known version is the Abhidhamma Pitaka, formulated by Buddha during the fourth week after his Enlightenment. The three Pitakas (basket) are Abhidhamma, Vinaya, Sutta. cf Davids, Rhys: ibid., p. 370 believes that the sutta pitaka is the earliest. cf '*Abhidhamma Pitaka, The Basket of Abhidhamma*' Texts and Transla-

tions. Access to in insight.org.2005–2013 also Harvey, Peter '*Buddhist Ethics*' Network. Web Source.

25. Dutt, Nalinksha. HCIP p. 378
26. Mookerje, Radha Kumud. HCIP, Vol II pp. 18–35
27. Thapar, Romilla, '*Asoka and the Decline of the Mauryas*' Oxford University Press. Second edn. p. 46. Ibid., p. 379, Refutes this on the basis of the edicts of Ashoka saying that Mahindra was converted to Therâvâda in Ceylon.
28. A Srivathsan, 'Buddha at the Cross-roads'; '*The Hindu*' Magazine, 10 June 2012.
29. Dutt, Nalinaksha HCIP p. 385
30. Paramitas meant liberality *dâna*; righteousness *sîla*; forbearance or endurance *shânti* mental strength *vîrya* mental concentration *dhâyana* realisation of the truth *pragyâ* skillfulness in expedients *upayakaushalya*, vow or resolution *pranidhyâna* attainment of certain powers *bala*; knowledge *gyâna* HCIP. p. 386
31. Dutt, Nalinaksha. HCIP Vol II p. 386
32. Bently, H. Jerry. '*Old world Encounters Cross Cultural Contacts and Exchanges in Pre-modern Times*' pp. 43–44 New York: Oxford University Press, 1993
33. '*The History of Buddhism Silk Road*' www.upf.edu/materials/historia
34. cf. '*Confucian Philosophy*' www.chinaculture.org/gb/en_made_in_china/2005. Web Source
35. Analects 12.3–12.22. Wale, Arthur 1938. London: George Allen and Unwin, rptn Knopf Alfred A. 2000
36. London, Scott. '*Understanding Change. How it happens and how to make it happen*' Web Source www.scottlondon.com/ report/ change.htm.
37. Dee Finnery (compiled) *The Life of Lao Tse Tung. The Art of War. The Dream and the Reality.*'
38. cf London Scott. cf. Denville, Pau 'Philosophy and Religion from Hanto Sui' *Cambridge History of China'* Vol I: The 'Chin and Han empires: Ed. Twitchett, Deenis & Lowe, Michael.
39. Giles, Wade '*I Ching*' Web Source wikipedia.org.
40. Beal, Samuel '*Travel of Fahhian & Sungyan*' – 'Buddhist pilgrims from China to India 400AD–518AD'. British Library. edn. 1869
41. Ray, Harprasad '*Understanding Xuanzan and the Xuanzan Spirit*'. Ch. 16. '*Across the Himalayan gap*' edited by Tang Chung. Indira Gandhi National Centre for the Arts (IGNAC).

5

The *Memsahibs*

Transcending Boundaries

Bandana Chakrabarty

> One is not born a *memsahib*; the dignity is arrived at later through circumstances, processes and sometimes through foresight on the part of one's mamma.
>
> (*Simple Adventures* 1)

Thousands of British women travelled to India during colonial times forming an important segment of Anglo-Indian community. They first arrived as wives, sisters and mothers and later as teachers, doctors and missionaries. Both fiction and non-fiction portray these women as *memsahibs* and they have been portrayed as heroines, martyrs and villainesses. Male writers like Rudyard Kipling have disparaged British women travelling to India during Victorian times as 'frivolous, vain, selfish and snobbish flitting from bridge to tennis parties in the hills' (qtd. Barr 197). Many women writers, like Barr, have taken offence to Kipling's depiction of the British *memsahibs* that has lived in the annals ever since, 'as being truly representative of the whole species' (159). Alan Blackstock states that the *memsahib* is a staple caricature in literature related to the empire, 'resented by British and Indian alike; and from Kipling to Orwell there is little change in the stereotype' (35). This consistent denigration of the *memsahibs* has caused feminist writers to attack what Jenny Sharpe calls 'a male-generated image that misidentifies the relative powerlessness' (2). The present paper takes into account the Canadian author, Sara Jeanette Duncan's *The Simple Adventures of a Memsahib* and British author Pat Barr's *The*

Memsahibs: Women of Victorian India to explore the lives of *memsahibs* who travelled to India and faced the challenges of a new and alien environment and how they gradually contributed to empire building by transcending boundaries of race, culture, gender, economics, politics and history. Writers and historians have largely ignored the role of British women in 'defining, directing and maintaining imperialism' as I shall later discuss in this paper that their role has been underplayed. Duncan is an outsider in the arena of imperial representation of Anglo India whereas Pat Barr, focuses on contemporary historical constructions as well as on those women who wrote about their experiences in India. Barr has set right the omissions made by early historians who judged the actions of thousands of British women living in India as unworthy of recording. Both writers position India as a paradigmatic space of colonial rule through which their ideas of British colonial intervention are explored.

In the eighteenth century English women were sent by the shipload, in what were called 'fishing fleets' to search for husbands in India. It took nearly six months to accomplish this journey. Later with the invention of steam power and the opening of the Suez Canal in 1864 the trip was reduced to four weeks. When they arrived in India, British women were not expected to know or learn much of India or Indians. But as she took over the management of the house she had to learn the local language or Hindustani to order her servants about. 'It took little time,' says Margaret Macmillan 'for most women who came out to India at the height of the Raj to become *memsahibs*' (55). They tried to adapt themselves to the needs of their new environment and society where the rules were very strict.

Simple Adventures narrates the evolution of young Helen Peachey from an English vector's daughter to wife of an Anglo-Indian clerk, George Browne and her story is narrated by the omniscient Mrs. Macintyre. On every five years' leave in England Mr Browne met Helen and eventually they get engaged. Soon Helen embarks on her journey to India to meet her future husband. 'Helen was the first bride that Canbury had contributed to India, in the social memory' (10). Their marriage, too, is not an elaborate affair and Duncan writes ironically that Canbury sent hearty wishes for the future Brownes 'as if they had behaved properly in every respect' (11). In the nineteenth century, women who returned home without husbands or fiancés were known as 'Returned Empties' (*SA* 305). Duncan, at the very beginning of the novel warns readers not 'to expect anything extraordinary from Helen' (26).

After settling down in Calcutta, the 'domestic arrangements' of Helen and George were taken care of with 'unobtrusive smoothness that can be fully experienced only in India' (68). Their meals appeared and disappeared as by magic and the rooms swept and dusted 'while there was no eye to see' (69). Mr Browne and Helen wanted to see their servants. She is gradually introduced to the *kitmatgars,* the *mallie,* the *bawarchi,* the syce, the *dhoby,* the *bheesty,* the sweeper (who doesn't venture in their presence), the *ayah,* etc. A week after Helen was introduced to her servants; she takes charge of the accounts. She wanted to prove to George that she was 'capable of more than driving in a tum-tum and writing enthusiastic letters home about the beauties of Calcutta' (81). Very soon she learnt to count rupees and annas, pi and pice and also a few words of that language in which orders are given. She decides to 'assume discipline, righteousness and understanding' (81).

Duncan has interspersed the text with anecdotes where Helen takes charge and tries to keep an account of the cook's expenditure. Once when he tells her that seventeen eggs were consumed the previous day, Helen's outburst is: 'Seventeen eggs, *bawarchi*? When did we eat seventeen eggs? How did we eat seventeen eggs yesterday?' (82). Though Kali Bagh, the cook, accounts 'circumstantially for every egg' Helen makes up her mind to see whether he actually put four eggs in the soup or not from the next day onwards. Soon the golden age of the cook wanes when Helen has particular knowledge of the bazaar. When Helen finds an enormous quantity of rice being prepared for not only the cook but also the *mussalchi,* the sweeper and the syce, Helen is furious but she had 'no language with which to circumvent it or remonstrate with it' (86) but she decides to discipline the cook. As days pass by Helen and George visit Her Excellency's Drawing Room where 'she had the opportunity of taking a lesson in social astronomy' (125).

Imperialist historians considered imperialism as a masculinist construct with women placed in it as victims to be safeguarded and protected and as mates for imperial husbands. Imperial culture provided British women a new social space in which they could assert 'their value, authority and domestic roles'. According to

Rosemary Marangoly George, 'A *memsahib's* triumph, was to replicate the empire on a domestic scale' (108). She further says that it included 'caring for, disciplining and controlling the native help'. Thus women like Helen exercised authority over the domestic space as well as the people working within it. This could be managed only when one 'conquered the language' (13).

According to Mrs. Macintyre the *memsahib* has no concern for accuracy: 'she gathers together her own vocabulary ... from the east, west, north and south, from Bengal, Bombay, Madras and the Punjab, a preposition form Persia, a conjunction from Cashmere, a noun from the Nilgherries' (227–28). Helen discovers that it is more desirable to speak like a *memsahib* than a native. For Helen, Hindustani being the tongue in which orders are given helps in domestic administration. For her, she makes her own rules. Her constructions in the language are such as she pleases to place upon it (228). In the course of her *memsahib* apprenticeship Helen masters a new 'language'. She learns the art of bartering and commanding and becomes 'an entrant into the secrets of social astronomy' (125). She also acquires the accompanying body language needed for commanding the servants. If anything, Helen has 'acclimatised too soon' (247). She is a *memsahib* like another (310). Like Helen in *Simple Adventures* many Englishwomen began in the so called 'safe' and 'feminine' areas such as the home and their interactions with Indian domestic servants. An October 1886 article by J.E. Dawson in the *Calcutta Review* cited Englishwomen responsible for upholding domestic order in India:

> Each Englishwoman, in her own bungalow, is the centre of an influence and the cynosure of an argus-eyed criticism even to her most insignificant acts, to which her English life offers no parallel. The smallest establishment will contain from ten to a dozen, the larger from a dozen to twenty or thirty servants. With every one of these the *Memsahib* is more or less in contact and the happiness and comfort of their lives depends largely on her supervision. (363)

When Helen makes efforts to learn Hindustani, Mrs. Macdonald warns her that she is 'going the wrong way about it in studying a Hindustani grammar to learn the language' (230). She learns Hindustani by immersion, in the same way that she acquired her native language and thus loses the comparative objectivity gained in a systematic approach. Having graduated to memsahibship Helen 'takes the easiest word and the shortest cut' (308–09). Flora Annie Steele wrote in 1904, 'An Indian household can no more be governed peacefully without dignity and prestige than by an Englishwoman'. In a conversation with Mrs. Toote, Helen asks her if the ladies in India are all frivolous to which there is a vehement 'no' by Mrs. Toote but she sarcastically says that the unfrivolous ones either go in for 'society or philanthropy – that's the way everybody ends up' (114).

The garden is a significant space in most books about *memsahibs*. Helen, in the novel, finds solace in the garden because English flowers were grown by the *mallie*. The Brownes planted a vast amount of 'interest and affection and expectation in it; and it all grew' (165). Their love for the garden began by counting them. 'The bungalow, the club, the garden thus become sovereign English spaces within an 'alien' landscape, a locus of English culture embedded within a 'foreign' cultural setting', writes P.K. Nag. He further adds that from the 1850s, the cultivation of the garden became a visible sign of inscribing English authority over the Indian landscape. Several books on gardening in India were published for instance, *Indian Gardening* (1872) and *Gardening: A Guide for Amateurs* (1903) by W.W. Johnstone. These books offered advice on how to grow English-style gardens with Indian plants thus bringing about 'an indigenization of English culture as well as an assertion of control over colonial space'.

Foucault uses the term *heterotopia* to describe spaces that have more layers of meaning or relationships to other places than immediately meet the eye. A garden is a heterotopia because it is a real space meant to be a microcosm of different environment with plants from around the world. Eugenia Herbert gives several reasons for the penchant of colonials for English gardens besides clubs, cricket and hunting. Initially it was a need on the part of these people to replicate 'home' as much as possible in an alien environment. In an effort of 'creating an oasis of Britishness in an alien land' they made gardens. Wherever the men were posted they tried to create lawns and gardens and above all 'English gardens with English flowers'. When the Duchess de Dino visited England in the nineteenth century she felt, 'Green lawns and flower-beds with superb trees which obscure the view is what the English like, what one finds everywhere here'. (115) Hence gardens were very much a part of English identity. Another reason was that the colonial rulers personified a masculine ideal. They first came as merchants and later as administrators. They lived, worked and played in a largely male environment, married late and often bore long periods of separation from wives and children. Gardens were largely a female contribution to imperial life and thus it made India a place which was 'more familiar and more acceptable'. By the nineteenth century gardens and gardening became a part and parcel of English life. The garden has been a sort of happy universalising heterotopia since ancient times. In the opening pages of *The Memsahibs*, Emily tells one of her friend, Lady Pamela Campbell that even at Barrackpore, 'a secluded private garden filled with familiar English flora to remind them of dear Greenwich' (10) was set up by the subservient natives.

There is also mention of the Brownes' experiment with economy when they enclosed a fowl-yard and stocked it because they thought that when the cook used such a quantity of eggs why shouldn't they produce it on the premises. Later in the novel Helen also learns the art of thriftiness to make both ends meet. When she realises that five hundred rupees a month is not enough she saved on the *dhurzie* and on family darning (205). At the same time Mrs. Browne, that is Helen has the ability to appreciate the rains of India which had 'quite an extraordinary quantity of moisture about them' (251). In the closing pages of the novel, Duncan states, 'Mrs. Browne has become a memsahib graduated, qualified, sophisticated, that was inevitable ... she has lost her pretty colour, that always goes first and has gained a shadowy ring under each eye, that always comes afterwards' (308).

Lady Wilson in *Letters from India* writes about her first experience of Anglo-Indian housekeeping when she first came to India in 1889. She says, 'If I wished to give orders about the fire, about the flowers, about the arrangement of the dinner table, about purchases, about breakfast, lunch or dinner, not one Hindustani word could I say that they could comprehend' (6). Further, like Helen of *Simple Adventures* Lady Wilson, too had thirteen servants including groom, waterman, sweeper, milkman and house servants (9) but she soon realises that despite having so many servants that if one wants a thing done one must do it one's self or at least superintend that it's being done properly. She then gives a paraphernalia of the daily chores that needed supervision:

> One must look after the filter, see to the milk, the feeding of the cows, sheep and poultry, the making of butter, bread and asks to the careful trimming of lamps, to the dusting of books, pictures, furniture, to the tinning of pots and pans to the way the cook uses his dishes or his dusters. (9)

Memsahibs like Lady Wilson were not restricted to flippant attitudes. Rather her great ambition was to establish a school for girls. The garden, as I have mentioned earlier, was a significant space in most books on the Victorian women. Lady Wilson, too, spent most of her day in the garden, 'which is shaded by willows and by apricot trees, laden with fruit (35) with the scent of roses in the air. In an article entitled 'Nineteenth Century Memsahibs in India' Margaret Case writes, 'The lives of the *memsahibs* were taken up with running the household – providing food and clothing for the family, furnishing their home, overseeing the servants and raising the children' (133). The wives of the administrators, the *memsahibs*, had to often tour with their husbands and the camp was moved every two or three days. It was not as easy task for these women to accompany the husbands on such tours. 'We have three tents – two for living in, and one for Jim's office-work. While we are using one, the other goes ahead, and is pitched at our next halting-place. We generally move on every second or third day' (Wilson 13).

Women who left the supervision of housework to the servants were forced to live idle and bored lives. Such women were criticised by Kipling and other male writers. But at the same time there were other British women who were more energetic and as Case writes, insisted on keeping control of their households (138). Many *memsahibs* sent their children to England and this was yet another reason that these women showed strength and fortitude. The death rate of very young British children in India was appalling. In the early 1870s, about a quarter of the children born in army families died within six months. Emily Eden wrote, 'it feels like death and all the poor mothers here who have to part with their children are more to be pitied than it is possible to say'. British women went to India to help the men recreate the same life that they had experienced back home and they succeeded in doing so to a surprising degree.

The second book *The Memsahibs: The Women of Victorian India* by Pat Barr discusses the effect of the male dominated imperial scenario on British women. She is of the view that Kipling did not broaden his canvas to include as much diversity of character among these women as he developed in his male characters. Early in the book she writes of the entourage of Lord Auckland and his sisters. To gain some first hand experience of the real India they had to undertake onland journeys. They left Calcutta on 21 October 'for eighteen months of travelling by steamers, tents and mountains' (21). The Imperial Cavalcade consisted of government secretaries and scribes, army officers and their wives and children, soldiers, sepoys, servants and servants' servants, drummers, guards, laundrymen and loaders, messengers and tent pitchers, cooks and mahouts and grooms. To transport this multitude and their equipments between ten and twenty miles a day overland in strictly hierarchical degrees of comfort required an array of elephants, oxen, camels, horses and ponies. In this entourage, a Lady called Fanny Parkes believed, 'Travelling about the country is very amusing, (26) and whenever the rains stopped she left her husband working and 'took to wandering – by camel, boat, horse, to the north, east and west' (26).

Barr then talks of one Henry Lawrence, a senior lieutenant in the Bengal Artillery, and his wife, Honoria Henry. Being a revenue surveyor, he had to 'map long distances and Honoria accompanied him and enjoyed every hour of it' (36). She wrote home, 'Our life in camp teaches us how many 'indispensables' we can do without' (36). Even with an advanced pregnancy, Honoria had to follow after Henry on his journeys in a *dhoolie*, as if 'she were another item of baggage' (37). She missed riding freely at her husband's side. She narrates an incident that tells readers of the plight of pregnant women and mothers for whom life was so difficult. When Honoria's son is born, she had to carry her three weeks old child to Cawnpore with her husband. Barr says 'It was not any easy introduction to life for Alec' (30) and Henry had to get goat's milk for his son's survival. Despite having to face discomforts Honoria was not troubled by them and she sought to be by her husband's side all the time and she also brought to motherhood 'the same spirit of earnest endeavour' (43) that she had brought to India and to Henry himself, for the sake of her son's debilitating health Honoria did go to Simla but she resolved not to 'fritter away' her days on Simla's normal social round.

Pat Barr also gives us an example of Lady Sale who arrived in Kabul in 1840 when she was fifty-two years old yet like 'most women she settled down quickly and competently in the alien environment' (58). She brightened her bare bungalow and cultivated gardens. 'By the second summer, her flowers were the admiration of all the Afghan gentlemen' (58). The rebellion in Kabul is another example in the book where white women and children had to face abandonment and hunger. These women suffered the ordeals of the retreat from Kabul and their long captivity in states of increasing pregnancy survived which is a testimony to the toughness of the female body. Lady Sale and many others like her proved that they had been soldiers' wives too long to sit down tamely when their honour was being tarnished. When the Lawrences were moved to three different districts in rapid succession in 1843 Barr comments that it was not only frustrating for an ambitious man like Henry but equally troublesome and expensive for the wife that is Honoria. In a letter Honoria wrote, 'People at Home can scarcely picture the small vexations of this roving life' (73).

When Henry was posted as the new British Resident in Nepal, Honoria could not accompany him but later she 'went Dak' which was the customary method of travelling long distances before, the arrival of railways. Thus she journeyed in a *Palki* carried by bearers mostly by night alone with her five year old son. When finally she was waiting to sail from Bombay for England she reflected upon all the 'varieties of experience Englishwomen could have in India according to whereabouts they lived, what their husbands did, how their luck and love spun up and down' (78). As long as Honoria lived, she was full of zest, fervour and intelligence.

The 1857 Mutiny and its accompanying civil rebellion made things worse for the British women living in parts of central and northern India. For them it was like a nightmare and as Barr says, they were thrust hard against the 'barbarities of war' and suffered extremes of 'thirst, hunger, fatigue' (106) and the first British women to die violent deaths were in Meerut. After the siege things were harsher for women as they had to fight a constant battle against rats and insects to preserve what stores they had (134). In their refuge called Begum Kothi, the women ground *dhal* between stones and made a paste of it to wash clothes in the soapless and candleless place. A lady called Katherine Bartrum wrote, 'But we have so little that it is a question of whether we shall use it to wash with or to eat' (134). Though many women like Katherine became widows and wandered aimlessly like refugees, a few thousand British soldiers killed yet the British continued with their 'subsequent expansion of their imperial role in India' (138). With Queen Victoria coming to power in 1858, there grew an edginess, an unease between the rulers and the ruled in India. With the presence of more British wives, the domestic life became 'more self-sufficient and elaborate' (144).

There were many British women who were endowed with 'above-average determination and energy, who sought to wrest more from their Indian experiences' like Flora Annie Steele. When her husband fell ill she wrote his reports for him and she was never afraid to speak her mind. The first thing she did was to try and acquire some knowledge of the local languages. This gave her an opportunity to enjoy the inspection tours she accompanied her husband to. In Kasur, a sub division of the Lahore district, Flora took delight in her garden and soon made gardening fashionable there. At the same time she was a creative and versatile cook and later compiled her personal experiences and advice in *The Complete Indian Housekeeper and Cook* dedicated to these 'English girls to whom Fate may assign the task of being Housemothers in our Eastern Empire' (152). She believed that the memsahib's only remedy is to 'equip herself with sufficient knowledge to assert her authority and bring Western-style order out of Eastern-style chaos' (153). The book also contained instructive chapters on gardening and cookery. This book as Barr says was the 'distillation' of twenty-two years' experience of India and it run into ten editions.

A woman like Flora not only had domestic sagacity but she also paid attention to community affairs. In her later years she paid great attention to the education of the Indian female. Both husband and wife engaged themselves with the planting of road-side gardens and with the opening of girls' schools. She became the first woman member of the Punjabi Education Board. Even after leaving India, she wrote several novels, the best known was *On the Face of the Waters* which was hailed as a classic. Maud Diver, the author of *Englishwomen in India* paid a tribute to Flora in the following words: 'a shining example that might well prove profitable and stimulating to lesser *memsahibs'* (160). Besides women like Flora Annie Steele, British women whose careers in India parallel the development of British imperial power from firm self-confidence are such as Mary Carpenter, Annette Ackroyd Beveridge, Margaret Gillespie, Margaret Noble and Eleanor Rathbone. They promoted social reforms within an imperial relationship. Edith Brown qualified as a Doctor of Medicine and was a very enterprising and dynamic lady. She remained in Ludhiana for over thirty years 'winning hearts' (184). British women travelled to India as doctors, missionaries and teachers.

The white woman's burden in nineteenth century India was cumbersome yet she has received no praise for it. Maud Diver explained as Barr concludes in her book that the average *memsahib*'s career unfolded – 'as wife, mother-in-exile, hostess and housekeeper and she lived through them with a heart sobered by experience and self-knowledge ... till the years of her husband's work are accomplished and it is she herself who must go, leaving the younger generation to tread the same paths and uphold the same traditions after their kind' (201). These women in the British empire, in the nineteenth century serve as a recent example of travel outside the Home. They became a complete individual.

Both the books under consideration convey stories of triumph and tragedy but above all of extraordinary women who carved a new life for themselves away from the restrictions of their own prohibitive social customs and mores. They impacted upon the dynamics of the British society in the subcontinent. These books uncover the world of British India as seen and experienced by the British *memsahibs*. With the establishment of the English home outside England, 'there was physical repositioning of the hitherto private into what had been considered the most public of realms – the British empire' (George 99). By revising the relationship between the British women and British India, both Sara Jeanette Duncan and Pat Barr have made our understanding of the real efforts of these women significant as they undertook the roles of wives, mothers and missionaries. They have accentuated our understanding of the ideological work performed by gender in the construction of the empire. I would conclude the paper in Maud Diver's words:

> What would India be without England, and what would the British empire be without Englishwomen? To these women are due gratitude not only of their country but of the civilized world.

> Fearlessly the woman of British birth looks in the eye of danger. Faithfully and with willing sacrifice she upholds the standard of the King – Emperor – the standard of culture and of service to humanity. (154)

References

Barr, Pat. *The Memsahibs*: *The Women of Victorian India*. London: Secker and Warburg, 1976.

Blackstock, Alan. 'Beyond the Pale: Women, Cultural Contagion and Narrative Hysteria in Kipling Orwell and Forster.' ARIEL: A Review of International Literature. 36:2 (January–April 2005) 183–206.

Case, Margaret. 'Nineteenth Century Memsahibs in India' in *As Others See us Mutual Perceptions, East and West,* No. 13 (Fall 1985).

Dawson J. E. 'Woman in India: Her Influence and Position'. *Calcutta Review* 83 London. (October 1866): 347–70.

Diver, Maud. *The Englishwoman in India*. London: Blackwood, 1909.

Duncan, Sara Jeanette. *The Simple Adventures of a Memsahib*. Ed. Thomas E. Tausky. Ottawa: Tecumseh, 1986. Refered to as *Simple Adventures* or SA.

Foucault, Michel. 'Of Other Spaces'. *Diacritics* Vol. 16, No. 1 (Spring 1986).

George, Rosemary Marangoly. 'Homes in the Empire, Empire in the Home'. *Cultural Critique* 26 (1993–1994): 9512, Web Source. Viewed. 10.12.2010.

Herbert, Eugenia. *Flora's Empire: British Gardens in India*. Philadelphia: University of Philadelphia, 2011.

Kapila, Shuchi. 'The Domestic Novel goes Native: Bithia Mary Croker's *Nineteenth Century Anglo-India*. *Context* 26.3 (September 2004): 215–35.

Macmillan, Margaret. *Woman of the Raj*. London: Macmillan, 1988.

Nayar, Pramod K. 'The Disorderly Memsahib: Political Domesticity in Alice Perrin's Empire Fiction.' *Studies in English* Vol. 38, No. 1, pp. 123–38.

Sen, Indrani. ed. *Memsahib's Writings: Colonial Narratives on Indian Women*. New Delhi: Orient Longman Pvt. Ltd., 2008.

Sharpe, Jenny. *Allegories of Empire: The Figure of Woman in the Colonial Text*. London: Univ.of Minnesota Press, 1993.

Steele, Flora Annie. *The Complete Indian Housekeeper and Cook*. London: William Heinemann, 1888.

Stigall, Natalie. 'Memsahibs and Bo-kadaws: Representations of Feminine Imperial Authority in *Burmese Days.' Plaza: Dialogues in Language and Literature*. 2.1 (Fall 2011) 36–46.

6 Gandhi's Journey

Transformative Experiences

S. Asha

Travel is a human activity that has a great potential to alter one's perceptions or the directions one decides to take in life. In itself, travel has the potentiality to become a journey of life, as it opens up many doors and windows, and leads to self-reflection, primarily because it is an encounter with the 'other', the cultural other. This is what acts like a mirror. This resultant transformation from travel and travel related conditions in many literary writings offers an opportunity for extensive scrutiny to the reader. Does travel really bring about a transformative experience or not is a question one needs to address seriously. Is there a significant inter-cultural experience? The role of the active agency of the subject is a significant factor if meaningful transformation has to take place. In an autobiography the individual thoughts are the expression of the mind's journey and it is the hidden voice that cannot always be expressed in conversation finds release.

Gandhi's experiences can best be studied through his autobiography, biographical portrayal in literary writings as well as in cinematic mode. This paper seeks to explore how Gandhi's journey brought about a sustained shift in his thought, deed and belief in light of the various changed locations. Films like 'Gandhi, My Father' critique him. His book *An Autobiography or The Story of My Experiments with Truth* has a vivid account of his transformation resulting from the exposure to foreign locations. The autobiography chronicles the transformation of a young man full of internal struggle into India's spiritual leader. When we read his autobiography, the experiences are manifold and each one is different. Gandhian journey is a transformative experience for the subject as well as for the readers. Gandhi sought to narrate his experiments with truth which would gradually evolve into an autobiography.

Autobiography is a way to organise the story of a life and reflect on the past in order to understand the present. Both Anderson and Quigley justify the need to consider autobiography as a genre because they argue that it is always interesting to know about the actual lives of others. The autobiography is considered as a 'developmental narrative' which orders both time and the personality, a trait lacking in a journal or diary. The author attempts to justify his or her past actions to the reader. Quigley states that a 'related but not identical narrator and protagonist' are integral to the process of self-justification (107). The author establishes relationships to himself or herself in order to show causality. For example, because the narrator and the protagonist are not identical, the narrator has 'the ability to treat the self as other ... creat[ing] the occasion for self-regard and editing ... [Because of] the distance between self-now and self-then' (Quigley 107). These arguments further prove that there is a special relationship between the reader and the author. Both share common norms as the author constantly judges his/her past actions. The narrator speaking in the autobiography 'is always moral, even if the protagonist of the narrative is not' (Quigley 107). Autobiography is also a form of introspection. When authors write about their past, it is not free from emotions. Revealing character's intentions, thoughts, and emotions is another way that the narrator evaluates why events occurred as they did. By explaining what happened in the past, the author is able to express how the self evolved. This makes it a journey of the mind. An autobiography thus becomes either the starting point of investigation or a field force of analyses or both, questioning one's place. It records one's moral conflicts and the implications of choices made by the subject. The approach leads to a wider and theoretical development of issues within their multiple complex manifestations. The autobiography has become a site for critical insights because of its notion of multiple locations, incorporating the contexts of reading and positioning for the subject.

M.K. Gandhi's autobiography is a self-assessment in which he retrospectively looks at his past. The book was published in 1927. It is in five sections, beginning with his birth, up until the year 1921. The introduction reads, 'What I want to achieve – what I have been striving and pining to achieve these thirty years – is self-realisation, to see God face to face, to attain Moksha. I live and move and have my being in pursuit of this goal' (1). In the same introduction, Gandhi states 'a God-fearing friend had his doubts, which he shared with me on my day of silence. 'What has set you on this adventure?' Gandhi quotes the friend's expression of doubts:

> Writing an autobiography is a practice peculiar to the West. I know of nobody in the East having written one, except amongst those who have come under Western influence. And what will you write? Supposing you reject tomorrow the things you hold as principles today, or supposing your revise in the future your plans of today, is it not likely that the men who shape their conduct on the authority of your word, spoken or written, may be misled? Don't you think it would be better not to write anything like an autobiography, at any rate just yet? (1)

Gandhi responded by stating emphatically that he did not attempt to write a conventional autobiography. He wanted to tell the story of his numerous experiments with truth, and as 'my life consists of nothing but those experiments; it is true that the story will take the shape of an autobiography' (1). He wanted his work to be read as an account of his experiments. This clearly makes room for deliberation, after thought and the liberation to share experiences at will, much in conformity with the genre of autobiography. He compels the readers to travel through his subjective experiences which shaped his 'self' and his political career. According to translator Mahadev Desai, Gandhi's autobiography largely written during his tenure in jails, accounts for events from his childhood to later struggles in India. The jail which in its confinement becomes a space to evoke memories, Gandhi set forth his experiences objectively. It serves as a self-portrait of a man striving to bring about change in society. An experiment is an act of conducting a controlled test or investigation and Gandhi's experiments with truth find mixed interpretations. His autobiography lacks self-praise. It is marked by humility and truthfulness. He is harsh with himself, as he staunchly believed in the supreme principle of Truth. The essence of Gandhi's experiments with truth lies in his strife to apply the knowledge of truth to everyday life, to apply the spiritual to the practical at the same time enabling people to conduct their own experiments in the light of his principles. He did it in a scientific spirit. Gandhi's account of his childhood and youth clearly shows him in a progressive, even revolutionary light. His book contains a vivid account of incidents which shaped his thinking and cultivated the innate virtues of truth, honesty, loyalty and punctuality within him.

Experience can be defined as the state of having been affected by or gaining knowledge through direct observation or participation. Jasbir Jain indicates three determiners in the making of the Mahatma –'experience, analysis of that experience and the moral interventions in that analysis' (68). Gandhi narrates his embarrassments, his fascination for new experiences, his exposure to a whole new world, his initiation into public life, his experiments with diet and personal relationships. The autobiography is a formal recording of the action of writing his self. It is an evolutionary process and this is, 'gradual, preparing Gandhi through a constant fluctuation between vanity and withdrawal' (Jain 66). He takes us through his journey of struggles which bring about transformation. Gandhi's experiences can be divided into three segments – his stay in London, his return to India and his experiences in South Africa – which largely shaped his political career. These in themselves offered many challenges and exposed him to subordination and compelled him to work out solutions. In the last chapter he writes, 'My life from this point onward has been so public that there is hardly anything about it that people do not know …' Gandhi did not cover the period after 1920 for he felt that his experiments in that period were yet to yield definite conclusions. His childhood values were largely shaped by the teachings of his mother. On his first trip to England, he recalls having taken three vows – to keep away from meat, wine, and women. Gandhi took these vows in all solemnity and went to England. These vows shielded him from all kinds of temptations during his stay in England. However, as he recalls, during his stay in London he experimented with becoming 'English' in terms of food and dress. He could not savour non-vegetarian food and reverted back to vegetarianism in a big way by being associated actively with the Vegetarian Society. This implies that the will to conform to principles came about as the result of travel, changed location and experiment. His spirituality may be attributed to his mother's teachings earlier in life but his experiments with truth surfaced only after his association with the Theosophical Society during his stay there. He read scriptures from other religions and became influenced by writers like Tolstoy and Thoreau. He even translated Tolstoy's reply to the 'Letter of a Hindu' in 1908. The autobiography also gives insight into how he grew accustomed to the English ways which were apparently very different from the Indian. Adapting to new ways and initiating oneself into a new culture was a long journey for Gandhi.

Gandhi's return from England brought in disillusionment, frustration and boredom as it would be for any youth in search of adventure. The need for a stable means of livelihood coupled with the spirit of travel made him apply for a job abroad. He obtained a one-year contract to work in South Africa. Abdullah Sheth, a rich merchant invited him to resolve a dispute with his cousin Tayeb Ali. This trip resulted in significant transformative experience. It exposed him to British racism of Indians in South Africa. The film, *The Making of the Mahatma* by Shyam Benegal is a moving and powerful narrative of his transformation from a London – educated lawyer to a symbol of human dignity in the face of repression. His sojourn in South Africa shaped his thinking and widened his vision for a free India. Railways enjoyed a special place in Gandhi's journey of life, be it an inspiration for a struggle for human rights, evolution of an ideology, a measure to connect with the masses or his last destination unaffected by its surroundings. Even the most compelling scene of the film 'Gandhi' by Richard Attenborough symbolically begins with Gandhi's last journey and switches back to his shattering travel experience of being thrown out of the train carriage in Pietermaritzburg in South Africa just because of his colour, a scene, an experience which proved to be the turning point in Gandhi's life. The experience, experiencer and the changed location unite to act as 'a therapy for personal change' (Ross 54). The act of being thrown out of the compartment and forced to spend hours at the platform filled him with courage in the face of adversity. 'The travelling self thus creates firm ground to explore the dependency and intertwine with other selves,' as Melita Rechter states. Most of the biographers see this incident as a landmark in the transformation process that is, making of the Mahatma. South Africa is the country where Gandhi realised the vocation of his life. Travel in South Africa mostly, travel by trains, shaped Gandhi's fearlessness. He gradually matured from a reticent youth to a thinking, acting person. Repeated insults made him more and more defiant. Shyam Benegal, in *The Making of the Mahatma* shows Gandhi reading scriptures of all religions as The Koran and The Bible. Insights from these scriptures and quotes from the Bible as 'Forgive them for they know not what they do,' help him brave the insulting remarks like, 'filthy, black bastard' and bear the shiver and cold at the station all night. He also stoically faces the insults hurled while travelling by coach and walking by the pavement reserved for the whites. The film *Gandhi My Father* also has a similar scene in which Gandhi is thrown out of the carriage as his first experiment with passive resistance. The novel *Pehla Girmitya* gives a detailed account of Gandhi's nightmare at the station while it portrays the innate humanity of two *coolies* who spent the whole night taking care of Gandhi's belongings. Gandhi is defiant as he insisted on travelling by the same class because he had a valid pass. This incident gave him a vocation which was to serve people and to eliminate social discrimination in the country. He succeeded in bringing about reconciliation between the discordant cousins by persuading them for reconciliation. His ability to unite people is exemplified in another incident where he urges them to sweep the streets themselves in Pretoria, as a protest against racial discrimination. The success of this experiment in adopting non-violent means paved the way for several strategies which Gandhi adopted in later struggles both in South Africa and in India. Another incident which Gandhi states 'served as a catalyst for his activism' was the order to remove his turban in the courtroom on 22 August 1894. He refused to obey and opted to go out of the courtroom as it was a matter of national honour for him. But later when he registered as a barrister in South African, he removed the turban when asked to do so. This act was in conformity to the laws of the country. Later he took up the cases of Balasundaram and Jaduvanshi, two indentured labourers, ill-treated by their masters. He took up cases that dealt with inhuman treatment and racial discrimination. Gandhi resolved to actively participate in the civil rights movement which shaped his role as a leader in the making as is evident from his characteristic style of speech delivered at the Natal Indian Congress in 1894. He matured from a hesitant speaker to one who made wide impact. Transformation of the individual and transformation of society were inseparable for Gandhi. On the one hand, revolutionary social principles concentrate on changing the society while on the other, spiritual seekers concentrate on changing the inner self. Gandhi not only bridged the gap between these two extremes, but also fused them together. He was both a saint and a social revolutionary. Unity of life was the utmost Truth for Gandhi. His principle of non-violence stemmed from this conviction. Non-violence was a matter of faith which he applied to all departments of individual and social life. He despised aggression which is why he considered Gopal Krishna Gokhale his political Guru. He made the doctrine of non-violence, dynamic and creative and vouched for a civilisation to be built on the basis of non-violence alone. That is why he abandoned all resistance which turned violent in course of his struggle for freedom.

Travelling by train back home was in contrast a pleasant experience as Gandhi recalls the assistance offered by the authorities when he returned to India in 1896 for a brief period. He travelled back to South Africa for his mission was yet unfulfilled. His act of publishing a pamphlet further angered the white regime and he was pelted with stones and eggs when he returned with his wife and children. His stay in South Africa saw him blossoming into a journalist and author, leader and administrator. He assayed in London to equip himself with authorial skills however one would agree with Naik that 'none of these were marked by any literary distinction' (55). In addition to the launching of a journal *The Indian Opinion*, his pamphlets 'An Appeal to Every Briton in South Africa' (1895), 'The Indian Franchise' (1895) and 'Grievance of the British Indians in South Africa' created a great impact. The continuation of *The Indian Opinion* was in itself an experiment. Raising funds and maintenance of the printing press and equipments was a mammoth task. As Gandhi believed that 'the aim of journalism is service, not commerce' (*The Making of the Mahatma*), he experimented in practising economy to manage the newsletter which was the 'Indian Voice'. In South Africa Gandhi's battle for self-respect for the Indians found him experimenting with trust and betrayal. He reposed trust with General Smuts on the registration issue only to be betrayed and this action angered his fellowmen. Learning from this experience he sought a written statement when called for negotiation on the miners' strike and marriage registration issues. But as a goodwill gesture, he even presented a pair of sandals, made by him while in prison to the

General. As he announced his decision to leave for India, General Smuts expressed his concern for the British regime in India.

Gandhi, My Father (2007), is based on the biography of Harilal Gandhi, titled *Harilal Gandhi: A Life* by Chandulal Bhagubhai Dalal and examines the personal life of Gandhi. It is based on the theme that Gandhi managed to save the soul of the nation, but failed to save the soul of his son. It recounts his tumultuous relationship with his eldest son, Harilal who is presented as a troublesome offspring and who rebels against his father's aspirations only to suffer at the hands of the very society he tried to liberate. He is a case of parental neglect because Gandhi, who sees family ties as inimical to his mission, denies Harilal both his love and formal education. Although Harilal yearns to become a barrister like his father and earn fame and money, he is sacrificed to Gandhian principles. He is sent to battle against the oppressive South African authorities. As Gandhi's reputation soars both in South Africa and in India, Harilal's morale sinks. He strives to please his father in vain. His business schemes fail, he takes to drinking, is convicted of fraud and his wife with the children leaves him. He converts to Muslim faith, reverts back to Hinduism and is disowned by his parents. He dies in a Bombay hospital on 19 June 1948. The movie shot in South Africa and in several Indian cities including Mumbai and Ahmedabad seeks to portray Gandhi in a more vulnerable and humane light and brings out the price which Gandhi paid for the cause of humanity. The historical backdrop of Gandhi's struggle for humanity at the expense of his family is conveyed in both these films through scenes like Gandhi forcing Kastur to clean the chamber pot, his decision to practice abstinence in the prime of his youth, participating in the Boer war, refusing to give Kastur beef tea as medicine, forcing the simplistic farm life upon them and his perpetual state of dissatisfaction with Harilal. In *The Making of the Mahatma,* Kastur calls Gandhi 'a hard, uncaring man'. The director of this film also authored a play, *Mahatma vs. Gandhi*, which had a similar theme but was quite different from the film.

Gandhi undertook a long train journey to experience people's hardships despite having the privilege of travelling in special compartments in India. His first journey was from Calcutta to Rajkot with stopovers at Varanasi, Agra, Jaipur and Palanpur. The amount spent on the whole journey was a meagre sum of thirty one rupees, but it made him aware of the plight of an average Indian.

His experiences while travelling through India convinced him of the need for Swaraj. In one of the letters to the editor of *The Leader* Gandhi expressed his concern for people travelling in third class compartment under pathetic conditions. Though travelling through India brought him face to face with the masses and grim realities of their life and this went a long way in shaping his political ideologies yet in *Hind Swaraj* his seminal work, he expressed that the railways, lawyers and doctors had impoverished the country and railways had a great role in enslaving the country. His insight into the economic condition of farmers is also attributed to the railways. He further calls it a dangerous institution. According to him, 'If we do not rush about from place to place by means of railways and such other conveniences, much of the confusion that arises would be obviated' (24). But Gandhi used the rail to traverse the length and breadth of the country to align with ordinary people. The ugly face of colonialism which he witnessed gave him the required attributes to further the cause of independence. Ironically, it was a third class compartment which carried his ashes to Allahabad in 1948. The space of the compartment thus assumes a special place in Gandhi's journey through life, be it an inspiration for a struggle for human rights, evolution of an ideology, a measure to connect with the masses or his last destination unaffected by its surroundings. Of the several non-violent agitations which Gandhi led was the Salt march to Dandi in 1930. This travel by foot, covering four hundred kilometres from Ahmedabad to Dandi, aroused the masses. Travel in this case goes beyond the purview of individual experience to become a collective one. Raja Rao and Mulkraj Anand have also depicted these non violent incidents of collective experience in their literary writings.

For Gandhi the very act of experiment with truth was a difficult, arduous journey for the soul. It was truly an eternal journey for a man seeking his own little 'paradise', which could be discovered with self-realisation. Sabarmati ashram, though static becomes a space of transformation, a place for training for National service for the community and the country. His ashrams were energising centres and training grounds for civil disobedience, non-cooperation and 'satyagraha' campaigns. This space symbolised the nation in miniature. His first ashram was established in December 1904 after eleven years since he first came to South

Africa. During an overnight train journey from Johannesburg to Durban he read Ruskin's *Unto This Last* which influenced his thinking. He immediately resolved 'to change [his] life in accordance with the ideals of this book'. (273–75). He established an agriculture settlement on an area of 100 acres, fourteen miles from Durban, Natal's largest city and its principal port. Known as the Phoenix settlement, it 'marked an important stage in Gandhi's progressive self-disentanglement from city life and from the ordinary circumstances of secular life' (273–75). *The Making of the Mahatma* shows how the people in the settlement led simple lives by doing their own work. They did not earn wages. In 1910, Gandhi founded Tolstoy Farm, an ashram for satyagrahis. Located in the Transvaal, 21 miles from Johannesburg near Lawley, its 1100 lush acres were donated by Herman Cullenbach from Germany and a young Jewish intellectual Polak from England. The three young men, Gandhi, Polak and Cullenbach, quickly became intimate friends. Along with the two Jewish immigrant intellectuals, Joseph Doke is frequently credited with deeply influencing Gandhi's early thought and practice. Of the Satyagraha ashram, Gandhi said that it 'set out to eliminate what it thought were defects in our national life' (509). His travel and stay at Sevagram can be equated with the journey of the Buddha, an enlightened mind, in search of Truth. Gandhi's visit to the Kumbha mela prompted him to impose certain acts of self-denials. Travel can evoke the idea of cultural assimilation too. During a brief passage through France in 1931, Gandhi witnessed Ravi Shankar's first ever performance on the sitar on 3 March and his brother Uday Shankar's dance performance. The success of these performances convinced Gandhi of the potential of Indian spectacle in Europe. He saw 'Charkha' as a representative of national identity and a symbol of empowerment.

Transformative travel can be defined as the journey of self discovery. 'Transformation on account of travel thus becomes a dynamic, socio-cultural and uniquely individual process which involves choice' as stated by Susan Ross (53). In *A Tale of Two Cities,* Dickens asserts his belief in the possibility of resurrection and transformation, both on a personal level and on a societal level. This is possible when the traveller immerses himself in the new culture stepping outside the known and the familiar. Ward very rightly remarks that transformative travel involves attitude more than the actual act of travelling. Ross believes,' It's an attitude of being open to new people, new ideas, new cultures; a willingness to let go of assumptions, judgments and pre-conceived ideas. Most of all, it is being ready – and even more than ready, eager – to allow yourself to feel your experiences and let them change you'. One would agree with Ross's observation that 'Transformative travel renders a sustained shift in the form of one's thinking, doing, believing or sensing due to the novelty of the intersection between the experience, the experiencer and the experiencer's location in time (54). On the therapeutic uses of transformative travel Kottler states, '... no other human activity has a greater potential to alter your perceptions or the ways you choose your life' (24).

Gandhi's ideas, ideals, and methods of practice developed organically, in relation to real-life influences and travel experiences. Accounts of his transformative experience throughout his life impart a new understanding of Gandhi – not as a saint or as a person who was somehow 'different' from the rest of us, but as a person who responded with immense creativity and conviction to the challenges of his time.

References

Anderson, Linda. *Autobiography: The New Critical Idiom*. New York: Routledge, 2001.

Dickens, Charles. *A Tale of Two Cities.* New Delhi: Penguin Books, 2007.

Gandhi, M.K. 1927. *An Autobiography: My Experiments with Truth*. trans. Mahadev Desai, Ahmedabad: Navjivan Publishing House, Reprinted 2008.

——. 1938. *Hind Swaraj.* Ahmedabad: Navjivan Publishing House, Rpnt. 2008.

——. *Third Class in Indian Railways and Other Essays.* Google ebooks Web Source www.floatingpress.com2009, viewed on 18 June 2012.

Giriraj Kishore, Acharya. *Pehla Girmitya* (Hindi). New Delhi: Jnanpeeth, 1999.

Jain, Jasbir. 'The Difficulty of Writing/Reading the Self' in *Literary Constructs of the Self.* Eds. Santosh Gupta and Mini Nanda. Jaipur: Rawat Publications, 2010, pp. 63–80.

Kottler, J. A. 1998. 'Transformative Travel'. *The Futurist, 32* (3), pp. 24–29.

Man, Paul de. 'Autobiography as Defacement', in *Deconstruction: A Reader*. Ed. Martin Mcquillan. Edinburgh: Edinburgh University Press, 2000.

Naik, M.K. *A History of Indian English Literature*. New Delhi: Sahitya Akademi, 1982.

Quigley, Jean. *The Grammar of Autobiography: A Developmental Account*. Mahwah, NJ: Lawrence Erlbaum Associates, Inc., 2000.

Ross, Susan. 'Transformative Travel: An Enjoyable Way to Foster Radical Change', *ReVision*, Vol. 32, No.1

Ward, Mariellen. Web Source http://www.BreatheDreamGo.com. Viewed on 20 June 2012.

Filmography

Making of the Mahatma. Dir. Shyam Benegal. Perf. Rajit Kapoor, Pallavi Joshi.

Gandhi. Dir. Richard Attenborough. Perf. Ben Kingsley, Rohini Hattangadi, Roshan Seth.

Gandhi: My Father. Dir. Firoze Abbas Khan. Perf. Akshaye Khanna, Darshan Jariwalla, Shefali Shah.

7 Dynamics of Evolutionary Reflections

A Study of Iqbal's Select Urdu Poems

Samina Khan

> One has to make a great journey of transformation to realise that divine spark which Iqbal calls *Khudi* (selfhood). (*Stray Reflections*).

Iqbal, as Nicholson observed, is a man ahead of his age. Obvious at times he seems to be in disagreement with his age. The statement aptly discloses the temperament and philosophical urges of the poet. The Sufi tradition was the main dominating influence on the cultural and intellectual life of the then society. Iqbal received the same impression from his father Noor Mohammad, who was a saintly man and used to move mostly in the company of sufies. Before 1905, Iqbal too reflected the same mystic and existential approach to life and poetry. Allama Mohammad Iqbal went to Europe for academic advancement, he studied there for three years from 1905–08 and acquired a law degree at Lincoln's Inn, a Bachelor of Arts degree at Cambridge and Doctor of Philosophy at Munich University. About his stay and academic ventures at Munich, Germany, Iqbal records passionately, 'Germany was a second home to my spirit: I learnt much and thought much in that country. The home of Goethe has found a permanent place in my soul' (*Stray Reflections*). This tour to Europe refined his intellect and widened his mental horizon. Upon his return from Europe in 1908, Iqbal embarked upon a career in law, academics and poetry.

He was highly impressed by the action–oriented Western society. This reminded him of his own community's (Muslims) stagnation and thus his idea of Sufism or Mysticism underwent a radical change. Here one should not forget that though Iqbal drew inspiration from the works of English authors and teachers, his background was essentially Islamic. Iqbal wanted to bring the life giving waters of love to the arid intellectualism of the West and dynamics of the Western life to the static and often ascetic Eastern view of life. This change in his attitude for Sufism was the result of the gospel of everlasting activity which he wished to preach to his fellow men. It was the education received in the west that enabled Iqbal to arrive at a correct and more vital interpretation of the Quran. With the vital illustrations of the Quran, Iqbal explained the uselessness of traditional Sufism. It was not only his visit to the west but the impact made Iqbal aware that in the path of his vital urge for dynamics; the concept of Sufism was a main hindrance. In addition, it was not in harmony with the real spirit of the Quran as well.

Iqbal is a poet of love, passion and *Ishq* which is the most emphatic aspect of Sufism. Sufi cults stress the need of frenzy and madness of love for union with God. They refute the claims of 'Reason' for the seeker's approach to the infinite. Iqbal here too objects the negation of reason *Aql*. Love is not baseless emotion or madness in Iqbal, it is a passion to lead a life of action and purpose. Iqbal was an admirer of the active and practical Sufism of Rumi. Poetry and philosophy coexist in Iqbal. His contact with the western vitalistic philosophy of Henry Bergson helped him save Sufism to be reduced to an objectless philosophy of contemplation through his popular poetry as a blend of passion and intuition. Here it is in the fitness of things to record that Iqbal only attacked the ascetic, world neglecting and life destroying theory of Sufism. The real sufistic order, according to Iqbal, is dynamic, pragmatic and inspired by spiritual vision. It does not ignore the natural motives before humanity and aims at evolving a civilisation which is socially just, aesthetically beautiful and spiritually integral.

In 1905 Iqbal travelled to England for higher studies. He studied philosophy and passed out with distinction. From there he went to Germany and received a doctorate for his work 'The Development of Metaphysics in Persia' from Munich University. Iqbal qualified as a barrister from Lincoln's Inn, London, and was called to the bar in 1905. While in Europe, Iqbal was so occupied with his studies that he got little time to write poetry. Iqbal, at one stage thought of giving up poetry altogether, calling it a 'useless pastime'. Instead, he wanted to be active in the overall upliftment of the Muslims. Sir Abdul Qadir and Sir Thomas Arnold convinced Iqbal that the kind of poetry he was writing could contribute greatly in the well being of his country and community. Iqbal started writing in Persian after he came back from England.

Iqbal visited London to attend Second Round Table Conference in 1931, on his way back, he attended World Muslim Congress in Jerusalem in 1932, and he went back to London to attend Third Round Table Conference. After the conference he reached Paris, where he met Bergson, whose philosophy influenced him a lot. He visited Spain and from there he went to Italy. He met Mussolini and wrote a poem in which he saw a saint and devil combined in him. Iqbal had settled permanently in Lahore after his return from Europe. His following remark shows his indebtedness to them:

> Nietzsche was more negative and destructive while Bergson was more positive and constructive, Bergson's emphasis on the deeper levels of consciousness, or in other words, on the spiritual inwardness of human life and the part which intuition plays in bringing into play this dynamic experience that fascinated Iqbal. (Dar 39)

The years in Europe opened up new horizons to Iqbal. He saw for himself the great material and scientific progress that ruled such large parts of the world. At the same time, however he witnessed the dangers that Europe passed to the Eastern and Islamic culture. He saw also the superficial hedonism of leading circles in Europe and the growing gap between ideals of Christianity – of charity and love – and the daily life of individuals and communities. Capitalism had lost its progressive character and had become blatantly imperialistic. The nations of Europe were engaged in a fierce struggle against one another in their efforts to subjugate new territories. Nationalism and patriotism were being used to occupy and exploit the backward nations of the world. Iqbal supplied a ruthless critique of the western civilisation and considered German fascism as a product of these ideas. Iqbal summed up his reaction:

Tumhari tehzeeb apne khanjar se aap khudkushi karegi,
Jo shaqe – nazuk pe aashiyana banega napayedar hoga.
(Salil 20 Introduction)

Your civilisation will commit suicide with its own sword
The nest built on delicate bough is bound to fall.

Dayare magrib ke rehne waalon Khuda ki basti dukaan nahin hai
(Salil 20 Introduction)

You, the people of the West, God's kingdom is not a place of trade.

Iqbal's poetry transacted a vision of Islam that was not confined to national boundaries. Pan Islamic, global and human concern was the message of the East. Tarana-e-Hind *Saare Jahan Se Achcha* composed before his visit to Europe Iqbal mentions,

Mazhab nahi sikhata aapas mein bair rakhna
Hindi hain hum vatan hai Huindustan hamara
(*Kulliyat-e-Iqbal* 83).

Religion does not teach us to bear ill-will among ourselves
We are of Hind, our homeland is Hindustan

After he returned from Europe the reconstructed version of Tarana-e-Hind was released as Tarana-e-Milli (1910) in which he alters the tone by referring,

Chino Arab Hamara, Hindustan Hamara,
Muslim Hain Hum, Watan Hain Sara Jahan Hamara.
(*Kulliyat-e-Iqbal* 159)

China and Arabia are ours, Hindustan is ours,
We are Muslims, the whole world is our homeland.

Iqbal's stay in Europe was a watershed in the growth and development of his mind. He had drunk deep on the fountain of Eastern and Western thoughts, and as his talent gathered form, depth, beauty and majesty, his writing became a vehicle for humanistic urges. In this sense he is a secular poet. According to Sarojini Naidu, Iqbal's best poetry is essentially humane and touching. It strikes a deep cord in man's heart and mind. His great poetry is judged on the highest artistic standards. Some of his longer poems like '*Khizr-e-Rah*' (The Torchbearer), '*Shama aur Shayar*' (Flame and The Poet),

Masjid-e-Qurtaba (The Mosque of Cordoba) and *Waalda Marhooma Ki Yaad Mein* (Dedicated to the Memory of My Mother Who Passed Away) dealing with lofty themes, bring to our mind the grandeur of Milton. They carry the full soul force of the poet. According to A.J. Arberry both Milton and Iqbal are poet Prophets.

After his return from Europe, when Iqbal was writing mainly in Persian, he was persuaded to write in Urdu for the masses. His first collection of Urdu poetry *Bang-e-Daran*, (The Sound of Bells) appeared in 1924. The book has three parts, the first part contains poems which he composed before he left for Europe in 1905, the second part contains poems which he wrote during his stay in Europe and the third contains the poems written after he returned from Europe. *Bang-e-Daran* was followed by *Bale-e-Jibrail* (The Wings of Gabriel) in 1935 and *Zarb-e-Kalim* (The Staff of Moses) in 1938 published after his death.

It is surprising that in his early poetry Iqbal was attracted by platonic and neo-platonic philosophical attitudes. But even while dealing with this neo-platonic attitude in his poetry, Iqbal reflects a great affinity with the kinetic imagery and moving symbols of traditional Persian and Urdu verse style. His constant mention of yearning, restlessness, burning and discontentment with the limited scope of human desires establish him to be a poet of vital possibilities and greater promises for the future of mankind. It is not passive but active prophecy that creates history. This poetry tends to release in the soul a productive process for the growth of human consciousness. Poetry, for centuries has been a vehicle of information and the poet has also functioned as a preacher, a prophet, a thinker and a journalist. But Iqbal invested the traditional poetic images with a new revolutionary content and intended to establish the poet as a commentator and initiator of life in all spheres of understanding. Neo-platonism in his poetry does not lead to 'quitism' or stasis. On the contrary, one becomes vehemently aware of the yearning and questful nature of his inner self as evident by this couplet from his lyrical poem *Ishq aur Maut,*

> *Kahin shaakh-e-hasti ko lagte the patte*
> *Kahin zindagi ki kali phoot ti thi*

(*Kulliyat-e-Iqbal* 57)

Somewhere twigs of life bear leaves
Somewhere life's bud sprouts

This quest is discernible in his noteworthy poems of the early phase ' Himalaya', *Gul-e-Rangin* (Colourful Flowers) ' Mirza Ghalib', *Aql-o-Dil* (Reason and Heart), *Sada-e-Dard* (The Echo of Pain), *Aftab* (Sun), *Mah-e-Nau* (New Moon), *Ishq aur Maut* (Love and Death), *Mauje-Dariya* (Waves of the River), *Chand* (The Moon).

Thus the poem of the first section of the collection *Bang-e-Daran* (The Sound of Bells) written till 1905, which have been discussed so far reflect a peculiar kind of unity of themes and repetition of the same wandering spirit in search of absolute truth of life. The collective significance of the titles, *Jughnu* (Glow Worm) *Chand* (The Moon), *Abr* (Cloud), *Sitare* (Stars), *Parinda* (Bird), *Bachcha* (The Child), etc. is self evident. They symbolically unmask the poet's urge for freedom, knowledge, and light in this world. These poems which belong to his early poetic ventures, show Iqbal's temperamental vitalism and creative urge to interpret life.

Iqbal seems to be moving ahead to achieve a more deliberate vitalism of a philosophical nature in the second section of *Bang-e-Daran*. These poems belong to the period when Iqbal was exposed to the western thinkers during his visit to Europe. His outlook on life underwent two important changes about this time: he conceived an utter dislike for the narrow nationalism and developed an admiration for a life of action and struggle. This philosophical idea of vitalistic will has been pronounced in the following couplet,

Hai Daurta ashhab-e-zamana
Kha kha ke talab ka taaziyana

(*Kulliyat-e-Iqbal* 119)

Swift runs the shadowy steed of time
Lashed by desire's whip into foam.

Mohabbat (Love), 'Haqiqat-e-Husn' (Reality of Beauty), *Chand aur Tarey* (The Moon and the Stars), *Koshish-e-Natamam* (Endless Striving), confirm how Iqbal had emerged as a poet of love, action and dynamism. He had developed his concept of love. Though ultimately derived from the Quran and the Islamic tradition, this had been reinforced by his reading of Western philosophy. Iqbal had also been recognised by then as a poet of vision. In fact his poetry of this phase shows a shift of mood and even a complete transformation of thematic concern and symbolic interpretations. Traditional symbols are used with greater precision and intensity. Union, separation, endeavour, struggle, striving, solitude and other themes take a very peculiar dimension in his poetry that was more or less philosophical in its appeal. It is remarkable to note that in his poetry Iqbal assimilates the vitalistic and voluntaristic insights of Schopenhauer and Nietzsche into his own personal vision of *Ishq* (love) and *Husn* (Beauty).

Ulajhne sulajhne mein lazzat ise
Tadapne phadakne mei rahat ise,
Samajhta hai tu raaz hai zindagi
Fakhat zauq-e-parwaz hai zindagi

(*'Saqi Nama', Bale-e-Jibrail* 418)

Life derives its pleasure from tangling and detangling,
from yearning and mobility
You consider life to be a mystery
But it is merely a will for flight

There is a constant growth towards an ideal and greater deliberation and transmutation of experience into the symbolic modes of imaginative traditions. To some extent, there is no discontinuity of evolution from *Bang-e-Daran* to *Bal-e-Jibrail* (The Wings of Gabriel). Iqbal's representative works in the present context where he uses foreign locations and mentions them as sub-titles are *Khizr-e-Rah* (The Torch Bearer), *Masjid-e-Qartaba* (The Mosque of Cordobe, Spain), 'Hyspania' (*Hyspania ki Sarzamin Mein Likhe Gaye, Wapas Ate Huuye*), *Sarzameen-e-Andolus Mein, 'Abdul Rahman Ka Khajoor Ka Pehla Darakht', 'Tariq Ki Dua'* (Written in Andolus), *Saqi Nama* (To the Cupbearer), 'Mussolini' (Written in France) (Ghazal No.41), *'Lenin Khuda Ke Huzur Mein' Zouq-o-Shouq* (Written for Philistine). Iqbal makes ample use of locations and his vocabulary express a peculiar geoscape that fall very close to his intuitions and aspirations to make poetry universal and significant.

Iqbal forms his concepts of '*Khudi*' (selfhood) after meeting Bergson visiting Europe reading his *Time and Free Will*. His concept of '*mard-e-momin*' or '*mard-e-kamil*' (complete man in Islam) too has a close affinity with Nietzsche's superman. Iqbal's superman cultivates a rationally directed self creative will to understand the universe and render his services to be successful in the struggle for existence. The concept appears in one of his representative poems '*Lal-e-Sahra*' in *Bal-e-Jibrail:*

> *To shaakh se kyun phoota, Main shaakh se kyun toota,*
> *Eak jazba-e-paidai, eak lazzata-yaktayi'*
>
> ('*Lal-e-Sehra*', *Bal-e-Jibrail* 413)

> The flower has a passion for being while he himself has a passion for individuality. The root of both is the same

Nietzsche's 'Will for Power' and 'Live Dangerously' appear in many symbols of *Baaz* (Hawk), *Shahin* (Falcon) in Iqbal. Thus, Iqbal's poetry reflected a movement of mind and spirit, an evolution of philosophical nature. The implication of the religious framework that Iqbal brought to bear on western vitalism has been taken into consideration here and his transformation in his view of life had also been discussed. Iqbal's geoscape of mind made ample use of his visiting of places he mentioned in his poems, a disciplined metaphysics of Iqbal reconstructed the classical spirit of Islam and his poetry became action-oriented. His active contact with the Western ideologies made him realise the pan-Islamic vision of Islam. *The Reconstruction of Religious Thoughts in Islam* helped in the rediscovery of the dynamic spirit and will-oriented vitalistic existence of human beings. Fundamentalist's approach to consider Sufism as deviation from Islam was rejected by Iqbal. His poetry made a significant contribution in establishing the passionate and creative energy of Love as the basic spirit of Islam that is enhanced by Sufi traditions and cult. To quote from Iqbal's ghazal '*Kabhi ae haqiqat-e-muntazar*':

> *Jo main sar-b-sijda hua kabhi to zamin se aane lagi sada*
> *Tera dil toh hai sanam ashna tujhe kya milega namaz mei*

> Whenever I bend in prayer, a voice from the earth I begin to hear: Your heart is enlightened with sublimity of love, what'll you gain out of prayer?
>
> (Salil 50)

Iqbal was both a philosopher and poet whose revolutionary poetry was aimed at inspiring the Muslims to get rid of their backwardness. He wanted to reform the Muslim society of its illness and awaken them to the new challenges of the world. Iqbal's message of revolution is meant not only for the Muslims but for the entire mankind, as he was a humanist whose poetry advocates universal human values and self-development, freedom and equality among human being. Iqbal left for us a mystic-human thought and an endless metaphor of journey to the unknown worlds:

Sitaron se aage jahan aur bhi hain
Abhi Ishq ke imtihan aur bhi hain

There are worlds beyond the stars too
And many more trials in love still to go through.

(Salil 40)

References

Ansari, A.A. ed., *Iqbal Essays and Studies*, New Delhi: Ghalib Academy, 1978.

Bergson, Henry, *An Essay on the Immediate Data of Consciousness*, London: Allen and Unwin, 1959.

Dar, B.A. 'Iqbal and Bergson', *Iqbal Review*, Lahore: Bazm-e-Iqbal, 1954.

Iqbal, A.M. *Kulliyat-e-Iqbal* (Complete Works of Iqbal), Aligarh: Education Book House, 1989.

——. *The Reconstruction of Religious Thoughts in Islam:* A Collection of VII Lectures, Lahore: OUP, 1944.

——. *Stray Reflections: A Notebook of Iqbal*, Lahore: Iqbal Academy, 1961.

Kiernan, V.G. *Poems from Iqbal*. London: John Murry, 1955.

Salil, Kuldeep. *The Best of Iqbal* (Selected Ghazals and Nazms with their English Translation), Delhi: Rajpal & Sons, 2011.

8 Northrop Frye

A Poetics of Seasons

Pooja Joshi

14 July 2012 marked the centenary of Northrop Frye's birth and this provides an excellent opportunity to revisit and explore the arena of Frygian theory and criticism twenty one years after his death. Whenever Frye is mentioned, he is referred to as a Western literary theorist or a myth critic. His magnum opus *Anatomy of Criticism* (1957) too is read and discussed as a text on the theories of literature, specifically 'archetypal criticism'. Doubtlessly Frye is a critic and a theorist and *Anatomy* the most influential work on criticism by a twentieth century author. Yet both Frye and *Anatomy* are much more than this. 'Norrie' as Frye was popularly known among his friends and campus colleagues was a highly imaginative and romantic personality. *Anatomy of Criticism* can also be interpreted as a travelogue in the sense that archetypes travel across boundaries of genres, symbols, images, etc.

In the two decades post First World War critics felt that the isolation of critical thought from the reading public was rapidly increasing. In this scenario 'archetypal criticism' came as a phase of revival to rekindle this bond between academics and the public. According to Douglas Bush, Frye appeared on the scene as 'the chief contemporary theorist' of this phase with his extra-ordinary 'range of active knowledge, inexhaustible fertility of ideas and taxonomic genius' (168). M.H. Abrams places *Anatomy* in the tradition of Kanes, Coleridge, Richards, and others who have reformulated 'literary theory from first principles, in order to accommodate existing materials to new concepts' (209). In Frye's case the new concepts come from psychology, anthropological theories of myth and ritual, and medieval symbology. Frye has explored these theories in the third essay of *Anatomy* – 'Archetypal Criticism', which is the heart of the matter.

Archetypal patterns are most clearly discernible in myth, because mythical stories present a world of pure, abstract literary design. The third essay of *Anatomy* 'Archetypal Criticism' develops this thesis in detail. Here Frye provides an elaborate taxonomy of the structure of archetypal imagery, classifying it from the perspective of both meaning (*dianoia*) and narrative (*mythos*). The diagrammatic framework of the theory of myths, especially Frye's treatment of the basic narrative patterns (romance, comedy, tragedy and irony), is the fullest and most elaborately conceived section of the book. The present paper focuses on the four basic narrative patterns or genres – romance, comedy, tragedy and irony or satire that Frye compares with the seasonal cycle of the year – spring, summer, autumn and winter respectively.

Mythical stories of gods in which characters have the greatest possible power of action are the most abstract and conventionalised of all literary modes for they have space for the highest degree of stylisation in their structure. For the reason that archetypal criticism has larger context of literature than other approaches, the structural postulates of literature are likely to be derived from this category. In this essay Frye charts a grammar of literary archetypes drawing heavily from the Bible and to some extent from classical mythology. Myth, as Frye observes, is 'an abstract or purely literary world of fictional and thematic design, unaffected by canons of plausible adaptation to familiar experience' (136). As realism is an art of indirect simile, myth is an art of indirect metaphorical identity. However, when we use certain technicalities in a realistic fiction of mythical framework to bring it close to the tenets of plausibility we create a displacement.

The narrative is a process of cyclical movement from one structure to another. Success and failure, effort and repose, life and death, are part of this pattern that forms the rhythm of process. Frye identifies the four basic categories of literary narratives: the romantic, the tragic, the comic and the ironic or satiric. These categories are not to be specified as a poem or a drama but as one term to describe general characteristics of a literary work. Tragic, comic or romantic, is also a kind of structure and mood other than being a genre. We employ all these terms as elements of the literature of experience in place of 'realism' here. Thus the four narrative pre-generic elements of literature are termed as a 'mythoi' or generic plots by Frye. Frye's classification of archetypes is based on the natural cycle of the year that is real and powerful. It touches poetic themes, imagery, and characters along with verbal and visual rhythm. Comedy is the *mythos* of spring season because the genre of comedy is characterised by the birth of the hero, revival and resurrection. Spring symbolises the defeat of winter and darkness and arrival of a newly formed ideal society. The most popular source for comic form is New Comedy, provided by Platus and Terence through the plot structure of Greek. Comedy, in the formation of the dramatic story also includes some fictional elements. Very often the story is of two young lovers whose union is objected to by their parents. Some twist in the play marks a turning point and everything is settled through a happy ending. This twist is not a miraculous transformation, a conversion or an unbecoming metamorphosis of character and hence, is not brought all of a sudden. The people in a comedy belong to different societies. When the play opens the opposed party is seen gaining the upper hand and a new society appears on the scene with some development in the plot. The hero shines in the light of this newly formed society and at this juncture the comic discovery *anagnorisis* or 'cognitio' takes place (163). The new society is recognised with some party or festive occasion or even weddings. In Shakespearean comedies the play generally ends with the bells of marriage almost in wholesale capacity.

The action in a comedy originates from the impediments that come in the way of the hero's longing. The comic resolution is brought through overpowering the hurdles which are usually parental. Hence, the fact that comedy is written for the young audience in the theatre. Other than the parents the antagonist may be a contestant who is aged but wealthy. The comic act consists of innumerable characters. Among these the scapegoat ones are exposed and ridiculed to arouse *pathos* but not expelled from the society. In *The Merchant of Venice* however the overdone tragic elements upset the charm of comedy at various places though the play comes to be in a class apart as tragic-comedy. Sometimes it becomes necessary to penalise the characters but the author, carrying the purpose of comedy on his shoulders has to transform the mind of his characters. The comic society aims at inclusion rather than exclusion as perceptible in all good comedies. Many times comedy begins with some absurd or irrational law as the law of compulsory marriage in *A Midsummer Night's Dream*, the law that approves Shylock's bond and the like. Some common tricks are employed to bring the comic discovery such as hero's old nurse recalling his birthmarks or over hearers of communications, etc. Frye suggests two ways of developing the form of comedy:

> One is to throw the main emphasis on the blocking characters; the other is to throw it forward on the scenes of discovery and reconciliation. One is the general tendency of comic irony, satire, realism, and studies of manners; the other is tendency of Shakespearean and other types of romantic comedy. (166–67)

Comedy is generally understood to be a mode of art that ends happily; it doesn't include enmity or hatred of any kind as in tragedy. In comedy of manners, the characters interest the audience for their absurdity. Ben Jonson's theory of the 'humor' attempts to explain this absurdity. The humor's dramatic function is to express a state of what might be called ritual bondage. The character that is obsessed by his humor has to repeat his obsession in the play. But the essence of the humor is that the literary initiation of ritual bondage is funny. The law of repetition is another basis of humor that provokes laughter in comedy. The society that emerges in the final act of comedy produces both social and moral judgments. Though the real life of the hero begins at the end of the play, we are made to believe the popular dictum 'lived happily ever after'. Ideals are left undefined and everything hangs in the air of predictability. Frye feels that it is not necessary that the total *mythos* of comedy is to be narrated or presented on the stage. Often the first phase is simply understood by the later course of action in the play. Finally, comedy restores the current of energy and memory combining everything in a harmonious action.

Characterisation is another important factor that depends on the structure and category of the play. What is Frye's method and structure of comic mythos? It is evident in this passage from *Anatomy:*

> In drama, characterization depends on function; what a character is, follows from what he has to do in the play. Dramatic function in turn depends on the structure of the pay; the character has certain things to do because the play has such and such a shape. The structure of the play in its turn depends on the category of the play; if it is a comedy, its structure will require a comic resolution and a prevailing comic mood. (171–72)

The hero wins his ladylove against all odds at the end of the play. Thus, the typical comic structure exhibits the triumph of reality over illusion. What is real in the comic ending, then, is actually the ideal, even though the nature of the ideal is seldom precisely defined. Spring season is the harbinger of happiness and prosperity. Frye keeps returning to the issue of what the comic action moves toward: the new society created at the end.

Romance, the *mythos* of summer cannot be defined and classified in periodical terms. In any group, society, community, State, or nation, it exists in different forms and shapes and is always looked on with new hopes and desires. The fundamental element that characterises all types of romance in all ages is 'adventure' (186). It involves a series of actions, which is purely imaginative, and this aspect of romance is carried better in fictional works than in drama. Quest is the most significant adventure that provides literary form to the romance. Romance and summer are paired together because summer is the culmination of life in the seasonal calendar, and the romance genre culminates with some sort of triumph, usually a marriage. Frye outlines three main stages for the successful quest of romance: minor adventures followed by a perilous journey (in Greek terms the *agon* or conflict), struggle between the hero and the enemy where either or both, must die (in Greek the *pathos* or death-struggle), and the exaltation of the hero (in Greek the *anagnorisis* or recognition of the hero). This three-fold structure can be seen repeatedly in most of the comedies and the works of fiction. Two main characters, the hero (the protagonist) and the enemy (the antagonist) focus on a conflict that is involved in their quest. This conflict concerns 'our world' which is in the middle and subjected to the cyclical order of nature. Whatever seems unpleasant in the pursuit can be associated with the opponent such as winter, darkness, sterility, old age, etc. The hero enjoys spring, dawn, fertility, vigour, and youth.

The quest-myth is the supreme method to show the displacement of romance and its main form is the dragon-killing theme. Leviathan, a sea-monster is prominently featured as the enemy of the Messiah in the Bible and stands out as a symbol of social barrenness. The Leviathan, Satan and the Edenic Serpent, the three figures in the Book of Revelation serve as elaborate dragon-killing metaphor in Christian symbolism: the hero is Christ; the dragon is Satan, the impotent old king Adam, whose son Christ becomes, and the rescued bride the Church. The Leviathan is assumed to be the complete fallen world of sin and death, and torture where Adam is a victim. Consequently, Adam's issues must get born, live and die inside his belly. Therefore, by killing the leviathan in 'the day of the Lord', the Messiah will rescue us. This theme has been dealt with in many folk tale versions and even in the later stories of Henry James in its most intricate form. Frye identifies two concentric quest-myths in the Bible:

> ... a Genesis-apocalypse myth and an Exodus-millennium myth. In the former Adam is cast out of Eden, loses the river of life and the tree of life, and wanders in the labyrinth of human history until he is restored to his original state by the Messiah. In the latter Israel is cast out of his inheritance and wanders in the labyrinths of Egyptian and Babylonian captivity until he is restored to his original state in the Promised Land. (191)

Water is a powerful element from the beginning of literature. The Leviathan is the sea-monster so he stands for water metaphorically. Being denizens of his belly we are metaphorically too under water. If we go deeper in literature looking into this context we can find the significance of fishing in the Gospels, in *The Waste Land* the impotent king referred to as an ineffectual 'fisher king', many quest heroes as popular and old as Beowulf attain their great feats under water, and even Christ commanding the sea also fall in the same category of symbolism. If the Leviathan is taken to be a symbol of death then the hero's quest ends in the last stage with his death and cyclically it is the process of rebirth and dialectically, resurrection. Thus Frye arrives at the conclusion that the quest myth has one more notable aspect of it other than the *agon*, the *pathos* and the *sparagmos*. This fourth feature is 'the reappearance and recognition of the hero, where sacramental Christianity follows the metaphorical logic' (192). Those who in the fallen world have partaken of their redeemer's divided body are united with his risen body.

In this way, the four *mythoi* of comedy, romance, tragedy and irony appear together as four aspects of a central unifying myth. *Agon* or conflict is the archetypal theme of romance as it is a series of fantastic adventures. *Pathos* or catastrophe, either in success or in failure is the archetypal theme of tragedy. *Sparagmos* or the sense of lacking in heroism and true action leading to confusion pertain to the archetypal theme of irony and satire. Finally, *anagnorisis* or recognition of a newborn society with a hero and his bride corresponds to the archetypal theme of comedy. In romance, the quest for hidden treasure is a popular theme that may imply not just wealth but in mythic terms power and wisdom for the hero as well. The bride is an additional reward in this quest that is rescued from the clutches of another male figure. Prof. Denham comments: 'each of these four aspects of the 'central unifying myth' appears also in the quest-myth which has a romantic structure, indicates that Frye conceives of romance, formally speaking, as the fullest or most comprehensive literary type' (72).

Tragedy of all literary forms is nearest to real life. Frye observes in this connection:

> In romance the characters are still largely dream-characters; in satire they tend to be caricatures; in comedy their actions are twisted to fit the demands of a happy ending. In full tragedy the main characters are emancipated from dream, an emancipation which is at the same time a restriction, because the order of nature is present. (206–7)

Autumn is the dying stage of the seasonal calendar, which parallels the tragedy genre because it is known for the 'fall' or demise of the protagonist. Tragedy is the study of an isolated individual who is caught in the tragic process. The conception of Greek tragedy is the basis of tragic action which doesn't offer any explanation for anything that happens. The primary motif of tragic structure is revenge that is both powerful and intricate. Nature is conceived as an order running two kingdoms of the visible and the invisible and the tragic hero has to keep the balance known as *nemesis* in Greeks. Still, tragedy can be explained with two contradictory devices: firstly the overpowering role of fate that determines the limit of human effort and the second theory revolves around a violation of moral law. Fate as an element of tragedy is associated with irony and the 'moral' factor is Aristotle's 'tragic flaw' that has connection with something unjust (210).

Paradise Lost is an example of Milton's faith in the archetypal myth of tragedy. Adam is in a perfect heroic stage where the destiny of the gods is under his control. His act of exchanging a fortune of unrestricted freedom brings him the fate involved in the repercussion of the act of exchange. With his fall Adam enters another world of nature which itself is tragic. Frye therefore calls Aristotle's *hamartia* 'a condition of being, not a cause of becoming' (213). Time plays a crucial role: in comedy it discloses what is required for the happy ending but in tragedy the *cognitio* is the realisation of the inevitability of a causal sequence in time. Tragedy and sacrifice are paradoxical in nature: in tragedy we pity the hero who must suffer and sacrifice unites people for something that actually belong to a greater power. The total pattern of a quest-myth is formed of all the four elements – romance, tragedy, irony and comedy. Tragedy may contain comic episodes and comedy can move on to serious action but they are introduced only on episodic levels. The hero of a tragedy stands helpless, miserable and all alone like the barren trees of autumn. Revenge, role of fate and destiny, and passion are some of the vital elements that characterise the course of tragedy in a narrative pattern.

Irony and satire predominate as the *mythos* of winter season. Satire is metonymised with winter on the grounds that satire is a 'dark' genre; satire is a mocking form of the three other genres. It is noted for its darkness, dissolution, the return of chaos, and the defeat of the heroic figure. Irony results out of complete realism of context and the author's suppressed attitude. In satire, at least a minimum of imagination is required to show the subject as weird. The selection of absurdities by the satirist involves an implicit moral attitude. Frye differentiates the two as 'satire is irony which is structurally close to the comic: the comic struggle of two societies, one normal and the other absurd, is reflected in its double focus of morality and fantasy. Irony with little satire is the non-heroic residue of tragedy, centering on a theme of puzzled defeat' (224). The two essentials of a satire are wit and an object of attack. Invective or pure denunciation is one of the forms of satire but we must agree that mere private or even social hatred cannot be expressed, as an attack in literature for the range of words for expressing hatred is too narrow. Humour comes with convention and fantasy. Moving to a further extent, Frye identifies six phases or stages of each of the *mythoi* and they correspond to the adjacent *mythoi* as well. These phases are in fact 'broad narrative movements' to quote Denham's words, 'which extend beyond, as well as cut across, individual literary works' (83).

Frye's conception of how literature fitted together with the myths of romance, irony, tragedy and comedy linked in a unified *rotary* vision is central to *Anatomy*. John Ayre points out that, 'it was a cosmology, a vision of literature as a totality' ('Geometry' 825). Since his undergraduate years in the early 1930s, Frye had been looking for a unified form that would compress key aspects of history, culture, and religion into one vision. He was initially fascinated by Spengler, who had attempted to demonstrate in *The Decline of the West* how civilisations rose and fell in a cycle alike to nature. As a student, Frye thought of Europe's rebirth in a cultural and political spring. In an essay written in graduate school, 'The Jewish Background of the New Testament', he noted:

> The sun dies every day and is reborn; vegetable life dies every year and is reborn; rivers flow continually into the sea but are continually replenished at their source. All art, we have seen, originates in man's attempt to express this rhythm of recurrence. (148)

In the playing out of this rhythm in art, there was an unquestionable release of emotion. Critics attacked Frye on the circle schema and diagrams in the *Anatomy*. M.H. Abrams, who reviewed the book for the *University of Toronto Quarterly* declared, with a touch of sarcasm, that what the book needed was a chart illustrating Frye's schema: 'the whole is reminiscent of the medieval encyclopedia tables designed to comprehend the *omine scibile*; instinctively though in vain the reader looks for an appendix that will open out into a square yard of tabular diagram' (191). Oddly enough, Frye gave every appearance of abandoning the circle schema once the

Anatomy was out. He certainly was 'very cautious about the schema himself. Although he continued to use categories and 'polar' concepts, Frye almost never identified works of literature by his own *Anatomy* terminology, least of all with the numbing array of phases in his Great Wheel '... this was unfortunate because theory free of application is simply unscientific' (Ayre 265).

Although Frye is unable to avoid an element of reductiveness in his archetypal categorisations but he is certainly unique about the theory of myths and the seasonal cycle of the generic phases. Whatever difficulties his theoretical approach presents, it is only to his credit that the study of archetypes has attained such an ordered and schematic structure. Though today 'archetypal criticism' as practiced by Frye and others has fallen out of favour, the archetypes remain, as is their nature. Frye's exploration of the genres of comedy, romance, tragedy and irony and their relation to the natural cycle of spring, summer, fall and winter has proved enormously fruitful. Many teachers have echoed Geoffrey Hartman's view about the usefulness of this concept in the classroom: 'it is empirically sound: it works; it is teachable; above all it reveals the permanence of romance' (126). Commenting on Frye's contribution as an archetypal critic Jean O'Grady observes:

> Frye has sharpened the critic's awareness of archetypal patterns such as the hero's journey, the descent or catabasis, the struggle with the dragon and rescue of a heroine and the eventual happy marriage or recovery of a lost paradise. Unlike other workers in the same field, such as Jungians and anthropologists, he has dealt with these in a specifically literary framework. Largely because of his work, it is impossible for any self-respecting critic today to ignore genre, or to read it without sensitivity to myth and metaphor. (16)

Even today Frye appeals us and holds us close when we begin a study of literature, no matter from which corner of the earth. One is bound to realise that even after such a long period since *Anatomy of Criticism* first came out in 1957; there is hardly any other text that deals with the theories of literature in such an elucidating and convincing manner. Literature is an order of words and there are elements of similarity and even unity that connect and mutually illuminate works of literature. What Frye aims to pinpoint simply is that what literature is and how it works.

References

Abrams, M.H. Rev. of *Anatomy of Criticism,* by Northrop Frye. *University of Toronto Quarterly, Vol.* 28 (1959), pp. 190–96.

Ayre, John. 'Frye's Geometry of Thought: Building the Great Wheel.' *University of Toronto Quarterly,* Vol. 70 (2001), pp. 825–38.

——. *Northrop Frye: A Biography.* Toronto: Random House of Canada, 1989.

Bush, Douglas. 'Literature, the Academy and the Public.' *Daedalus,* Vol. 107 (1978), pp. 165–74.

Denham, Robert D. *Northrop Frye and Critical Method.* University Park: Pennsylvania State University Press, 1978. Web Source. Viewed on 13 April 2012.

Frye, Northrop. *Anatomy of Criticism: Four Essays.* Princeton: Princeton UP, 1957.

——. 'The Jewish Background of the New Testament'. *Northrop Frye's Student Essays. 1932–1938.* Ed. Robert D. Denham. Toronto: U of Toronto Press, 1997. Vol. 3 of *The Collected Works of Northrop Frye.* Alvin A. Lee, Gen. ed. 30 Vols. 1996–2010.

Hartman, Geoffrey H. *'Ghostlier Demarcations: The Sweet Science of Northrop Frye.'* in *Northrop Frye in Modern Criticism.* Ed. Murray Krieger. New York: Columbia University Press, 1966, pp. 109–31.

O'Grady, Jean. 'The Poetic Frye.' *Journal of Canadian Studies,* Vol. 34 (1999), pp. 15–26.

9 The Essence of Spain in Hemingway's Work

Shahla Ghauri

Among a long list of foreign writers enamoured of Spain like Washington Irving, Richard Ford, George Borrow and many more, perhaps the greatest and certainly the most famous is Ernest Hemingway. Hemingway was not only besotted with the country but took it as a central theme in works like *The Sun Also Rises*, *Death in the Afternoon* and many of his short stories which brought him both popular success and critical acclaim.

Of all the places in Spain, the dearest to Hemingway was Madrid, which he first visited in 1923 to experience bullfighting, acting on the advice of Gertrude Stein, and to which he constantly returned for the next forty years. It was during his first visit that he experienced the fervour of Feria de San Fermin in Pamplona. In fact it was Hemingway's writing that made San Fermin the internationally renowned festival that it today is. His passion for bullfighting was such that he stayed at the Pension Aguillar because that was where the bullfighters lived. Although Hemingway never ran with the bulls in the San Fermin festival, he competed in amateur bullfighting competitions. The trip marked a watershed moment for Hemingway, beginning his love affair with bullfighting, an affair that ended when he allegedly took his life in 1961. Although, Hemingway's love for outdoor sports like fishing and big game hunting is well known, his greatest *afficion* was the bullfight and he made himself an expert in it and in the bullfighters and their troupes whom he admired almost limitlessly. His fascination with bullfighting can be seen quite early in the vignettes inserted between his short stories in the volume *In Our Time* dealing with such matadors as Maera and Villalta. The memorable account of Manuel Garcia in the *Undefeated* has close ties with an unpublished story *A Lack of Passion* as Susan F. Begel points out. According to the critic both stories were apparently begun in the autumn of 1924, and both have common sources in the bullfights that Hemingway witnessed at Pamplona, both have protagonists named Manuel. Whereas *The Undefeated* is about an ageing matador whose only gift is passion – his genuine willingness to kill his bull or die in the attempt; *A Lack of Passion* is about a young and gifted torero who does not care whether he kills his bull or is taken alive out of the ring: 'I'd have killed him. Or let them take him away alive. I don't care. Let them take them all out alive' (Scafella 69).

But it was *The Sun Also Rises* (1926) which gave Hemingway a certain monopoly of the bullfighting theme, at least in the English language which he later exploited in *Death in the Afternoon* (1932) where he uses it as a mechanism to set out his view of the country and the people. Besides being what it has often been called a treatise on bullfighting and the bible of the sport, *Death in the Afternoon* is indispensable for a study of Hemingway's development as a writer of fiction. In this Hemingway has made many theoretical comments regarding his method of writing among which the most famous and oft quoted is, 'If a writer of prose knows enough about what he is writing about he may omit things .... The dignity of the movement of an ice-berg is due to only one-eighth of it being above water' (*Death in the Afternoon* 192).

Hemingway's matter and manner were both profoundly affected by his traumatised experience of World War I which coloured his writing right from his first significant work *In Our Time* to his posthumously published novels and other writings. Although in his interview with George Plimpton, Hemingway rejected the 'traumatic' theory of Philip Young, there seems to be some truth in Young's assertion that trauma and wound acted as both cause and effect in respect of his literary productivity (Carlos Baker, 32). It was the First World War that separated Hemingway, as also some other writers, from the genteel and baroque stylistic American tradition. To convey the irony of war through simple, unadorned statements was a choice in keeping with his attitude to language right from his formative years. He wrote, for the most part, in a seemingly allegory manner with a marked allergory for all manner of ornamentation. He adopted an idiom which the peculiar reality of his time demanded but even otherwise this mode of writing was closer to his heart as he had an instinctive preference for a no nonsense use of language. His mode of writing suited most the themes he took up in his works, particularly the nuances of bullfighting.

The main action, which forms the latter half of Hemingway's first novel *The Sun Also Rises*, takes place in Pamplona where the bullfighting forms the central attraction of the fiesta. The festival goes on for about a week where Brett's passion for Pedro Romero, the young bullfighter carries forward the action of the plot. Pedro Romero is the perfect 'code-hero' of the novel. He is a man rooted in the Spanish tradition and soil with the past. He is given a physical identity through descriptions of his physique and controlled movements. He is not given to sentiments and proceeds rather cautiously in his love for Brett and does not loose self-respect in loving her. He is presented as a perfect bullfighter dedicated to his work and possesses a spirit the events of the world cannot touch. In fact, in portraying the character of Romero, Hemingway gave us a picture of an ideal artist, passionately in love with his art.

Melvin Backman in his essay entitled 'The Matador and the Crucified' treats the act of bullfighting as synonymous with the sexual act. According to him, 'both are experiences of controlled violence that demand a tight holding of self until the last moment, then the yielding, merging and flooding ecstacy ... that leads to the climax, the final thrusting' (qtd in Baker 248). But Hemingway's intention does not seem to equate the uniting of the bullfighter and the bull with the sexual act. He himself objected to Waldo Frank's interpretation of the bullfight as 'a searching symbol for the sexual act' (235). His description in *The Sun Also Rises* reveals his devotion to present the truth as it is and also the emotional and spiritual intensity of the fight:

> The bull charged as Romero charged. Romero's left hand dropped the muleta over the bull's muzzle to blind him, his left shoulder went forward between the horns as the sword went in, and just for an instant he and the bull were one, Romero way out

over the bull, the right arm extended high up to where the hilt of the sword had gone in between the bull's shoulders. Then the figure was broken (218).

In *Death in the Afternoon*, Hemingway writes, 'The beauty of the moment of killing is that flash when man and bull form one figure as the sword goes all the way in, the man leaning after it, death uniting the two figures in the emotional, aesthetic, and artistic climax of the fight' (84).

Bullfighting, thus, was a subject which attracted Hemingway right from the start of his writing career. His first writing about bullfight is an article published *in The Toronto Star Weekly* in 1923, nine years before the publication of *Death in the Afternoon*. This early article reveals that Richard Ford influenced Hemingway's earliest writings about Spain and the bullfight. The influence is apparent from the article's title, 'Bull Fighting a Tragedy', a homage paid to Ford's comparison of the bullfight to Greek Tragedy. Hemingway also uses the word 'amphitheatre' repeatedly in reference to the bullring, as does Ford in the two chapters of *Gatherings from Spain* devoted to bullfight. At the beginning of *Death in the Afternoon*, Hemingway tells us that he went to Spain to watch the bullfights because that was the only place, after the war, where he could study violent death, a subject he most wanted to write about. He also came to believe that bullfighting was 'not a sport but a tragedy'. In his article in the *Toronto Star Weekly*, Hemingway writes, 'I am not going to apologise for bullfighting. It is a survival of the days of the Roman Coliseum. But it does need some explanation. Bullfighting is not a sport. It was never supposed to be. It is a tragedy. A very great tragedy. The tragedy is the death of the bull. It is played in three definite acts'. Ford in *Gatherings from Spain* embellishes his theatrical analogy by comparing the animals in the bullring to actors in the play. He calls the bull the hero of the bullfight, 'The bull is the hero of the scene; yet like Satan in *Paradise Lost*, he is foredoomed' (20). David M. Wyatt is of the opinion that while watching a bullfight, Hemingway unconsciously identifies with the doomed animal. The protagonist, Jake Barnes speaks for his author when he says that 'people went to the corrida ... to be given tragic sensations'. The consolation for ironic life depicted through the 'lost generation' can at least be tragic death. Bullfighting, thus becomes a tragedy in the realm of art where the artist is made aware of the precious brevity of life in the face of death. When Robert Cohn in *The Sun Also Rises* complains that his life is 'going so fast' and that he is 'not really living it', Jake Barnes declares, 'Nobody ever lives their life all the way up except bullfighters' (10). Regarding the fear of death as the ultimate test of manhood, Hemingway puts death at the centre of nearly all his works. It is the nearness of death which becomes all the more reason for the Hemingway protagonist to cultivate his personal view of how he has played or misplayed the game of life.

Hemingway journeyed to Spain several times just to watch numerous *corridas* (bullfights). However, 1937 saw him return to this country for a totally different reason. When the Spanish Civil War broke out during the last week of July 1936, Hemingway was a staunch supporter of the Loyalists, helping their cause and covering the war from Madrid as a correspondent for the North American Newspaper Alliance. He translated these experiences into newspaper articles, a flurry of short stories, the 1938 play *The Fifth Column* and his famous 1940 novel *For Whom the Bell Tolls*. He also helped produce the propaganda film 'Spanish Earth'. The political issues of the Spanish Civil War were more important for Hemingway than were those of the First World War. The canvas on which Hemingway painted the Spanish Civil War is very large and densely crowded. Unlike the First World War novel *A Farewell to Arms*, the author has employed here an altogether new technique of extending proportions, associating the Spanish Civil War with the American Civil war and all wars against tyranny. Almost all the characters realise their duty to the Republic or to their own separate band and resort to some level of self abnegation, which again is an entirely new direction in the thematic pattern of his novels.

Besides the novels and the non-fiction work with Spanish background, there are some short stories the action of which takes place in Spain. Almost all the six Spanish stories are narrated in the first person. The narrator of these stories has been identified as Edwin Henry, an American writer, filming the conflict in Spain and showing us the several faces of war. The usual setting of these Spanish stories is Chicote's bar which was 'one of the best bars in the world' before the war. The action of the story *The Denunciation* takes place at Chicote's where Luis Delgado, a friend of Edwin Henry, now turned a Fascist, comes to recall old times. A Loyalist waiter reports him to the authorities. The story ends with the narrator Henry calling Delgado's captor to request him to tell Delgado that Henry, not the waiter had betrayed him: 'All we old clients of Chicote's had a feeling about the place .... I did not wish him (Delgado) to be disillusioned or bitter about the waiters there before he died' (CSS 423).

'The Butterfly and the Tank' is a story, which again took place at Chicote's where a young Spaniard was shot by Loyalist soldiers who mistook his joke of spraying people with perfume from his flit gun as real. In telling the story the narrator reveals his compassion as well as his understanding:

> I took a sip of the gin and tonic water and looked out the sandbagged window and thought of the wife kneeling there and saying, 'Pedro. Pedro, who has done this to thee, Pedro?' And I thought that the police would never be able to tell her that even if they had the name of the man who pulled the trigger (CSS 420).

'Night Before Battle' is the longest of the Spanish war stories based exclusively on talk – talk of an evening and night before battle and Chicote's serves as an ideal place to carry on the discourse. These Spanish Civil War stories are a pointer to the Spanish traditions and values which the people hold dear even during disturbing times.

Hemingway's settings evoke a mood in the reader, which may stand in contrast, or sometimes be analogous with the characters. His geographical descriptions and physical settings show the existence of subterranean currents of meaning and implication, which help understand the psychology of his characters. Although much has been said on Hemingway-heroes and the code-hero, they are not always the true focus of the author's attention. Through his characters, Hemingway brings out his thematic concerns, his vision of life, and above all his distinctive style of narration.

The political issues of the Spanish Civil War were definitely more important for Hemingway than were those of the World War I. In *For Whom the Bell Tolls*, for the first time, we find people, united voluntarily acting by mutual consent for their good and the good of the Republic. In *A Farewell to Arms,* in so far as it dealt with the war, the projection was limited to its negative or unattractive aspects, leading the protagonist to declare his 'separate peace'. The Spanish war novel deals with inner conflicts and the characters' sense of duty. Almost all the characters realise their duty to the republic or to their own separate band and resort to some level of self-abnegation. This is an entirely new direction in the thematic pattern of Hemingway's novels.

The protagonist of *For Whom the Bell Tolls,* Robert Jordan, is an expatriate – an American on the Spanish soil, yet is as authentic as any Spaniard for his love of Spain and its people: 'He fought now in this war because it had started in a country that he loved' (45). He is given the task of blowing a certain bridge, behind the Fascist line. After realising that this might mean death both for himself and for the aged Republican Anselmo, he says to himself: 'Neither you nor this old man is anything. You are instruments to your duty. There are necessary orders that are no fault of yours and there is a bridge ... and you must do it'. Discipline and duty are no longer felt to be restraints, as was the case with the previous protagonists, but rather a means of tying together the community, so that each character experiences an increase in the strength and the resolve to make sacrifices. For the first time Hemingway projected a multitude of variegated characters in this novel contributing to the main mission of fighting for the good of humanity. These characters are mostly ingrained in the soil and in their cause. Sheridan Baker finds the book alive with Spanish characters, each of whom seems to illustrate some facet of the Spanish character:

> Pilar gives us its best, its lustiness, decency, and fatalistic steadiness; Pablo its worst, its brutality and selfish cunning; Anselmo, its simple decency; El Sordo, its bravery and courtliness; the gypsy, its whimsicality (111).

Hemingway's choice of language in *For Whom the Bell Tolls* is also in keeping with the themes emerging from the spectacle of purposeful life. The simple language of everyday speech, with monosyllabic words, which had become a marked Hemingway style, would not suffice for the new material. He had to create an impression of breadth and inclusivity. He, therefore, gave an archaic tone to the language, affecting both a distancing from the real historical background and a broadening of the novel's scope of suggestion. The frequent use of the pronouns 'thou', 'thy', 'thee', not only took the language away from modern English, sweeping it back to the language of the Bible or the Elizabethan era, it also helped the novel's language acquire a tonal effect of spoken Spanish. To enhance the calculated effect, Hemingway used directly and distributed proportionately many Spanish words throughout the book in such a way that the reader could clearly make out their sense. Through these stylistic adventures, the writer has tried to produce the impression of translated Spanish speech in most of the conversation among the characters.

In October 1936, in the hostilities of the Spanish Civil War, the nationalist General Emilio Mola and his supporters besieged Madrid with four columns of troops. Mola claimed he had additional within the city. Explicit mention of the hidden troops as the 'fifth column' was reported in the Fitchburg Sentinal newspaper on 14 October 1963. Hemingway wrote a play *The Fifth Column* in 1937, in which he expressed his opposition to the Spanish fascist regime. In the Preface to the 1938 publication, the audience could hear Hemingway read in a recording that played after the lights went down to start the show explaining that 'the Hotel Florida, where we lived and worked was struck by more than thirty high explosive shells. So if it is not a good play perhaps that is what is the matter with it. If it is a good play perhaps those thirty some shells helped write it'. Hemingway diffidently points out that the play is a product of a specific historical moment and this timeliness may account for its failure on Broadway. Hemingway's love for Spain is also evident from the fact that he gave his voice to narrate the so called 'propaganda' film *The Spanish Earth* written by him and John Dos Passos, made during the Spanish Civil War in support of the democratically elected Republicans.

Andalusia was also a frequent stop on Hemingway's visits to Spain and it was again because of the bullfights. He watched numerous fights in the bullring of Malaga. In 1959, he decided to return to Spain, not only to write a book on bullfighting, but also to chronicle what was known as a 'mano a mano' (hand to hand). These are series of bullfights which pitch two great matadors against each other in an attempt to show their superior skill at fighting. They are very rare occurrences since it is not often that there are two matadors of this calibre fighting at the same time. It was this rarity that Hemingway hoped to capture, originally for a 10,000 word article for *Life Magazine*.

Interestingly enough the *Life Magazine* article mushroomed in size from the originally commissioned words to an unwieldy 120,000 words and was never published. It was reduced to 45,000 words and eventually published as *The Dangerous Summer* in 1985 after his death. The work describes the rivalry of two Spanish matadors, brothers-in-law, and their competition in one season of bullfights. The two matadors were the veteran Luis Miguel Dominguin, the most famous bullfighter in Spain since the death of the mythical Manolete and his opponent, the younger upstart Andalucian, Antonio Ordonez, who was born in Ronda. Hemingway was good friends with both.

Hemingway celebrated his 60th birthday in Spain but this trip was his last. The depth of his love for Spain and bullfighting can be judged by the fact that he had in his home where he took his life, tickets for the bullfights in Pamplona. They would begin a week later, without him. The recent ban on the bullfighting sport by lawmakers in the Catalonia region of Spain thrust a sword deep into Spain's centuries old tradition of bullfighting. The Animal Rights Activists may succeed in completely bringing to an end this blood-soaked pageant that has fascinated artists and novelists from Goya to Hemingway, but the sport has already attained immortality in Hemingway's work.

References

Baker, Carlos. ed. *Hemingway and His Critics*. New York: Hill and Wang, 1961.

Baker, Sheridan. *Hemingway: An Introduction and Interpretation.* New York: Holt, Rinchart and Winston, 1967.

Ford, Richard. *Gatherings from Spain*, Paris, 1849.

Frank, Waldo. *Virgin Spain: Scenes From the Spiritual* Drama *of* a *Great People*. New York: Boni and Liverright, 1926.

Hewingway, E. *The Sun Also Rises*, New York: Charles Scribner's Sons, 1926, pp. 218.

——. *Death in the Afternoon*, New York: Charles Scribner's Sons, 1932, p. 192.

——. *For Whom the Bell Tolls*. New York: Charles Scribner's Sons, 1940.

——. *The Complete Short Stories*. The Finca Vigia Edition, 1987.

Plimpton, George, 'An Interview with Ernest Hemingway', in Carlos Baker ed. *Hemingway and His Critics*, New York: Hill and Wang, 1961.

Scafella, Frank. ed. *Hemingway: Essays of Reassessment*, New York: Oxford University Press, 1991.

10 Microcosms in R.K. Narayan's *My Days* and *My Dateless Diary*

Prerna Vanjani

Travels in the realms of the mind may appear to be lucid descriptions of inward journeys but the fact is that they are embedded with meaning and play a significant polysemic role in the growth of a text as well as the psychology of the writer. Most of these digressions camouflage inherent symbolic interpretations of the inner mind. Despite the fact that the author is the real designer, the movement of travelling is a process which creates a pattern. Travels symbolise any change in the location or geography of context. It is the travels of the person to the geo-scapes within and without that shape his perceptions. Each change of movement in the outside environment provides an opportunity to the writer to discover the depths within his soul. Every journey is unique and it holds a different significance for each individual. The situations, locales and the people involved in that equation define whether it is a journey of discovery or recovery of the soul. John Steinbeck talks about the mystery of travelling as 'A journey is a person in itself; No two are alike. And all plans safeguard, policing, and coercion are fruitless. We find that after years of struggle that we do not take a trip; a trip takes us' (72). A trip continues long after movement in time and space has ceased to occur, as the process of travelling involves expanding of mental and emotional horizons. The exercise of locating, gathering, evaluating and then using available information analytically with the newly felt experience ignites the creative process of any writer. Creative sensibilities of a writer are transformed when the existing ideas are fused with diverse real-time experiences resulting in shaping the memory patterns of a writer.

The writer explores the inner spaces of the mind, through his imagination. He crosses the borders of past happenings and reinvents the present experiences in the mind. Writing about the self is often superfluous, since he has already, in rearrangement and disguise written out the material of his life many times. It becomes a daunting task as it represents not only the writer's life but also uncovers a large matrix of his personality, age, culture and society. Such an exercise unfolds a life pattern reshaped by recollections, omissions and distortions with lucid interplay of memory and emotions at various levels of existence. As Plekhanov has observed 'No work of art is entirely devoid of ideas, but not every idea conforms the basis of an artistic work' (59). Raymond Williams expresses a similar view 'All writing carries references, meanings and values. To suppress or displace such details are in the end impossible' (92). The borderlands between reality and fantasy open-up inexpressible possibilities of discovery. The awareness of other worlds, mapping real spaces, present symbolic cobwebs of memory revealing the fragility of reality. The real, though present seems to be always out of the reach of the writer's brush. Weaving reality into fantasy means that the symbolic order is re-affirmed keeping the real at bay and making the 'Self' interact and survive in the end. Zizek Slavoj in *Looking Awry* suggests that 'ultimate banishment of the real is impossible. The symbolic must always be hooked, onto a thing, some piece of the real (23). The interplay of memory is thus involved in the work of any artist. An artist's own confrontation with social problems shapes his artistic awareness in representing a realistic portrayal of life. No creative work is totally free from the prejudices and preferences of the writer. In all the writings of the 'self' memory plays a significant role. The disruption of time leads to the un-sequential order of incidents. The actions of ones life move forward and backward in an unchronicled order. Spaces in the mind involve memory of the past and the actions of the present to inextricably mix into one another. 'Memory', not only signifies the retention of the past actions and moments which are according to Freud the material of dreams, but also revolves around physical, geographical and emotional spaces juxtaposing feelings, suggestions, interactions and associations. It is the memory that haunts the writer with multiple impressions as he travels through different definitions of reality which are in constant flux. Such an art becomes a collage of segments of the real and perceived illusions thus providing a unique charm to the subject at hand. The writer's uncharted sojourns retrieve impressions from the cross sections of his memory and provide ready material to his imagination. The movement from real to fantasy is so smooth that there seems to be a transparent border line overlapping the real experience with fictional associations.

In the scope of this study, I wish to take up two writings of R.K. Narayan where travels have brought about an evolution of the self and have also given shape to his writings. His vision and his characters have both improved with his awareness to learn from his adventures to distant lands. R.K. Narayan's memoir – *My Days* (1973), presents the evolution of an eminent Indian writer of the twentieth century writing in English language with India as the background. The book registers the simple and uncomplicated life of Narayan and his evolution as a writer when he struggles to find himself in his literary quest. The second text that will be included in the scope of this paper is *My Dateless Diary: An American Journey* (1960). This book was written when R.K. Narayan was 50 years of age when he left India for the first time to travel through America. It is an account of his experiences in America when he spent a few years there.

Narayan's own life story as a resident in Mysore is clearly projected in *My Days,* his memoir. Conscious projections of his life from childhood dreams to the final recognition of his work find a place in the book. The autobiographical outpourings of Narayan reflect his constant urge to unravel the universal riddle of mankind. Most of his characters reveal this drama of life in a largely realistic manner in his work. This memoir speaks of the common and substantial human nature. Narayan's fascination for complex associations, sincerity and deceptions of human life and his keen observation of Indian mentality all find a place in his writing. Thus, *My Days* becomes a running commentary on his life and times as he witnesses it and enriches it with his personal reactions to it. Consciously and unconsciously, Narayan weaves his own life story in the web of activities of social importance. He works through multidimensional levels of experiential boundaries to understand the feelings he has grown up with. The creative urge brings in the written form his fascinating and fictional world of Malgudi and gives shape to a wide plethora of memorable characters. To understand the mind and the heart of this writer correctly it is indeed mandatory to understand the evolution of his self that is in constant interplay with his memory and consciousness. A meticulous study of the novels of R.K. Narayan also holds the same implication. The responses of his characters, their thinking patterns and their preferences in particular situations, invariably reveal Narayan's own commitment to life and his deep connection to Indian values.

R.K. Narayan was born in 1906 in a middle class Brahmin family of the second generation immigrants from rural Madras. Living with his uncle and his grandmother, he had a lonely childhood with only pets for company. He hated school and disliked the system of being prescribed a set of books to be evaluated at the end of a year without giving any importance to real learning. His imaginative mind wandered free to experiment with different forms of reading. His quest as a writer grows with each and every influence of his early life as he points out in *My Days*:

> Tagore's poetry (although I may be somewhat more critical today) swept me off my feet in those days. When I read: 'In the deep shadows of the rainy July,/with secret steps, thou walkest,'. I felt I was induced into the secrets of Nature's Glory. Palgrave, Keats, Shelley, Byron, and Browning also spoke of an experience that was real and immediate in my surroundings, and stirred in me a deep response. Perhaps I was in an extremely raw state of mind. My failure at the examination, and seeing my classmates marching ahead induced a mood of pessimism and martyrdom which in some strange manner, seemed to have deepened my sensibilities. (12)

When he failed in English he was left with one complete idle year and it was during this time that he stumbled upon his interest as a writer. With time he started weaving stories deriving his raw material from almost all his associations and embellishing it with the impressions from his memory. While his mind fed on daydreaming and irresponsibility, his heart found nurturance in the idle contemplation of life with no restrictions of any kind. The license to day dream made him naturally attracted to the freelance writer's life. While struggling to make a decent living he took up teaching as a vocation but with not much success. It was during this difficult time that *Swami and Friends* came out in the year 1935. It was due to his strong association with Graham Greene, an English author and critic of repute that his work was published. The small confusions and dislocations of a child reaching the end of an idyllic childhood and facing the grave task of adulthood find an apt representation in the novel *Swami and Friends*. 'Malgudi' as envisaged by him becomes the new world of 'urbanising India' that Narayan could relate to. While writing *Swami and Friends,* the writer began the Malgudi saga which grew to take shape in fifteen volumes presenting an imaginary landscape. As a prolific writer Narayan further went on to publish thirteen other novels, almost as many story collections, retold legends and various essays after a difficult start. He was totally uninterested in the world's praise and in the prestigious awards and the countless scholarly appraisals of his writings. Narayan wrote this memoir in 1974 in his sixty eighth year.

What is indeed interesting is that Narayan's quest as a writer draws strength from the reality of his simple life. He seems to be un-bothered by problems of political reform and cultural conflict though the undercurrent of all the situations is felt in his writings. Often the realism in his work as in his own life comes to the foreground when people around him acting in situations of social and cultural change do not fit in the newly changed parameters. The petty psychological and emotional identifications of his characters become the readily available raw material for his work. Compared to the writers of his age, R.K. Narayan never posed to be an intellectual. In fact he hated school education the most and was against all kinds of control. He did not like the idea of educating individuals through a system of regular exams in strictly controlled system. His focus was on learning through one's own individual journey. As compared to many of his contemporaries, he followed no literary theory except that every writer should be grounded in his cultural roots so that he becomes an authentic representative of his times and situation. Though most of his work takes shape from imagination, the true inspiration comes from the reality of his life. His imaginative literary talent has made him a natural story teller and his obsession of remaining connected to the cultural roots of India has given his writing style a unique flavour. The contrast between East and West encounter comes alive in many of his works. According to Meenakshi Mukherjee, 'In the novels written during the Gandhian era, we find the East-West theme operating as the conflict between pre-industrial mode of life and mechanisation' (69) while writing the novel *The English Teacher,* Narayan makes one of his character Gajapathy say 'The whole of the West is in a muddle owing to its political consciousness and what a pity that the East should follow suit ' (*My Days* 16).

My Dateless Diary: An American Journey was written when R.K. Narayan travelled to America for the first time. The book is an unusual and witty account of his experiences in America with a miscellaneous collection of his visits to different places in the US spanning over a period of few months. At the age of fifty, when most people have settled for the safety of routine, he has ventured to distant and strange lands to appreciate life in general. Though it is a dateless document of Narayan's journey through America, the stories somehow fall into sequence. His daily travels from one town to another in America are documented graphically in the book. The difference in attitude, as well as the temperament is very clear between the Indian and the Western mindset. Though most of his other work depict Indian society, its customs, traditions, culture, ostentations, superstitions and religious faith, this particular book presents a conflict between the traditional and modern values. Though the two works taken up in this paper present a conflict between the Eastern and Western culture yet the differences seems to merge in the mind of the creator. Narayan points out that 'one has to go to the West in order to come back to the East' (Yadav 28). In this account of his journey, the writer's pen unerringly captures the clamour and energy of New York City, the friendliness of the West Coast, the wealth and insularity of the Mid-West, and the magnificence of the Grand Canyon. The book becomes a record of his experiences on every day themes with America as a focal point with no unifying theme. It makes an interesting reading as it captures small details of places and people. The American attitude presented in an enjoyable manner highlights the stark difference with the Indian mentality. His narration is pleasant and his inquisitiveness towards human sentiments has a unique charm when he effortlessly brings binaries side by side.

The cultural difference between the two countries become evident right in the beginning of *My Dateless Diary* when he draws a contrast between the restaurant etiquette especially in that section where he waits for his coffee in an American self service cafeteria and ruminates about his experiences back home in Mysore (11).

My Dateless Diary showcases a host of delightful characters – from celebrities like Greta Garbo, Aldous Huxley, Martha Graham, Cartier Bresson, Milton Singer, Edward G. Robinson and Ravi Shankar to the anonymous business tycoon on the train who dismissed the writer when he discovered Narayan had nothing to do with India's steel industry. As a bonus, there are wry snapshots of those small but essential aspects of American life-muggers, fast food restaurants, instant gurus, subway commuters, TV advertisements, and American football. It is an entrancing and compelling travelogue about an endlessly fascinating land which stands for a space which is always tempting in its appeal. There were definitely interesting moments and observations, but on the whole the author simply comes across as self-centred, self-absorbed, somewhat denigrating of women, highly susceptible to flattery. Sometimes he is not very 'objective' in his observations. That Narayan was a competent writer can be gauged from the fact that all his novels and short stories, despite being set entirely in the fictional South-Indian town of Malgudi, never seem claustrophobic. That he is a great writer becomes clear when he ventures out of his Valhalla to not just another country, but another continent. This book is the story of Narayan's America. It is a testament to Narayan's humanist philosophy that he did not see what other people often see in America: the greed, the excess, the crass materialism, the disjointed family system. No doubt all this must have jarred against Narayan's strict sensibilities. Yet what he presents in *My Dateless Diary* is the other side of America, the true freedom of speech or religion it offers to all, the entrepreneurial spirit that is the foundation of its very existence, and the breathing space each individual gets being a part of this country:

> Religion is not a thing that anyone can openly avow – Its like one's underwear. You may make oblique reference to it or joke

> about it ... You may joke about God, but that's as far as you go in civilized societies ... Thou shall or Shall not may sometimes have to be elastic. (111)

The shocking difference in mindset is further aggravated in the living style of two cultures. Religion is a serious matter in India which has to be followed with exact minuteness as an ancestral responsibility. The individual quest does not matter. While in the West, awakening of the soul is given utmost priority over social obligations. Though India has endearing qualities of its own, but one of its irritating qualities is its claustrophobic closeness. One is surrounded wherever one goes by a heterogeneous mass of humanity, family, friends, relatives, engagements upon engagements. There is no escape. Indian culture itself does not permit breathing space. It can be seen that his going to America may have been to explore what it is to breathe on a foreign soil. His journey provides him with fresh awareness and creative vigour which is clearly reflected in this travel document.

Both the works of Narayan present contrasting landscapes and mentalities. The tug of war between India and America is on in the mind of the creator as he becomes a converging point. He sometimes uses the raw material from his experience sometimes from his imagination and many times from the present condition of his times. Travels have given him more clarity to understanding human nature. An apt example is when Narayan points out the difference in the attitude between Americans and Indians in *My Dateless Diary* about individual choices of pride and prejudice:

> Americans ... have a trembling anxiety lest they should be thought of badly. We Indians take it as a matter of routine to be roused to indignation when we find India attacked and ... it is never more than a passing indignation, nor do we honour our detractors by saying that we are pained by such and such comments ... it is different with Americans, who seem to feel genuinely pained by ill-informed criticism. (37)

Narayan's grasp of people and situations present the reality of situation in the same light as it exists. Another less humorous but more illuminating account of this contrast between the East and West is during Narayan's tenure as a professor in an American university. When Narayan asks his students to question him about his own novel and not hold themselves back, they rise to the occasion and fire him with a volley of questions about, among other things, gender profiling in his novels; these straightforward questions take him aback and leave him stuttering. And these are not high – schoolers having their fun, but adult students genuinely interested about the state of women in India in general, and Indian writing in English in particular. Would an incident like this ever occur in India? Never and not many Indians will react like this. Thus through the travels Narayan has become more genial in his appreciation of human life in different continents.

C.H. Lewes highlights how art will always have a slice of the real, 'Art is a representation of reality ... Art always aims at the representation of reality, i.e. of truth, and no departure from truth is permissible ... Realism is thus the basis of all Art, its antithesis is not idealism, but falsism' (56). Also Eudora Welty, points out the significance of a place in fiction by arguing that the named, identified, concrete, exact and gathering spot of all that has been felt constitutes the real essence of narrative. The artistic self-consciousness of Narayan compels him to make 'things of truth' from 'things of fact' by adjusting them to the new content. His imaginative delineation of Malgudi does not highlight just beautiful scenery but becomes a portrayal of the entire environment that is country, district, urban or rural location, climate, customs, economic levels, and moral value, intellectual and cultural life. What is indeed interesting is that the place in his fictional writing however artistically and tactfully disguised or concealed is usually the real one, which has a close connection to 'Lalgudi'. This place that has become famous through his novels is a queer admixture of real and the imaginary. It is partly actual and partly a dream country. Thus the writer through mental travels has given shape to a geographical area which has come to breathe a character of its own. Each one of his characters seems to belong to this geo-scape of his mind and is bound by the roots of existence.

Reflecting on the expanse of Narayan's art, the canvas of all his novels is a miniature of the cosmos. References intersecting memory and real experience come in vying forms to present the whole matrix of the creative work. The digressions of the mind overlap with the experiential life to present a composite picture in his work. The story moves forward when most of his characters are subjected to the vagaries of fate and are reacting to fate according to their own perceptions. Apparently it was the real life encounter with *The Vendor of Sweets* and his greedy, unruly son who were in the midst of a lawsuit, when Narayan decided to immortalise them. Narayan is not just a keen observer of human nature but also a person ready to learn from the lessons provided by life. Many a times he showcases his own experiences. *My Days* becomes a running commentary on the episodes of his life. The most famous of his work *Swami and Friends* reflects much of his childhood, his long college days and the beginning of his career as a writer. Yet again *The English Teacher* echoes a part of Narayan's adult life as a teacher. In 1939 Narayan's wife Rajan, died of typhoid. Narayan was devastated after her death and he has described this part of his experience of her sickness and death in *The English Teacher.* More than any other book, *The English Teacher* is autobiographical in content, very little part of it being fiction ...' (150), writes Narayan in this novel, the tragedy of Krishnan in losing his wife is also his creator's loss and the description in the second half of the novel, of Krishnan's communication with his wife's spirit acutely records Narayan's own experience of loss and suffering. As the sorrow of Krishnan merges with the sorrow of Narayan, the author ventilates the pent up feelings in *My Days* and tries to make sense of the experience of life and death:

> Perhaps death may not be the end of everything as it seems – personality may have other structures and other planes of existence and the decay of the physical body through disease or senility may mean nothing more than a change of vehicle. (151)

Narayan is acutely perceptive of the human condition which is often brilliantly funny and always forgiving regardless of the country the person belongs. The simplicity and uncomplicated directness of Narayan's style makes the presentation of his subject realistic. Narayan's unaffected natural sincerity makes him a very straight – forward writer. His memoir and his travelogue, transport the reader into a different world, with no self-conscious style to tempt the way. The man behind the novel is very much at one with himself and his creations. There seems to be no dichotomy between the two roles. Narayan all through his life seems to be graduating to the knowledge of the difference between present day India and its mystic past. Narayan however maintains a constant realistic vision.

In *The Guide*, Raju the protagonist is a saint or a charlatan is not clearly stated. Nor does Narayan want to identify him with a particular trait. Narayan just records the representative confusions of modern life and points to the difficulty of separating the true from the false in Indian spirituality. The rest is left to the liberty of the reader to judge the intentions of the characters and their situations. His works display the Indian sensibility with complete ease. The quest of his characters in different novels is actually his individual quest in the journey of life. It is in fact the discovery of his own self and he becomes one of the favourite writers of the common people who find their own reflection in the novels of Narayan. In spite of being a hard core Indian R.K. Narayan wrote in English. He wrote all his novels with India as their background. In Narayan's own words 'To be a novelist, anywhere, one must have roots, both in religion and in family'.

Much has been written about Narayan's English. What is true about it is that this south Indian novelist has enlarged the frame of writing in English in India. Drawing a comparison with the eminent writers of his age Mulk Raj Anand's provocative style and Raja Rao's philosophical inclinations are balanced by Narayan's gentleness in writing. Narayan's characters project a slice of their personality when they speak. While others were busy writing about Indian freedom struggle and Gandhi; Narayan was busy revealing the secrets of common man's life, in his own style and language. For him English was a way of expressing, he never tried to emulate his western idols but wrote and created forms of his own and became an icon of Indianness. His English was Indian in feel and appeal.

His most beautiful creation is the imaginary town of Malgudi, it is like any small town in South India with beautiful landscape, some recognisable buildings and simple people enjoying sitting under trees and discussing about each other's life, womenfolk celebrate their rituals together and children playing in natural environs. Everyone knows everybody else; any new entrant is easily recognisable. Malgudi shows growth and development with time,

British bring their impressions, to it and the new India brings its own symbols to it. Malgudi is the setting of most of his novels and though he made it world famous as a synonym of small town life of India but actually it is nowhere to be found on the map of India.

Though both the works of Narayan have different background settings, the essence of the journey of the human soul is same. His uncanny imaginative capability and his keen interest in human nature have made him a master of characterisation. His creations have become immortal. Swami, one of the earliest of his characters is the best of the lot. This small boy has a world of his own, he warts to eat, play, sleep and enjoy in the safe confines of his home, for him this means the world, he belongs to a typical South Indian Brahmin family, the description of his home, family and the town Malgudi (first introduction to this imaginary town) give us a feel of South India. Swami is like any of us in our childhood, full of mischief and curiosity, his friends, adventures and outlook towards life. The characters from his pen have kept growing over the years and have became memorable, they could be anyone from a doting mother, to a college student, a school boy, married man, a tortured wife, an unhappy son, a sad father or our very own village postman; all of them had their own peculiarities and characteristics, beautifully sketched and inspired from life.

In most of Narayan's work memory plays a pivotal role and journeys of the past entwine with the present. Almost all of his novels revolve and end around an unfulfilled dream of freedom and the dream of his own enchanted childhood. There comes a point in the development of his novels when his characters finally turn away from the challenges of the self-creation and individuality and seek re-absorption into the orthodoxy of the old Indian tradition. He is a master of miniature as his uniqueness lies in writing from his deep and shrinking world. Through his writings, Narayan has developed a special intimacy with his material which takes him to the deeper and subtler truths that cannot be perceived by analytical intelligence. He is a more accurate guide to the inner life of Modern India than any self-conscious maker of historical narratives as Salman Rushdie and Rohinton Mistry has ever been. His realistic irony is peculiar in his writings as it is rooted not in skepticism and disbelief but in faith in human nature. His portraits imbibe an exposition of cultural radiation. Narayan has tried to search his own self through his varied characters and his memoir *My Days* becomes a compelling account of this development graph. His novels can be seen as social histories or social documentaries echoing the dichotomy of individuality and social commitment in a newly modern setting. As in *My Dateless Journey* he writes about the different value systems between Americans and Indians. In India, joint family system is very important while in America it has no relevance:

> This whole American life is based on getting rid of parents ... A son when marries likes to live independently, and a modern house is so built that except that immediate family no one else can dwell in it without becoming a great nuisance. (113)

Narayan's uncanny sense of comedy and his glowing and effervescent humor are the products of his awareness of the gap between the dream and the reality. It becomes a dividing line between what is and what ought to be. His memoir clearly presents how his fiction invariably suggests a consistent thematic pattern which molds the vision of his protagonist's life. But the reality is that his imagination derives nurturance from real experiences freezed in his memory. Apart from his novels, which are well known and distinguished for their sense of form, his delightful autobiography *My Days* and his travelogue *My Dateless Diary* both are restrained, evocative and exemplify his art as a writer, the writer as citizen. Narayan's subjects and characters are universal and this appeal has carried over years and continues because time and technology can change but basic human nature remains the same and that is what Narayan captures the best. His popularity has surpassed many of his contemporaries because of his simple language and worldwide appeal of plot and characters. Thus, to sum up, R.K. Narayan's contribution to the genre of Indian English Novel has been extraordinary. His simple style, malice-free and infectious humor has made him the favourite novelist of the country. The calm and balanced attitude with which his characters evolve is extraordinary. We see India in his plots, situations, characters and also story. He has become a common man's writer in the true sense, he provides pure entertainment and in the words of Hillary Spurling, 'A treat ... he is an enchanter' (79).

References

Freud, Sigmund. *The Interpretation of Dreams,* Third Edition. Trans. A.A. Brill. New York: The Macmillan Company, 1913.

Lewes, C.H. 'Realism in Art: Recent German Fiction', *Westminster Review* 70. 1858.

Mistry, Rohinton. *Swimming Lessons and Other Stories from Firozsha Baag*. New York: Vintage International, 1997.

Mukherjee, Meenakshi. *The Twice Born Fiction,* New Delhi: Heinemann Educational Books, 1971.

Narayan, R.K. *A Critical Study of His Work.* New Delhi: Young Asia Publication, 1968.

——. *A Writer's Nightmare: Selected Essays 1958–1988*. New Delhi: Penguin, 1988.

——. *My Days: A Memoir*. New Delhi: Orient Paperbacks, 1986.

——. *Swami and Friends.* New Delhi: Oxford, 1983.

——. *The English Teacher*. Mysore: Indian Thought Publications, 1989.

——. *The Guide.* Mysore: Indian Thought Publications, 1978.

—— *The Vendor of Sweets*, 1967, Rpt. Indian Thought Publications, Madras, 1994.

——. *My Dateless Diary: An American Journey.* New Delhi: Penguin Books India, 1964.

Plekhanov, Georgi. *Selected Philosophical Works*. Volumes. Moscow: Progress Publications, 1981.

Rao, Raja. *Kanthapura.* USA: Oxford University Press, 2011.

Slavoj, Zizek. *Looking Awry.* Massachusetts: The MIT Press, 1992.

Spurling, Hillary. 'On R.K. Narayan: Shifts and Fiction'. Encounter, 1983, pp. 76–79.

Steinbeck, John. *Travels with Charley: In Search of America*. United States: Penguin, 1969.

Welty, Eudora. 'Place in Fiction'. *Critical Approaches to Fiction*. Eds. Shiv Kumar and Keith Mckedn. New York: McGraw Hill Book Company, 1968.

Williams, Raymond. *Marxism and Literature*. Oxford University Press, 1977.

Yadav, B.S. '*The Guide:* A Psycho-Philosophic and Socio-Ethical Study.' *Indian Writings in English.* Vol. 4. Ed. Manohar K. Bhatnagar. New Delhi: Atlantic Publishers and Distributors, 1999, pp. 24–28.

11 Geoscapes of the Mind

Unravelling Naipaul's *The Enigma of Arrival**

Jasbir Jain

The Enigma of Arrival is one of Naipaul's most highly acclaimed work that combines his anguish as a colonial with his anguish as a writer. Placed on the autobiographical – fictional intersection, it is actually none of the two. It carries within it several burdens: of recent and ancient memories, of history, of origins and expectations and of dreams and nightmares. Its five-part division is deceptively simple and its classification as a novel is an experimental move. The 'enigma' hides within it the many failures of the 'arrival' theme. In many ways, Naipaul lives out his travelogues in this work. *Enigma* was reviewed by Rushdie, soon after its publication and the review was titled 'A Sad Pastoral'. In this Rushdie expresses the view that the work suffers from a dominant tone of unbroken melancholy and lacks affection for the human race, as it moves from idyllic surroundings to one of decay and wildernesses.[1] Other critics like Richard Allen and Gillian Dooley have commented on the novel's aesthetic pleasures. Allen looks at it as an engagement with European modernism and the bringing together of 'immediate communication' and 'deferred meaning'. Placed as it is between the Modern and the Romantic, echoes from both James Joyce and

*First published in a slightly different version in *Journal of Caribbean Literatures,* Volume 5, Number 2 under the title 'Landscapes of the Mind: Unravelling Naipaul's Enigma of Arrival', 115–124.

Marcel Proust are visible in the *Enigma*.[2] Gillian Dooley pursues a somewhat similar argument and quotes a long passage from an earlier essay of Naipaul's 'On Being a Writer', where he specifically refers to the associative power of words, 'the differing meanings or associations of words, garden, house, plantation, estate', words that carry different backgrounds, self-perceptions and perspectives.[3] Dooley uses Alan, the other writer in the novel, as a counterpoint and the telling of the tale itself as an exercise in self-reflexivity.

In the present paper I propose to look at *The Enigma of Arrival* as an outsider's way of belonging to a culture and the difficult process of this belonging, a process which actually takes place as a geoscape with geographical images mingling with histories, reaching back in time and overladen with multiple experiences concretising the writer's perceptions. There are many kinds of travels overlaying one another. In pursuance of this belonging the different perspectives and experiences of history become significant and there is a constant parallel with his travelogues. Nature and landscape also happen to be major concerns with Graham Swift, a 'native' British author in several novels, particularly his novel *Waterland*, but he does not approach them through written texts or paintings. Again, Kazuo Ishiguro in *The Remains of the Day,* travels over almost the countryside as Naipaul but he places his narrative in the interiors of both minds and spaces. Though an immigrant, Ishiguro does not have to contend with a sense of homelessness that has become rooted in the unconscious of the people with histories of indentured labour. The persistent encroachment of a past on the present, one that can never be erased, leads Naipaul to continue his engagement with his many pasts – personal, family, Trinidadian, Indian and that of a traveller. The to and fro movement, carries a different baggage with it and each repeat trip leads the neat five-fold division to become a manoeuvre that seeks to camouflage rather than to reveal.

Both Naipaul's fiction and non-fiction are, in the main, written through a constant reference to earlier readings and observations. He finds the task of revising his ideas pretty trying. His characters are not initiators of action. They allow things to happen to them. Their energy is spent in other occupations of the mind or of self-indulgence. The posture of being outside all observed reality allows the observer to notice small details, which otherwise as an insider one may fail to note. It also allows the observer to turn himself into a conduit for communicating his thoughts (with commentary), to the reader. All external interventions of memory, recollection, comparison, contrast, parallelisms are allowed to infiltrate. One of the main interventions is the story-book version of a culture/country that he begins with, in preparation for his encounter. This shapes his approach. In his travels to India, the reading of books by western writers loads him with prejudices that form a frame. Later, he turns to primary material, which again is the written word: Gandhi's autobiography, Vijay Tendulkar's plays, R.K. Narayan's novels. *An Area of Darkness* shows a dependence on peripheral writing, *India: A Wounded Civilization* a dependence on literature and in *India: A Million Mutinies Now,* Naipaul gets hold of a book by William Howard Russell, *My Diary in India in the Year 1858–59.* Written by a correspondent of the *Times,* it voices the conqueror's perspective Naipaul finds it 'Victorian and wordy ... the writer is too much of an imperial figure, travelling too easily through a world made safe, and taking that world for granted' (*Mutinies* 393). Naipaul's own identity, as it begins to move towards self-definition, is marked by its separateness from both the white man and the Indian; it is anchored in his Trinidadian childhood in 'the vanished world of sugarcane fields and huts and barefoot children' (*Enigma* 265).

The frameworks for *The Enigma of Arrival* are more complex than whatever he had employed earlier. He works through texts and intertextualities. And, this time, he works with a strong inclination towards the visual. Towards this end he calls forth the recollections of paintings, a recalling that supports an interaction between memory and imagination. Then there is the framework of history, of the imperial past, symbolised by the manor house representative alike of feudalistic remnants and colonial exploitation. Despite its constantly declining state it continues to be the centre around which smaller mortals place themselves –Jack, Pitton, the Phillipses, Brenda and Les, Bray and Alan– all. Each one of them is, in some way or the other connected with the Manor House.

A sizeable portion of the novel is devoted to Jack's garden. This is a periphery of all peripheries and carries within it echoes of the childhood poem many of us may still remember, 'The house that

Jack built'. Instead this is a garden, symbolic of Eden, a paradise that is slowly slipping away. Jack is its timekeeper as it slides into wildernesses. Jack's garden is wild (*Enigma* 43) and is contrasted with the pruned pear tears (64). Placed against the marshy swamps, and the wildernesses, memories of Gray and Wordsworth's literary world are summoned forth. Poems are imagined. Later, Ruskin and William Cobbett also surface in a subsequent section. This garden evokes his imagination of England and its imperial glory as well as the Trinidadian memories of the plantations as places of hard labour. Words, their meanings and their associations change with the shift in context, their signification is unstable.

The Enigma of Arrival begins with the narrator's arrival into this world of the manor house. He has hired a cottage amidst these fields and open country with a river flowing through it, a country of 'flat fields and flowing river' and a walk that leads to a hilltop from where he can get a view of Stonehenge, the heathen temple (3–7). If the flat lands remind one of Graham Swift's Norfolk country and the River Leem, Naipaul's references to a fairytale world take us back to Swift's constant harping on the fairytale world of *Waterland,* Stonehenge is a journey back to Hardy's *Tess of the d'Urbervilles.* The ending of the Hardy novel is unforgettable. Stonehenge, the pagan temple, becomes the site of Tess's capture (Hardy 440–444). Stonehenge is a recurring reference in the *Enigma,* and each time it prods different kinds of memories – the tourists who throng in to see Stonehenge are in themselves a matter of interest to the narrator. The temple gives one a sense of the age of the earth, of antiquity, and of the past (*Enigma* 19–23).[4] At a later point, standing outside himself and the literary act, he observes 'Literary allusions came naturally to him' (189). The past is always close to the surface as he gets involved deeper and deeper into his surroundings. The river bed seems to him to be 'almost something from another geological age' (27); then there is the tenth century antiquity of Amesbury, and tales of Guinevere and King Arthur (280). A constant presence is also the Trinidadian experience. Romance, fantasy and memory together build a collage of myths, legends, literary and visual representations.

The novel's narrative structure functions in a curious manner, like a kaleidoscope where the objects are never stationary, like rings that intersect with each other variously. Divided into five sections, it begins from the peripheries, gradually making its way inwards, only to move out again. The prelude to the central section 'Ivy' is as different from the postlude in its concerns as it possibly could. These peripheries are manifested at several levels: areawise, it is the fringe, class happens to be the worker's, Jack is an out-door person. But this engagement with the surroundings, with Jack (who never really gets the prefix Mr to his name) and his garden, is his first lesson at *knowing*. It is through the garden that he learns to respond to seasons, to the changing gardenscape, to derive pleasure from those flowers that could grow (like the author) in both the climate of England and the tropical climate of Trinidad (31). Here he encounters the many faces of change – the change of seasons, the shrinking area of the garden vis-à-vis the growing one of wilderness, and face-to-face confrontation with mortality. Jack dies. The dampness in the cottage kills him and with this melancholy and illness descend on the author.

Then as he moves on to the cottages, their demolitions and reconstructions, he also sets the ground for the second section 'The Journey'. This journey is a prelude to the arrival talked about in the first in terms of time. Thus, the narrative prelude and the temporal prelude work from opposite ends disrupting linear progression. It is one of Naipaul's habitual interludes of autobiographical confession and analysis, the self-reflexive voice keen to lay bare his innermost dreams and nightmares. The second part is the emotional, structural and thematic centre of the novel just as the third is the physical centre of the grounds. 'The Journey' is about his literary developments, the many journeys that expanded his world and through many a hesitant beginning, wrong turnings, and mistaken withholdings back, taught him to confront his prejudices. He has learnt through being an outsider, ill at ease in the unfamiliar world, and he has learnt through rejections (of his manuscripts as well as his own acceptability), and through self-revisions. During this process of learning, he rejects stepping into a fabricated or imagined world (159), as he also learns that he would have to acknowledge more of himself (167), and finally to grow out of what he was:

> The noblest impulse of all – the wish to be a writer, the wish that ruled my life – was the impulse that was the most imprisoning, the most insidious, and in some ways the most corrupting, because refined by my half-English half-education and ceasing then to be

> a pure impulse, it had given me a false idea of the activity of the mind. The noblest impulse, in that colonial setting, had been the most hobbling. To be what I wanted to be, I had to cease to be or to grow out of what I was. (267)

'The Journey' is a recognition of his alienness, another of the many frames Naipaul employs. This section serves many needs, it helps in coalescing history and memory; it also contains within it the summaries of almost all his works written up to that moment. It works through his dreams and nightmares and his proposed future projects in an embryonic form. There are also references to a travel diary he had maintained on his first journey abroad. This facilitates a double reading of the events: as they were then 'noted' (with all the omissions), and as they are now read with his more reflective self coming into play. The diary, in its skeleton recordings, also allows him to measure his present 'writerly' consciousness using it as a map. His current 'arrival' as a writer brings the observer and the narrator together. Naipaul's acknowledgement of 'objectivity' may in itself reveal several gaps, and cannot be taken at its face value. How much of it is real and how much a façade, still remains a question. His whole narrative style, the inability to get away from the centre of the 'self', is itself a severe limitation. It almost permanently fixes him in the role of an observer obstructing a going across. In *The Enigma of Arrival* as in several of his works, Naipaul is engaged in negotiating the difference between the two 'gazes', imperial and colonial. The first is a controlling image, dependent upon Foucault's theory of the panoptic, the all – seeing gaze, expanded upon in *Discipline and Punish: The Birth of the Prison* (1977)[5]. George Orwell in *Nineteen Eighty Four* (1949) had attributed this control to Big Brother's surveillance. As the colonial gaze is merely stated as a parallel and not worked out by Naipaul, primarily as he occupies a mid-ground, he reverses the imperial gaze by adopting it as a narrative strategy, an all controlling one of characters and narration. This position does not allow interaction, it also does not necessarily empower but it becomes a route towards knowledge of both the self and the other.

The landlord who has so far been hovering in the background makes an appearance only in the third section. The narrator catches a glimpse of him on one of the rare car-rides the landlord indulges in. He is the direct opposite of this man in the fringe. Inherited wealth and social privilege, a protected childhood and a young manhood of artistic talent ... and social frivolity' place him in a different category. The two men have begun life from different ends and are from different cultures. The kinship that is momentarily felt is one based on a shared sense of withdrawal and seclusion (207–209).

'Ivy' is at one level a continuation of all that has gone before, at another level a counterpoint. It continues the narrative through visual art. In 'Jack's Garden,' it is Constable's landscape paintings, specifically the one of Salisbury Cathedral, which form the basis of his narration, in the second section we have the explosive effect of Chirico's painting 'The Enigma of Arrival' – two different kinds of artists, representing two different centuries and sensibilities: Constable (1776–1837), a British landscape painter and Giorgio de Chirico (1888–1978), an Italian surrealist painter. While one makes a visual impact, the other works on the mind and the unconscious. In 'Ivy' it is the landlord's poems of Shiva and Krishna and the accompanying drawings and sketches that form a continuity as well as a response to the writer's presence. Before and after we have E.H. Shepard's illustrations in Kenneth Grahame's *The Wind in the Willows,* a children's book about the wild woods on the banks of the River Thames[6] and Vincent Beardsley's sketches to finally culminate in the mention of Toulouse – Lautrec's (1864–1904) early surrealistic work.

Constable's paintings compensate the narrator for the lack of an ancestral memory as they present him with nature framed in an idealistic perfection. The writer's memories of Constable go back to a third standard reader when he had been first introduced to a reproduction (5). The coming to Salisbury is a homecoming: it corresponds to his imagined sense of perfection; it also provides a standard to use for the gradual decline that is now seeping in. Constable brings the past into the present: 'Shepard and Constable – they had imposed their vision on an old landscape' (203); 'the view through which I walked, was of a Nature almost unchanged since Constable's day' (222). And again the landlord's poems and sketches, the Indian divinities besides the river send him back to Constable and the landlord's messages help to make his settling in the cottage much easier (231).

Texts, writers and artists, become for Naipaul, the means of 'knowing' a society. The 'intuitive' knowledge that comes to those who are born in a culture or belong to it is not shared by the outsider. The 'conscious learning process', as Alan Durant labels the outsider's efforts, is served by a range of resources that include visits, 'expert' native informants, textbooks, and audio-visual and multi-media materials (20). For the native learner a process of defamiliarisation may have to be adapted in order to develop critical awareness, but for an outsider it is this strangeness that has to ameliorated. Constant contrast and comparison also become ways of knowing.

The Enigma of Arrival steps out of the fictional genre, to establish a way of 'knowing' a culture. The writer brings to it his school memories, texts, the authors that he has read, illustrations and paintings he has seen and looks for the correspondence to these memories first in the world of nature, then of power, and then of human beings and their failures. His linguistic knowledge (of which he is conscious, especially when he comments on the meanings of 'Avon', 'Walden' and 'Shaw') is another skill that enables him to approach the culture from outside. At first, he feels disadvantaged with his colonial nerves getting the better of him. But by beginning from the fringes of social life, through his association with gardeners and caregivers looked upon by him as a category of those remarkable people 'who caused the unremarkable seed to grow' (259), he is also nurtured into 'acceptance'. His other skills range over his earlier travels, his experiences and encounters, and his failures both as a writer and as a human being. In fact, his constant preoccupation with failure, in this novel as well as in his other writings, is also a learning process. In fact, all around him he comes across people who are on the downward slide, who have failed to achieve their aspirations – Jack, Pitton, the landlord, Alan – all of them. Like Samuel Beckett, failure is almost a fetish with Naipaul, except that he doesn't seek silences. Instead he uses confessions as a means of talking about his own failure and the failures of others.

Durant refers to the fact of representation as representations 'mediated by previous interpretation'. One needs to develop the skill to look beyond the surface. As the narrator/writer goes through this phase his perspective also undergoes a change. What he first views as change, as decay and decline, gradually is accepted as flux (*Enigma* 304). What he had imagined but had not found the courage to verify, becomes possible for him through observation. And as he begins to feel comfortable with the people around him his prejudices fall off. The process of belonging, of acceptance, is a gradual turning of the abstract into the real. The separation between man and writer, inevitable for the outsider, slowly and gradually disappears to finally come together through the process of knowing (*Enigma 1*60). In many ways a work seen as one overlaid by death and a sense of illness and decay, the *Enigma* is about the process of the bridging of gaps, of finally being at home and of being accepted. It is a novel which, through the process of writing explores the writer's growth and turns this inward knowledge into a written text as such it looks forward and achieves a fair degree of hope. It is also an acceptance of mortality.

The last two sections are rather slender in comparison with the other three. They are in the nature almost of appendices and are merely reinforcement measures. Part four is devoted to Alan, the 'other' writer in the novel, a native of the culture, who is used as a comparative yardstick for the writer 'the childhood, the man with the sensibility' and also with a whole range of material available to him with his 'deep knowledge of the setting'. But all Alan's plans come to naught. No 'book came from Alan' (313). Other writers, now of the twentieth century, of the thirties and the forties, surface in comparison with the earlier recalls of the Romantics, the mid-nineteenth and late nineteenth-century writers summoned up so far. Now the references are to Christopher Isherwood and Cyril Connolly. The narrator-writer, a person one finds difficult to separate from Naipaul, is of the opinion that Alan has 'knowledge' of his culture, the aristocratic command comes naturally to him, the house 'would have been a house without any kind of strain, making no demand on him, not requiring him to act or maintain a particular personality' (315), yet writing does not surface. Why? For Alan, the writer's landlord is merely a relic. The manor house and men like the landlord are no longer important either in social terms or in literary-artistic terms. Alan's character is a way of going-over the same ground for the writer from the opposite end. He sees in him the reflection of his earlier self. He, like Mrs. Phillips, forms another link for him with the landlord's world. And then Alan commits suicide. We come back again to Jack, to the Phillipses and to the

Doomsday painting of St. Thomas's in Salisbury, 'the sense of an arbitrary world, full of terrors, where men were naked and helpless and only God gave protectio' (329).

The final section is, once again, a personal narrative and links up with the second, which still awaits a detailed discussion. But it also reveals the structural experiment within the novel. There is no linearity; in fact all linearities are disrupted through return, repetition and spiraling memories. The first leads alike to the second and the third. The fourth is a counterpoint to the second. The third and the fifth are both a continuation of the second. The two stable points within this intricate structure are the writer/narrator and the Manor House. All figures – Jack, Pitton, Bray, Brenda and Les, Jack's wife, Phillips and his wife, Alan and the landlord, the old woman who visits him and fails to recognise her cottage – are conduits of experience, of learning; they are either reflections, distorted mirrors or appendices. It is the landscape that enables his 'rooting'. And it is the knowledge acquired through literary texts that is to be tested and re-formed. The novel is a curious mixture of autobiography, meditation and reflections on change. Despite its fringe populations, it is a one man story about 'how to become a writer'.

Triggered off by Chirico's painting 'The Enigma of Arrival', the title given to the painting by another poet-painter Apollinaire, who in his own right was an initiator into the absurd: 'The scene is of desolation and mystery: it speaks of the mystery of arrival' (106), the writer's imagination runs away with him. For once he wants to depend solely on the faculty of imagination: there was to be no research. Later, he realises that all human experiences work with similar frames, they express mystery and fear. He finds his African story reflected in this Mediterranean narrative. Moreover it doesn't occur to him that he was looking for a pattern to give coherence and meaning to a dream or nightmare haunting him for more than a year (108). Refusing to fabricate, and on this occasion refusing even to research he, perhaps for the first time, acknowledges the role of dreams and of imagination: an internal dramatisation as it was. There is 'a special anguish attached to the career, an ongoing one, not allowing one to arrive at one point of recognition and staying there' (*Enigma* 159). These metaphorical arrivals need to keep the successive physical ones company. Every physical move involves strangeness and a getting used to – of working one's way from the unfamiliar to a degree of familiarisation and every move requires a dismantling of the life put together. A hidden component of 'Jack's Garden' the silent reference to the 'house that Jack built', is that as gardens grow into wildernesses, houses fall into ruin. All strivings carry within them the fear of failure. The quality of imagination liberates him. It offers a release (111). Dreams and ideas linger in the mind to become obsessions. They stay buried for years until they force a manifestation.

The final section returns to the point when *The Enigma of Arrival* had surfaced in the idea of a Mediterranean fantasy. Between the birth of the idea and its realisation, a transformation has come about:

> The fantasy and the ancient world setting had been dropped. The story had become more personal: my journey, the writer's journey, the writer defined by his writing discoveries, his ways of seeing ... writer and man separating at the beginning of the journey and coming together again in a second life just before the end. (375)

The last section is also an obituary for a sister who is now dead, for a home that he has abandoned, for a ritual that he can watch from the outside without being a part of it. This farewell for the sister, is for the writer, the beginning of another arrival. Like a phoenix it rises out of the past. No wonder he is obsessed with the idea of antiquity and traces the cultural history of England through its writers, painters and artists. Ishiguro, also an outsider, and a comparative latecomer to England, in *The Remains of the Day* does it through character, the question of class, the pretensions not only of aristocracy but also of their staff and through the restraint that they display. Even as Stevens, the butler, travels through the countryside, more than the countryside it is the hotel rooms and the social interaction that are centre-stage. Through the sale and purchase of Darlington Hall, cultures are contrasted, memories unfolded, changes marked and ideological conflicts revealed. Stevens too passes through Salisbury, but through the main road, not through the woods.

Graham Swift's *Waterland* is steeped in the world of fairies, river barrages and woods. Naipaul shares with him, his feeling of the fairytale, fantasy, romance and mystery of the woods. But Swift, carrying within him echoes of his childhood readings of Charles Kingsley's *Water Babies,* creates a world full of children as they grow up carrying with them not innocence but manipulation and cruelty. The novel is about history and its master narrative, of the past as it lives on in the present. There is a constant movement to and fro like the ebb and rise of the tide, there is also a constant movement between memories of childhood and the classroom. Different ways of storytelling are contrasted; fairytales, stories, fables, myths, yarns and histories – personal, family, political –jostle with each other as facts and imagination mingle, destabilising and reflecting each other. But the 'knowing' is intuitive, it is a lived 'knowing', a 'growing-up with' kind of knowing. But for Naipaul 'knowing', is a process worked for and arrived at through other representations, it is a slow process of learning to distinguish seasons, of taking 'people' in alongwith the landscape. The 'almost instinctive knowledge' 'that had come to him as a child in Trinidad is missing. It is like learning a second language and is a second childhood (30). Thus characters remain portraits, singled-out, framed. They remain subjects of study rather than of relationships. And thus memory turns into several memories with the shrapnels of each hurting the other as self-reflection and mediation overtake fantasy and imagination.

Notes

1. See Rushdie 'A Sad Pastoral' (13 March 1987) *The Guardian* 'its subject is the narrator's consciousness ... the writer becomes the subject, the storyteller the tale'. Why then do we not compare it with Wordsworth's *The Prelude*? What is it that differentiates it from the poet's work? Direct communication, emotional restraint and inadequacy, lack of spontaneity, or the to and fro movement of time where memories intervene with responses? Rushdie refers to Naipaul's style as 'delicate, precise prose of the highest quality, but it is bloodless prose'.
2. See Allen, 146–147. He goes on to make the linkage with the travelogues, 150–151.
3. Quoted by Dooley, 155.

4. There are recurring references to Stonehenge strewn all over the narrative, a constant reminder of the past, of the heathen temple and of the presence of solidity amidst ruins.
5. Foucault develops this argument with reference to Jeremy Bentham's work *Panopticon* and examines the effect of rendering a subject conscious of permanent visibility that ensures an automatic functioning of power. In effect it is a total denial of privacy. For more details see Foucault 200–203.
6. Kenneth Grahame had spent his childhood in the countryside, later he worked in the Bank of England in London for many years. Finally he shifted to the countryside and began writing his novels. *The Wind in the Willows* is a children's book and creates a magic world full of toads, and rabbits and innocence. E.H. Shepard has provided the illustrations.

References

Allen, Richard. '*The Enigma of Arrival* and the Comfort of Influence', *V.S. Naipaul: An Anthology of Recent Criticism*. Ed. Purabi Panwar, Delhi: Pencraft International, 2003, pp. 146–151.

Dooley, Gillian. 'A Definition of the Writing Self: *The Enigma of Arrival*,' *V.S. Naipaul: An Anthology of Recent Criticism*. Ed. Purabi Panwar. Delhi: Pencraft International, 2003, pp. 155–172.

Durant, Alan. 'Fact and Meanings in British Cultural Studies,' *Studying British Cultures*. Ed. Susan Bassnett. London: Routledge (1997), 2003, pp. 19–38.

Foucault, Michel. *Discipline and Punish: The Birth of the Prison* trans. Alan Sheridan (1977). London: Penguin, 1991.

Hardy, Thomas, (1891). *Tess of the D'Urbervilles* Delhi: OUP, 1988.

Ishiguro, Kazuo. *The Remains of the Day,* New York: Vintage, 1988.

Naipaul, V.S. (1964). *An Area of Darkness*. Harmondsworth: Penguin, 1970.

——. *India: A Million Mutinies Now*, London: Minerva, 1990.

——. *India: A Wounded Civilization*, Bombay: Vikas Publishing House, 1977.

——. (1987). *The Enigma of Arrival*. London: Picador, 2002.

Orwell, George. (1949). *Nineteen Eighty-Four*, London: Penguin, 1962.

Rushdie, Salman. 'A Sad Pastoral,' *Guardian,* 13 March 1987. Web Source. Guardian co uk reviews/general fiction.

Swift, Graham. *Waterland* (1983). London: Picador in association with William Heinemann, 2002.

12 From Behind the Veil and Beyond

The Self in Transit in the Poetical Works of Imtiaz Dharker

Rimika Singhvi

Imtiaz Dharker, one of the major women poets writing today is a technically skilled poet, prize-winning documentary film-maker and an accomplished artist whose work has been widely exhibited in India and abroad. She has published five collections of poetry, all of which are self-illustrated. Born in Lahore, she grew up a Muslim Calvinist in Glasgow and married a Hindu Indian. Dharker now lives between Mumbai, London and Wales. Her incessant travels across the globe and marrying outside her faith twice (she was also married to a Scottish national) have added to the commingling of cultures in her. In fact, both her marriages outside her own religious community constitute an important crossing of borders. Her various cultural experiences of Pakistan, England and India have opened up her mind into problematising religion and culture, identity and belonging, as components of the self.

The poetic journey of Dharker is an interesting one to map. *Purdah and Other Poems* (1989), her first book, brings forth a somewhat disjuncted inner self through which explorations of the multiple resonances of the veil and the gender-subordination inherent in the purdah system are made. Dharker powerfully interrogates, explores, and exposes the gender-specific straitjacket, and the politics of women's clothing and their marginalisation. In several of her poems, she depicts the purdah as 'not just as a concealing garment but a state of mind' (de Souza 48). This comment, made in the context of her poem entitled 'Purdah II', brings out the purdah's physical and mental aspects and explains how a mere piece of cloth plays havoc with the woman's sense of selfhood. Dharker writes:

> the girls I knew,
> unwilling virgins who had been taught,
> especially in this strangers' land, to bind
> their brightness tightly round,
> whatever they might wear,
> in the purdah of the mind. (53–58)

Besides the spatial limitation created by the purdah by binding their 'brightness' (the face and the hair), the women have also to contend with mental boundaries which stunt their intellectual growth. It is a condition of the mind under social pressure and stress where eventually one loses a sense of being true to oneself.

Looking upon the purdah as 'the oldest form of colonisation, of domination and of control', Jasbir Jain argues that 'the purdah has many subtle forms, and dress is the most superficial and the most visible of these' (244). In her analysis, the claim of purdah as modesty, *izzat, laaj, sharam,* is actually symbolic of conformity, 'while the concept of independence, freedom and self are all relegated to a world outside it' (246). Viney Kirpal quotes Patricia Jeffrey who maintains, 'Meant to conceal a woman's face and body from public view, the purdah renders her anonymous; a non-person, unapproachable, just a silent being skulking along, looking neither to right nor left' (28). By defining the limits of freedom, demarcating the confines and outlining the margins, the purdah stultifies and annihilates, with the female being enclosed within it.

The initial location of Dharker in her first anthology thus is within the binary of centre and periphery within the Muslim religion – the religious leaders and the women in purdah. The purdah captures the claustrophobic fear and the objectification of Muslim women confined behind it and denied the powers of rational and imaginative agency. It is in this context that Sudha Rai states that the poems 'point to women's legacy of shame, sin, dislocation from their natural selves, alienated by their hostage positions within the scrutiny of the male gaze and its voyeurism' (101).

With her second volume – *Postcards from god* (1994) – Dharker's poetry journeys further. The landscapes of the self and a hostile city expand to embrace the world. In her search for a sanctuary, the speaker realises that anchor is sometimes to be found in the journey rather than the destination. Dharker's forte is rebellion. Be it religion, personal life or social customs, she registers her protest and disapproval as well as her bold criticism of tradition in an emotionally emphatic way by adopting a satirical stance and using telling images and symbols steeped in literal as well as metaphorical connotations. A continuation of such a position is seen in *I speak for the devil* (2001). Here, Dharker's persona shows a movement from questioning to assertion. Discarding identity and initiating a new subjectivity, hers is the voice of resistance against the patriarchal construction of women, and the codes of seclusion and feminine modesty imposed on their lives. Peeling her entire body and being, the speaker wishes to begin afresh by giving birth to a new self in 'A short detour from dying', 'You once had an idea/of yourself./Kiss it goodbye' (10–12). Her decision to take off her veil in 'Honour killing' – 'this black veil of a faith/that made me faithless/to myself' (9–11) – her silks and her skin, amounts to attempting a 'new geography' – both inner and outer.

The mood of rebellion continues in the poems included in *The terrorist at my table* (2007). Directing her gaze and attention to herself, Dharker makes a political statement in 'Opaque' by questioning others' '… right/to fight my outlines' (5–6). Refusing to be bound by clothes as indicative of a woman's identity, she verbalises her anger thus: 'Why should they have weight? Don't I have any say?' The question that Dharker raises is that being in-between, what does one do with that space. For instance, in her most recent collection entitled *Leaving Fingerprints* (2009), for the speaker who is always 'somewhere else', there comes a point when she realises in 'Carrying the ashes' that, 'I have stopped still/in the space between/coming in and going out' (10–12).

Alienation and a search for home thus serve as a premise for further exploration. The experiences of being dispossessed and displaced, of migration and cultural transplantation create a temporal and spatial distance between the poet and her material thereby adding to the creative tension. So, in 'Inspiration' (*The terrorist ...*), she asks for:

> ... railway stations.
> Voices on loudspeakers,
> people with their surfaces pulled away
> by travelling. Movement gives me words,
> carried in the carriages of trains. (7–11)

A closer analysis of Dharker's poetry reveals that her notion of displacement and exile, deeply embedded in memory and personal experience, does not only imply a state of unrelieved anxiety or despair; it is also perceived as a challenge and turned to strategic advantage. In fact, the experience of de-territorialisation works in her favour as it is seen to help, rather than hinder, assimilation and integration, leading to a kind of re-territorialisation.

This leaves us to wonder as to what effect does *not* staying in any one place/home (or all manner of other spaces wherein human relationships can occur) for a long time have on one's imagination and writing. Dharker's constant engagement with the significance of space as a formative aspect of the self is similar to such a poststructuralist redefinition of space in the recent years. Whereas staying within a space can confine and suffocate, moving out of spaces can liberate. In Dharker's poetry, both the processes are presented as she talks about the impact of inhabiting a space for some time, changing her perception, and then moving on. In doing so, she uses her emotional, ideological and cultural positions to recast, redefine and reconstitute herself. Her ideas change as she reconsiders, re-examines and responds to new experiences in 'other spaces' corroborating Michel Foucault's assertion that the present epoch will be 'the epoch of space. We are in the epoch of simultaneity: ... of juxtaposition ... of the near and far, of the side-by-side, of the dispersed' (22). In seeing ourselves located in and defined by a space, Foucault discusses how it takes for us the form of relations among sites. It is, however, his concepts of 'elsewhere' and 'nowhere' that allow us to make connections and see why Dharker is interested in a heterotopia without geographical markers.

Dharker's poetry is also an exploration of the interstitial space which women occupy and the way they use it to create a heterotopia. Set against a prescriptive religion and cultural constructs and the individual's rebellion against them, her poetry is found to move from anonymity and loneliness to a sense of self which stands outside these frameworks. The poems are seen to create a sense of betweenness of an alienated, isolated traveller shuttling between cultures, exploring the dilemmas of negotiations among countries, and fighting the devils of politics and religion. In fact, the self moves beyond the dictates of religion towards an intellectual understanding of its principles. The constantly shifting sense of place and landscape and the man-made divisions and boundaries – geographical, historical, cultural, social and religious – broaden the poet's vision into an all-embracing cosmopolitanism thereby expanding the dialectics of the self.

The claims of nationality, religion and gender are cast off to allow for an exploration of new territories. The gender-roles, references to other cultures and the pattern of spatial metaphors, are all concerned with the politics of the self on an existential plane and establish the feminist thrust of Dharker's poetry. Moreover, a sense of 'elsewhere' and 'nowhere' looms large in her work and the metaphors of travel and journey (such as the mention of trains, planes, stations and airports) suggest this 'elsewhere' or 'nowhere'. In fact, her poetry is that of the 'multiple outsider' (King 321). Such a state of being-in-the-margins-of-society suits Dharker for it affords her an objective distance; a unique vantage-point to observe and comment from afar. Her identity as the displaced writer is thus at once plural and partial; she straddles various cultures and the distance, the long geographical perspective, provides her with new angles at which to enter reality, and to write from a kind of 'double perspective' (Rushdie 19), as both insider and outsider.

Is it for this reason that Tabish Khair comments that Dharker's poems 'emanate from a liminal space, located on the border between cultures ... While her characters and speakers ... sometimes seem to be caught painfully in this liminal space, Dharker herself sees it as an advantage ... she enjoys the benefits of being an outcast in most societies ...' (72). As she moves from being in-between to being an outsider, she uses the changed perspective to her advantage rather than let her 'outsiderness' victimise or exclude her. Khair goes on to state that some of Dharker's best effects as a poet come from 'a subtle overlaying of images from different spaces' (73).

The physical fact of discontinuity, on account of travelling across national boundaries, may lead to alienation in the out-of-country writer. Such alienation inevitably means that the writer will not be capable of 'reclaiming precisely the thing that was lost' and will therefore need to create 'imaginary homelands ...' (Rushdie 10). For Dharker, however, the act of poetic creation is seen to be governed not so much by nostalgia for the past, a lost time, as by her desire to go beyond narrowly defined religious and cultural frontiers. The multiplicity of commingled faiths and cultural influences in her poetry points at the 'chutneyfication' of culture referred to by Salman Rushdie in *The Satanic Verses* (1988). There, however, seems to be no conflict in her of the self that is divided between cultures. For Nilufer E. Bharucha, such '... moving into wider places does not mean that women have to desex themselves and become male-identified in order to gain acceptance in an androcentric world. The circumscription and reduction of the inner worlds of women are undesirable and must be resisted ...' (106).

At the same time, it cannot be ignored that geographical dislocation or relocation to a new socio-cultural and geographical space creates an ambiguous, and often unsettling, effect on the mind of a sensitive poet such as Dharker. A sense of violence is seen as associated with the process for it involves a kind of decentring for the writer who carries herself everywhere. Wherever she is becomes her home, though she may continue to feel like a guest in the host/adopted country and everywhere else too. Moreover, there can be no going back to the native country for she has become a foreigner in her own land too.

This fact of 'belonging to multiple cultural spaces', argues Himadri Lahiri, 'may create a sense of belonging nowhere which may, in turn, create a sense of profound uncertainty' (118). The self-image thus created in diasporic locations is vulnerable and constantly exposed to a racist gaze. However, just as one finds women poets like Dharker voicing their concerns about patriarchal forces still at work in the new spaces, one can also sense their exhilaration at acculturating themselves in a new country, at finding a better opportunity for enjoying freedom not possible in the land of their origin. The liberation from the narrow confines of national space into a more globalised location is seen to lead to a kind of globalised self in turn.

Dharker dwells on her persona's experience of multiculturalism, which is seen as an oddity, but at the same time finds her multiple selves bound to, and co-existing peacefully with, multiple linguistic structures. She says in 'Stitched' (*I speak* ...):

> And so my mouth spoke Punjabi
> while my brain heard Scots
> My ears followed German
> and my tongue did French.
> It seems they were about to put me out
> in a garbage bag, I looked so odd. (5–10)

Another poem titled 'Minotiry' (*Postcards* ...) talks about the woman persona feeling like a 'foreigner' in a strange land on account of belonging to a racial/ethnic minority:

> I was born a foreigner.
> I carried on from there
> to become a foreigner everywhere
> I went ...
> I don't fit,
> like a clumsily-translated poem ... (1–4, 13–14)

This sense of being in a kind of exile; of non-belonging to a fixed location and/or not fitting anywhere; of being always on the point of setting off; on the brink of departure, is the fallout of living in fragile times, in an 'age of fire and blood' ('1993'). The personal constructs of 'home' and 'away' add to the complexity and flux that a writer has to grapple with. The situation is further compounded when the self is loaded with experiences of emotional distancing and lack of communication. The speaker realises that 'leaving a country' is not as traumatic as 'walking out of a door' ('Here'). With the passage of time, not so much the distance, there is an acute sense of loss. For, as the speaker says in an earlier poem in *Postcards* ..., that distances are not just 'made of miles' ('Absent Without Leave–IV'). The sense conveyed is that the poet's persona does not stop at these losses but gets over them eventually thereby strengthening the self in the process. Her spatial and temporal disorientation and dislocation help her to keep her sanity in this day and age when 'things fall apart' and the 'centre cannot hold'. Displacement as a trope, therefore, is quite evident in much of Dharker's poetry.

Displacement, for Dharker, however, does not spell exile. It can mean instead an exhilarating sense of life at the interstices. She shared at an interview given to Arundhathi Subramaniam: 'I may never be able to define my home, but the question is, do I want to? Where is my home anyway? In Scotland, under a particular group of trees? In the texture of a fabric? The feel of rain? In the end, you carry these things with you wherever you go' (*The Hindu Magazine* 5 May 2002). Dharker clarifies further in the same interview: 'Home for me is here [in India], but it's also in the smell of the south of France. And when I went to Punjab, I felt I was genetically programmed to know that landscape of flat sugarcane fields. I'm sure I shall feel the same shock of recognition when I bite into an olive in Tuscany'.

The experiences of postcoloniality and exile only add to the process of self-construction. This theme has preoccupied Dharker since her first collection of poems, *Purdah* ... in which some of the poems talk about the speaker's experience as an immigrant, of 'us' and 'them'; of transgression. There is a mood of nostalgia for the homeland; to return to one's roots, captured poignantly in 'Going Home' (*Purdah* ...):

> ... I've tried the world
> and found it wanting
> tell me
> how can I come home? (94–97)

She further says in 'Pariah' (*Purdah* ...):

> ... I may live their lives,
> but my feet will walk again
> on good red soil
> through fields of cane
> and sunlight delicately laced with flies. (29–33)

Dharker's sensory experiences thus form the basis of her attachment to a space in which she moves. She recalls a natural scene rather than a historical monument as she reminisces about her past. 'Home' or 'country' has a different meaning for her; it is a territory beyond boundaries. The metaphor of the pomegranate fruit reminds her of 'another home' ('How to cut a pomegranate'). The lush fruit, 'bursting with promises' ('Women bathing'), makes the speaker's mind, in 'Train to Granada', go in search of '... a safe haven,/peace, a promise of rest,/a hope of poetry' (26–28). The nostalgia for the distant homeland is thus evoked by an exotic fruit and its associations of nourishment and exotic beauty. Just as the seeds are packed together in the fruit, with each distinctly visible, so is the speaker's distinct individuality and sense of self in the midst of so many like her. The only difference is that in making her choices, she finds herself in 'The Women' like a seed 'flung a little further than the rest' (11).

There is thus in Dharker's poetry an upsurge of a longing for freedom, a vehement questioning of certain age-old socio-religious practices and prejudices, and an exposition of male chauvinism. Hers is not merely an emotional refuge in nostalgia for a lost homeland nor a bid to reclaim lost immigrant history. Rather, one sees an expanding intertextuality consequent on the female persona's discovery of the additional layers of being, obtained by living in other cultures; enjoying the sense of having local ties; valuing the links forged with other places; experiencing the contradictions of intersecting cultural locations; and, the dilemmas of the diasporic self. The finding that Dharker's displacement, born out of migration, is not a rupture but a continuum of geographic, linguistic and emotional landscapes, points at the impression of a constantly evolving, fluid self.

The multiple locations in which Dharker finds herself, her experiences of displacement, immigration and the several identities (religious, cultural, linguistic) are found to add to her self's growth which for her is a constantly developing process, never fixed or stable. Her hyphenated existence, the state of being in-between, is suggestive of a changing self. Her inner core has collected certain values which have gradually been released from the bounds of religion, community and nation. Moving out of narrow loyalties attached to an orthodox religion and a monolithic patriarchal system, her self is seen as belonging to a larger world. It is an experiential self grappling with multiple realities as she gives up the identity-markers against which a woman is traditionally and typically framed and defined.

A common thread running through much of Dharker's poetry is the commonality of women's experiences and a sense of collective identity. The broad aspects that Dharker foregrounds in realising the self include the body-as-territory, religion and culture, identity and location. The poet has come out of similar cultural spaces and uses the body to go against tradition. She also uses religion as a mode of confinement and oppression, to further use it as a testing ground for the self. There is in her corpus of poetic output an account of the relational development of the self; of a self located not merely in limiting familial constructs but also in the more open human ones.

Dharker's poetry further reminds us that the twenty first-century society is a world of mobilities and liquid experiences. On account of the growing fluidity and liquidisation of social networks, there is an emergence of new strategies of the self as well as life-strategies involving diversity, difference and discontinuity in interpersonal relationships and cultural pursuits. The postmodern self is identity set adrift, lacking in solidity, continuity and structure. All this is amply reflected in Dharker and it can therefore be inferred from her poetry that the self is realised and presented in terms of fragments and as being in a state of flux. In other words, the self is seen as becoming increasingly dispersed and multiple. Moreover, in our media-saturated world, different selves can now be adopted and discarded at whim. There is an avoidance of a fixed identity and an ordered, predictable structure. Such several forms of the self are better understood as simultaneous ways of living in contemporary culture, just as in Dharker's poetry as she moves away from inherited values and aspirations and speaks against the male appropriation of power.

Dharker's formulation of the self, therefore, does not emerge only from isolated experiences of her own self but also from the fact that it enlarges to become a part of the racial history of her people (women, in particular), their suppression and curtailment of freedom. A powerful poet, Dharker uses her many perspectives to create poetry which examines larger social problems and which is also concerned with political injustice. The experience of the other merges with her own thereby creating a collective identity. At the same time, what is important is that 'the specificity of the individual subject is foregrounded at the expense of a general theory of femininity and even of political engagement …' (Moi 169). In going beyond a gendered self to its (dis)location in time and space, Dharker thus allows her self to be perceived as an ever-growing, adaptive and fluid inner awareness vis-à-vis her experiences of constant travelling between the multiple realities of religions, cultures and boundaries.

References

Bharucha, Nilufer E. 'Inhabiting Enclosures and Creating Spaces: The Worlds of Women in Indian Literature in English.' *Post Independence Voices in South Asian Writings*. Ed. Malashri Lal, Alamgir Hashmi, and Victor J. Ramraj. Delhi: Doaba Publications, 2001, pp. 93–107.

de Souza, Eunice. ed., 'Imtiaz Dharker.' *Nine Indian Women Poets: An Anthology*. New Delhi: OUP, 2001, pp. 48–49.

Dharkar, Imtiaz *Postcards from god,* New Delhi: Viking, 1994.

——. *I speak for the devil*. 2001, New Delhi: Penguin Books, 2003.

——. *The terrorist at my table*. 2006, New Delhi: Penguin Books, 2007.

——. *Leaving Fingerprints,*Northumberland: Bloodaxe Books, 2009.

——. *Purdah and Other Poems,* 1989. New Delhi: OUP.

Foucault, Michel. 'Of Other Spaces.' *Diacritics*. Spring 1986, pp. 22–27.

Jain, Jasbir. ed., 'Erasing the Margins: Questioning Purdah.' *Women's Writing: Text and Context*. Jaipur: Rawat Publications, 1996, pp. 243–55.

Khair, Tabish. 'Speaking with Two (and more) Tongues.' *Indian English Women Poets.* Ed. Anisur Rahman and Ameena Kazi Ansari. New Delhi: Creative Books, 2009, pp. 69–73.

King, Bruce. 'New Women Poets: Shivdasani, Patel, D'Souza, Sambrani, Dharker, Divakaruni, Bhatt.' *Modern Indian Poetry in English.* 1987. Rev. ed. New Delhi: OUP, 2001, pp. 312–32.

Kirpal, Viney. 'Purdah in Indian English Writing.' *Margins of Erasure: Purdah in the Subcontinental Novel in English.* Ed. Jasbir Jain and Amina Amin. New Delhi: Sterling Publishers, 1995, pp. 24–32.

Lahiri, Himadri. 'Dislocation and After: Indian Women Poets in America.' *Indian English Women Poets.* Ed. Anisur Rahman and Ameena Kazi Ansari. New Delhi: Creative Books, 2009, pp. 106–124.

Moi, Toril. 'Marginality and Subversion: Julia Kristeva.' *Sexual/Textual Politics: Feminist Literary Theory*. London: Routledge, 1991, pp. 150–73.

Rai, Sudha. 'Beyond Purdah: Intersubjectivity and Interstitiality in Imtiaz Dharker's Poetry.' *Literary Constructs of the Self: Socio-Cultural Contexts.* Ed. Santosh Gupta and Mini Nanda. Jaipur: Rawat Publications, 2010, pp. 96–110.

Rushdie, Salman. 'Imaginary Homelands.' *Imaginary Homelands: Essays and Criticism 1981–1991*. London: Granta Books, 1991, pp. 9–21.

Subramaniam, Arundhathi. 'A poet's voice.' Interview with Imtiaz Dharker. *The Hindu: Magazine*, 5 May 2002.

13 Global Politics of Contemporary Travel Writing in Vassanji's *A Place Within*

Sangeeta Handa

The global world order has completely transformed the trends of contemporary writings both from the point of view of the reader as well as from the point of view of the writer. Due to the incessant border-crossings, contemporary theory is replete with metaphors of travel, displacement, diaspora, border, exile, migration, nomadism, homelessness and tourism to name a few. The twentieth century can be characterised as a time when increasing numbers of people have become disengaged from national, regional and ethnic locations or identities. As travel, changing locations, and leaving home become central experiences for more and more people in modernity, the difference between the ways we travel, the reasons for our movements and the terms of our participation in this dynamics must be historically and politically accounted for. This is not to say that the urge for travel has been just a recent trend, on the contrary, it would not be an exaggeration to say that the urge for travel has been as much a part of human need as the urge for food or urge for basic instincts. Travel has a unique complicity with adventure and knowledge. Hence it quenches many deep-rooted desires. It has also been unavoidable, indisputable and always necessary for family, love, friendship as well as work. Travel is also a great source of entertainment and a kind of relief from 'the rooted realities of dailiness'. (Kaplan Preface)

It is also a commonplace fact that the impulse for travel writing is very ancient and it dates back to the times of Homer. One of the earliest examples of travel literature is Pausanias' *Description*. Travel genre was also a fairly common in Medieval Arabic literature. Travelogues of Ibn Batuta and Marco Polo are still source great information for those involved in historical research. The purpose of travel writing is varied. One of the earliest known records of taking pleasure in travel for the sake of travel and writing about it is Petrarch's *Ascent to Mount Ventoux* (1336). He states that he went to the mountaintop for the pleasure of seeing the top of the famous height. Later while writing about his experience he makes an allegorical comparison between climbing the mountain and his own moral progress in life.

In the history of travel writing, worth mentioning are certain seminal texts like Richard Hakluyt's (1552–1660) *Voyages* which is considered a pioneer in tourism literature. During eighteenth century, travel literature consisted of the maritime diaries. In fact in eighteenth century Britain, almost every famous literary writer had written about their travel experiences. Captain James Cook's *Diaries* (1784) were the equivalent of today's best sellers. Besides these, the Americans, Paul Theroux, Bill Bryson and William Least Heat-Moon, Welsh author Jan Morris and Englishman Eric Newbay were widely acclaimed as travel writers, although Morris is also a historian and Theroux, a novelist. The history of travel literature would be incomplete if the names of the prominent writers like Jonathan Swift, Samuel Johnson, Mary Wollstonecraft, Charles Dickens, Robert Louis Stevenson, Joseph Conrad, Hilaire Belloc, D.H. Lawrence, Rebecca West and John Steinbeck are not mentioned.

The purpose of charting this selective brief history of travel writing from the times of Homer is to give a bird's eye view of the sporadic and scattered writings on travel that have been prominent and popular so far. Till the end of the last century, travel writing had not evolved as a genre and these writings did not attract that much reading public as the genre of fiction did. Interest in travel writing was first occasioned by the post-second world war resistance movements and the waves of liberation in the former

European countries as well as by the waves of immigration that followed. With globalisation and the dominance of corporate sector worldwide life has changed and with it the trends in reading and writing. The present generation has run short of time, because of long and demanding working hours. This passage from 'solid' to 'liquid' modernity has created, a new and unprecedented life setting for individual life pursuits which, in the words of Zigmunt Bauman is '... the collapse of long-term thinking, planning and acting ... lead[ing] to a splicing of both political history and individual lives into a series of short term projects and episodes which are in principle infinite, ...' (Bauman 3). Hence there is a general tendency in this new generation to enjoy life in spurts and snatches and that is why travel itself has become a fad of the 'Liquid Times'. This perhaps is the reason for the exponential growth of travel literature as a genre because it fits in very well with the imaginative tendency of the reading public. Along with policy documents, eye-witness accounts, newspaper stories and documentaries, travel writing has become a part of the discursive terrain that shapes the 'real' world of the global politics.

With the changes in the imaginative tendency of the reading public, the contemporary travel writing also reflects the changes that have taken place in global social scenario. As Colin Thubron points out, one of the most striking characteristics of contemporary travel writer is '... an awakened social consciousness' (Thubron 179). Thus even when authors choose to draw on traditional patterns of travel writing, such as exploration account, the dominant metaphor in such accounts is the rediscovery of the displaced self and re-evaluation of the ancestral place of belonging. It is from this perspective the M.G. Vassanji's travel narrative *A Place Within* is going to be analysed. The journey is both political and social and negotiates the conflicts that generated so much displacement in the twentieth century as an aftermath of the two world wars. Vassanji represents the progeny of his exiled ancestors who are 'men without country' (Kaplan 19). In this travel narrative *A Place Within* Vassanji visits certain important cities of India with an obvious intention to rediscover his identity. In fact, it is an attempt at exploration of the elusive notions of home and cultural identity, troubled as the author is by his own complex background-Carribean-born, US-raised and currently

Canada-based individual as he is. Charles Baudelaire's following statement seems to capture Vassanji's precarious circumstances:

> It seems to me that I would always be better where. I am not and this question of moving is one of those I discuss incessantly with my soul. (qtd Kaplan 28)

The systematic study of travel literature began as a legitimate field of scholarly inquiry and emerged most extensively in the late 1990s encouraged by the currency of Foucauldian criticism and Edward Said's *Orientalism*. Said has viewed the conjunction between fact, fiction, travel and Empire as a part of orientalist strategy for privileging the Empire:

> The increasing influence of travel literature, imaginary utopias, moral voyages and scientific reporting brought the Orient into sharper and more extended focus .... But all such widening horizons had Europe firmly in the privileged center, as main observer ... even as Europe moved itself outwards, its sense of cultural strength was fortified. From traveler's tales and not only from great institutions like various India companies', colonies were created and ethnocentric perspectives secured. (Said 194)

In the recent times travel writing has been involved in socio-political discourses. Travel books feature prominently among the texts Said handles in *Orientalism* (1978) as examples of the orientalist's discourse. Taking a cue from Said's *Orientalism*, many prominent critics of travel literature like Percy Adams, Mary Louis Pratt, Ian Bell, Inderpal Grewal, Barbara Kote have traced the complicity of travel writing (and travel writers) with colonial agendas and imperialist underpinnings. Grewal considers all kinds of travel literature written during the colonial span suggestive of '... the particular ways in which the knowledge of a self, society and nation was, and is, within European and North American culture, to be understood and obtained' (Grewal 4).

Some critics view contemporary travel writer's dubious role in implicitly carrying forward the 'legacy of Empire' and hence have established that it is 'virtually impossible to consider travel writing outside the frame of postcolonialism' (Musgrove 32). Another recent critic Debbie Lisle has in fact developed a full-fledged thesis on the politics of contemporary travel writing by establishing that in the very conscious efforts 'to abandon his/her colonial heritage' (Lisle 2) the contemporary travel writer is entangled in the surreptitious growth of neo-colonialism. A close reading of Vassanji's travel narrative also reveals this, in spite of his overt declaration in the sub-title of the book of his intention of the rediscovery of the self. Still, a clear-cut demarcation can also be seen in the ways of writing of the contemporary travel writer and their colonial masters. The 'tropes of power, control and exclusion at work' (Lisle 4) in the writings of colonial travel writers is substituted by 'emancipating possibilities created by an interconnected 'global village' (Lisle 4).

Contemporary travel writing, by and large, has a traveller-narrator, who is comparatively free to follow his own instincts and predispositions, rather than fill any political agenda of colonial expansion or any market strategy for inviting tourism. And it is this, so called 'traveler's eccentricities and extravagances – in the literal sense of wanderings off – which have attracted many readers (as well as the writers) to the genre of travel writing' (Youngs and Hulme 5). To establish this argument about the global politics at work in the contemporary travel writing Vassanji's *A Place Within: Rediscovering India* has been a very apt choice. It is a travel narrative based on several journeys made across India by the author over the course of fourteen years. In the introduction, Vassanji acknowledges his obsession with getting acquainted and rediscovering the land of his ancestors. He explains that the book is based on notes made while on a series of trips that began as a young man's pilgrimage to his homeland but which over a period of time developed into more nuanced explorations across private and public arenas. Kaplan's observation holds true in case of Vassanji's travel book:

> The act of border crossing potentially opens up wider epistemological questions about how truth claims are represented in language. In this sense, the discourse of literary genre regulates travel writing on two levels: firstly by trying to categorize a practice as diverse and ambiguous as travel; and secondly by trying to order the complex manner in which travel writing uses both fact and fiction to authorize self. (31)

Though Vassanji traces a spatially complex path, including Delhi, Simla, Orissa, Kerala, Punjab and Gujarat in his 'grand tour', history rather than geography is the dominant flavour of his book. Of course he has drawn on the historical references yet as

Lisle comments in another context 'the logic of identity/difference is secured by spatial divisions between home and away [as] travel writers repeatedly differentiate themselves from others by situating their authority in a stable, superior and unquestionable home' (Lisle 37). Propelled by the urgent sense of exploration of the land of his ancestors, there couldn't be a better choice than the format of a travelogue that Vassanji used for his visits and revisits to India. And then it is not just the travels and mere geographic descriptions that could do full justice to the rediscovery of the country of such enormous diversity and rich heritage. Wherever he travels whether it is Delhi or Gujarat, Amritsar or Kerala, Bombay or Simla, he analyses it historically as well. His excessive use of historical references has also invited negative criticism from the reviewers who consider it as a 'tedious distraction'. But Vassanji has justified his describing those historical monuments of Delhi which otherwise would remain neglected as he questions in the travelogue 'Isn't there a neutral, intellectual, dispassionate way to respond to history?' (56). In fact, Vassanji's avid references to the historical, mythological past of Delhi should not be taken as a distraction or an irritant to all of us who live in India and often visit Delhi; rather it is perhaps a reminder about the reason for its being the capital of the country. From being the site of the Painted Grey Ware pottery to the locus of politics for the legendary heroes of *Mahabharata,* to the centre of the politics during Mughal rule, Vassanji's historical diggings are a part of a well planned travelogue of a new kind.

Vassanji's relationship to India is enigmatic. As a third generation diasporic, he says, 'What was India to me? ... I was not born in India, nor were my parents ... yet how many people go to the birth place of their grandparents with such a heart load of expectation and momentousness, such a desire to find themselves in everything they see?' (vii). The query, a sort of nudging, that every sensitive diasporic might be experiencing some time, becomes an obsession with the author who feels, 'an uncontrollable and perhaps vain desire to know and record who I am' (46). Is his so-called rediscovery sojourn underlined by the above mentioned desire to 'differentiate' by situating himself in 'a stable, superior and unquestionable home' back in Canada? Is his 'return to roots' experience ennobling enough to make him desperate to settle back in India? He may be overwhelmed by the sensual reality but at the same time he is confounded by the country's contradictions, it's tragic instability, incomprehensible attitudes of India's intellectuals when faced with the mind-jarring violence of the riots that took place in 1993. Vassanji's neophyte fascination with India is also underscored by irony, which of course is guided by a kind of sympathy as well. But at the same time Vassanji's diasporic identity makes it difficult for the readers to locate his own position and stance with regard to India-the home of his ancestors. Lisle's observation in another context seems applicable in Vassanji's case in *A Place Within:*

> While the author is not actually at home for the duration of the narrative, home provides the geographical anchor from which he/she can make observations and judgments about foreign people and places. In other words, travel writing delivers 'us' and 'them' most successfully when it locates those identities in differentiated spaces of 'home' and 'away'. (137)

The travelogues written by diasporic writers like Naipaul, Vassanji and others make the genre of travel writing Janus-faced, partaking of both the empirical and the fictional, of truth and the tall tale. In such travel narratives, the identity of the writer is intriguing. Which 'home' do they belong to? The home of their search or their ancestors' 'home' where they are comfortably entrenched passing on judgments on their 'roots'?

The sections of the book devoted to places like Gujarat, Himachal Pradesh, Punjab, Kerala are written with the same intensity of the search for identity. In fact, this book might appear bland to the Western audience because, it seems Vassanji's intention is not to target any audience perhaps and neither to showcase Indian poverty. The travelogue has epic-like qualities though a few reviewers of this book have condemned it for being too discursive and seamless. That perhaps is the appeal of the book, because this renders it a more authentic flavour. Apart from being a travelogue, it is also an expression of 'homing desire', which merely remains a 'desire', a 'distant dream', which gives more pleasure in just being a desire and a dream which thankfully will not be translated into reality. Vassanji in the course of the narrative tries to authenticate or perhaps give justification for this as he says:

> Why this obsession with the past? I can only conclude that it reflects the deep dissatisfaction of unfinished, incomplete

> migrations, a perpetual homelessness in my life. My colonial existence-in which memory and the past were trampled upon in a rush to better our lot-and the insecurities of an unorthodox commercial culture, in the process of extinction and reinvention by exigencies of globalised living and modern politics have both created an incontrollable and perhaps vain desire to know and record who I am there are ways of the mystic and the scientist to answer this question and there is the way of history and fiction which I find more compelling. (46)

Vassanji is very clear and open about his inner urge to discover the land of his ancestors, but unlike Naipaul, his mindset is open to acceptance and even if, during the course of the narrative the comparison between Dar-e-slaam, the land of his birth and early childhood, or US where he spent nine crucial years of his youth in pursuit of higher studies, or Toronto (Canada) where he is presently living become inevitable, it is always with that sense of 'other' that he does it. During the course of the narrative Vassanji says, '… [he] believed we could shed our ancestral connections for a thin veneer of colonialness' (viii), but by writing this travelogue has he been successful in shedding this 'thin veneer of colonialness'. The tone and tenor of Vassanji's travel narrative is much more subdued and humble in comparison to Naipaul, but in this travel narrative he is not able to hide his judgmental attitude, placed as he is in a privileged position in a western society.

> The India I would find … seemed at once so startling familiar and yet so alien; so frustrating and yet so enlightening and humbling; so warm and friendly and yet so inhumanly cruel and callous'. Although again and again he also says, 'it (India) had reclaimed me', but that act of 'reclaiming' is never proved, it remains an abstraction, a feeling, a sort of 'bliss in solitude', enjoyed in the comforts of Canada his permanent home. It is another matter to say, 'What better way than to sit in a train responding to the ancestral homeland, every scene and every moment full of meaning and possibility, blooming epiphany?' The only torment: the wet washrooms. (Vassanji 16)

The 'torment' has to be borne; the price has to be paid for this journey of rediscovery. But this journey does not end here; it is in fact a metaphor of a travel that will never end. The book *A Place*

Within, cannot be simplistically viewed as a travel narrative conforming to the theory of travel genre. That, it is written by a third-generation diasporic author as a travel sojourn, ostensibly with a rediscovery agenda to the land of his ancestors makes it problematic. My conclusion is as open-ended as the genre of travel writing is '... [it] is best considered as a broad and ever shifting genre, with a complex history which has yet to be properly studied ... just as the ways and means of travel writing are constantly changing, so travel writing will continue to change in their wake: stories emerging from space travel, from virtual travel, and from the 'travails' of the world's refugees and migrants will doubtless continue to extend the genre in years to come' (Thubron 1999:12).

References

Bauman, Zigmunt. *Liquid Times: Living in the Age Uncertainty.* UK: Polity Press, 2007.

Grewal, Inderpal. *Travel, Home and Harem: Nation, Gender, Empire and the Cultures of Travel*. Leicester: Leicester University Press, 1996.

Kaplan, Caren. *Questions of Travel: Postmodern Discourses of Displacement*. NC: Duke University Press, 1996.

Lisle, Debbie. *The Global Politics of Contemporary Travel Writing*. Cambridge: Cambridge University Press, 2006.

Musgrove, Brian. 'Travel and Unsettlement: Freud on Vacation' in Clark, Steven H. *Travel Writing and Empire: Postcolonial Theory in Transit*. Zed Books, 1999.

Ropero, Maria Lourdes L'opez. 'Travel Writings and Postcoloniality: Caryl Philip's The Atlantic Sound' *Atlantic* 25. 1 June 2003, pp. 51–62.

Said, Edward. *Reflections on Exile*. Cambridge: Cambridge University Press, 2000.

Thubron, Colin. 'Travel Writing Today: Its Rise and its Dilemma'. *Essays by Diverse Hands: Being the Transactions of Royal Society of Literature.* New Series, Vol. 44. Ed. A.N. Wilson. London: Boyde 11.167–81, 1984.

——. 'Both Seer and Seen: The Travel Writer as Leftover Amateur' TLS No. 5026, 1999.

Vassanji, M.G. *A Place Within: Rediscovering India.* Viking: Penguin Books, 2009.

Youngs, Tim and Hulme, Peter. *The Cambridge Companion to Travel Writing.* Cambridge: Cambridge University Press, 2002.

14 Journeys to her Homeland

Lessing's *African Laughter* and *Under My Skin*

Preeti Bhatt and Manju Nemad

Doris Lessing was born in Persia, now Iran, in 1919 and spent her youth in Southern Rhodesia, now Zimbabwe – two countries that have undergone major transformations and are no longer known by their old names. The writer lived in Southern Rhodesia for twenty-five years before she immigrated to England in 1949. Having spent the best part of her life there, Lessing's writings, including her fiction and non-fiction are coloured by her memories of her past – of her childhood, adolescence and adulthood in Southern Rhodesia. Despite being a white with British origins, Lessing denounced in all her writings, the imperialist policy of racial discrimination and the oppression of the black natives by the white settlers, as she observed it closely during her stay in Africa.

Her opposition as a Communist to the racial oppression practiced by the Rhodesian government caused Lessing to be declared a 'Prohibited Immigrant' in 1956. She claims that this prohibition meant an exclusion 'from my own best self', since she considers Africa her hometown, and the place of her childhood memories (*African Laughter* 12). Her prohibition ended when Southern Rhodesia, which had been colonised since 1890, became an independent country in the leadership of Robert Mugabe in 1980, after the blacks won the war fought against white rule. She has described Rhodesia vividly in some of her best fiction, including *The Golden Notebook*, *The Children of Violence*, and in her African stories, and these works carry Lessing's perception of the beauty and richness of Africa in the 1930s and 40s.

Exiled for twenty-five years from her home country, Lessing travelled to Zimbabwe in 1982, 1988, 1989 and 1992. She published the travel book *African Laughter: Four Visits to Zimbabwe* in 1992, in which she recounted her experiences during these four visits and her conversations with the blacks and with the whites about the newly independent country. Her frequent journeys to Zimbabwe can be seen as her endeavour to reclaim the past as well as an effort to renew her strong emotional bonds with her home country. The first part of her autobiography titled *Under My Skin: Volume One of my Autobiography, to 1949* published in 1994 is again an imaginative journey to the past as Lessing recollects her childhood in the Bush, her personal relationship with the people around her, and the growth of her consciousness as well as of her political views in Southern Rhodesia. The two books together represent the writer's deliberate crossing over from the present to the past, in the quest to assimilate the fragments of her lost selves, lost during her forced exile from her homeland.

The present paper compares and contrasts these two works as journeys to her homeland: Doris Lessing's *African Laughter* as a description of the physical journey she undertook to the land of her memories, and her autobiography *Under My Skin* as a subconscious inward journey to her past. The paper attempts to examine the writer's views about home, memory and identity as presented in these two works of non-fiction – concepts which acquire a multi-layered significance in the case of the author due to her peculiar position of being both an insider and an outsider in her native land.

In the beginning of *African Laughter*, Lessing places a map of Southern Rhodesia alongside one of Zimbabwe to mark the difference in the names of the cities before and after the country's independence. The writer also includes a brief historical introduction of Southern Rhodesia, describing its gradual colonisation by the British, the coming together of nationalist forces, and the Liberation War (also called the War in the Bush), which brought freedom to the country in 1980. Throughout the travelogue, Lessing emphasises the optimism, the hopefulness and 'the creative energies of its people' (10). The book gets its name from this buoyancy, this self-respecting attitude of the Africans reflected in their spontaneous laughter 'the marvellous African laughter born somewhere in the gut, seizing the whole body with good-humoured philosophy' (80). The writer's admiration for the blacks and their simple unpretentious faith in themselves and in their country is revealed in these references.

During her four consecutive visits to Zimbabwe, Lessing keenly observes the transformation in the landscape, the perspectives of the people, and the political and economic situation of the country after the Bush War. As she subtly weaves in the element of time in the narrative, delving into her memories and conversing with the native blacks and the settler whites to compare the present with the past, *African Laughter* takes the shape of a reflective memoir. Lessing's journey to her homeland after a long hiatus involves a painful confrontation with a changed landscape, and a changed people who are learning to accept the responsibility of governing their own country. It also means facing once again her own beliefs, choices and decisions in the past which shaped her individuality and her life. In the following lines in *African Laughter* she describes the challenge faced by writers when they return home after a long sojourn, 'I know writers who very early build tall fences around theirs and afterwards make sure they never go near them'. Lessing continues, 'when the time comes for them to make the first trip home it means stripping off new skin and offering exposed and smarting flesh to – the past' (301). It is not an easy journey home and the writer is forced to review the memories of her childhood, adolescence and youth in Africa.

Early in the book *African Laughter*, Lessing discusses the fallible nature of memory when she describes a car journey during her childhood and a similar journey that she undertakes years later in 1982. As amazingly beautiful landscapes come into view, she tells us, 'I was cramming into my mind, like photographs in an album, these views and vistas that would never say put, but were changed by memory, as I would find out on the next trip' (19). As views change when she observes them after an interval, she wonders, 'Perhaps there had been a different 'view', and I had been mistaken?' (19). No, but that is not the case either. Lessing admits that she has always contested a battle against the ravages of memory. She states, 'I was obsessed with Time, always had been, and my very earliest memories are of how I insisted to myself, Hold this . . . don't forget it – as if I had been born with a knowledge of its sleights and deceptions'. The writer continues, 'Even now I hold a series of sharp little scenes, like photographs, or eidetic memory, which I refer to' (20). Lessing, in this description, problematises the complex nature of memory, which is neither reliable nor stable.

Lynda Scott in her article 'Similarities between Virginia Woolf and Doris Lessing' considers Woolf's and Lessing's autobiographical works to be nostalgic, 'since both writers seek to capture that which can never be regained. To a considerable extent, *African Laughter: Four Visits to Zimbabwe* (1993) is a lament both for the past and for the distortion of that past by the ravages of time'. This statement acquires relevance in the descriptions of Lessing's meeting with her brother after a long period of separation. She and her brother Harry, not having met for several years, now try to connect with each other again by recalling their shared childhood in Southern Rhodesia. Even though they were close at heart as children, they have different perceptions and different memories now. The siblings try to force each other to remember what they can. Too often, however, the question 'Do you remember?' has as its response, 'No, I don't, I'm afraid' (42). Lessing's travelogue, a written record of the writer's experience of revisiting her home country, in fact can be seen as an effort to freeze the frames of memory into an image of words which would not be affected by the passage of time.

The writer disrupts the conventional linearity of the travelogue by including the multiple voices of the black natives and the whites living there. It could be called a polyphonic book full of the voices of people from Zimbabwe – those of both, blacks and whites. Elizabeth Maslen points out, 'the whites in these pages speak with many voices, as do the blacks, some generous and big-minded, some bigoted and deaf to argument, some self-seeking and blind to their fellows' (56–57). While some voices captured in narrative by the writer are blatant in their dislike for the whites, or in their insistence to be heard, others are soft and hesitant like a murmur. Lessing puts down the views of farmers, teachers, extension workers, newspaper reporters, patrol leaders, and unemployed men in *African Laughter*. Melissa Walker notes: 'In *African Laughter*, recovery appears as neither an erasure of the past, nor an act of repression that inevitably leads to traumatic repetition, but as a process that promotes engagement with damaged environments and people, involving both white and black Zimbabweans' (31–2). Facts, opinions, memories of the past, rumours, jokes, and news clippings are interspersed in the narrative. The headings of the book's sections are equally interesting: Witchcraft, Television, Talk on the Verandahs, Giving Gifts, A Betrayed Lover, The Aesthetic Approach to Revolution, and several others.

Lessing observes the increasing sense of disillusionment of the natives as their leaders fail to fulfil the expectations of the people. The corruption, unemployment and the slow process of growth perturbs the natives who had expected good governance from their own leaders. In her first visit in 1982 which was just two years since Zimbabwe's independence, she 'could not understand why people expected things to change so quickly' (117). She feels pained to see that the country reeling from the bloodshed and destruction of the war had not been given time to recuperate, 'Every newspaper, television programme, or international expert talked about Zimbabwe as if it were an established country to be judged by the highest standards' (68). And yet, in every trip to Africa, she feels disheartened, unable to come to terms with the fact that Rhodesia's independence had failed to deliver its promise of progress and happiness for its people.

As she observes the vanishing green cover and its fauna, the narration adopts a nostalgic tone. She believes, 'Every writer has a myth country,' and for her it is Zimbabwe, explaining that 'Myth does not mean something untrue, but a concentration of truth'. In 1956, Lessing avoided visiting the farm she grew up in, due to 'a fear of tampering with her myth' (35). When, after much dithering she goes to see the farm in 1988, she finds that the hilltop has been flattened into a plateau and her house built of 'mud and thatch' (314) replaced by a 'graceless lump of a dark bungalow' (315). Lessing and her brother Harry lament that the bush, rich with varieties of flora and fauna, has been replaced by fruit trees. In the new bungalow an African family has been housed, and the writer notes that there are no books for the children 'not a book, toy, a magazine, an exercise book, a pencil, a picture' and realises that they are as remote from the civilised world as Lessing herself was in her childhood, yet her rooms were full of books and bookcases (315). The agony of having lost their paradise hits them and she tells her brother, 'We lived in Eden and didn't know it'. He replies, 'It's gone for ever' (37).

In his analysis of Lessing's African short stories, Dennis Walder observes: 'Nostalgia has a special resonance for people who have recently emerged from the grip of colonialism, whether we call them colonisers or colonised, although these are overlapping categories still far too often set against each other in a frozen binary' (100–101). Despite being a White, the writer feels the pangs of nostalgia when she returns to her homeland which is no longer a colonised country. In 1989, on her third visit to Africa, her 'myth country', she is dismayed to see a large notice saying 'Trespassers will be Prosecuted' (426), the place where her house had once stood. It is as if the harsh present deliberately distances her from her memories of the past. The writer's attempts to reach out to the past meet a sad end – she is now a complete stranger and a trespasser and her extradition from her homeland for twenty-five years is replicated in the prohibition notice that stares her in the face at the place where she had spent her childhood.

In her autobiography, *Under My Skin*, Lessing explains why the house made of mud and grass in which she had lived in Rhodesia did not interfere with nature, and was closer to her heart than all the houses she had lived in later, 'In London you live in houses where other people have lived, and others again will live there when you have moved or died'. Such houses can never be your own in the true sense. However, she feels, 'A house put together from the plants and earth of the bush is rather like a coat or dress, soon to be discarded, for it probably will have returned to the bush, from fire, insects, or heavy rain long before you die' (54). Commenting on the writer's comparison of a house with a dress, Pat Louw writes,' The image of the dress speaks of the intimacy of the domestic space of Lessing's childhood. She has the sense of being enfolded by the house in a very personal way, but at the same time being vulnerable to the surroundings' (166). Lessing's house in Rhodesia merges into the bush, and the writer states: 'What impresses me now is not how much effect our occupancy had on the landscape of the farm but how little' (55). In *Going Home*, she admits that the memories of her first home impinged on the houses in which she lived later and comments, 'I don't live anywhere; I never have since I left that first house on the *kopje*' (594).

The writer's visits to Africa help her to reconnect with the past, and with her own sense of self. Her physical journeys to her homeland turn into inward journeys as she recalls the memories of her childhood and youth in Africa. Lessing compares the rich past of Africa as she had experienced it, with the dreary present which has been encroached upon by civilisation and its trappings. Carol E. Leon points out:

> 'place/space, a fundamental category of human existence, is a source of our humanity and, consequently, our empowerment. Place and space lead us to see into ourselves, to feel a personal relation with something profound yet transitory and in the process to value ourselves anew'. (207)

Lessing's sense of belonging is replaced by a feeling of displacement, of having been exiled from her homeland. In 1990, Doris Lessing began writing *Under My Skin: Volume One of my Autobiography, to 1949* (*Under My Skin* 8). The volume was later published by Harper Collins in 1994 and won the James Tait Black Prize in the same year. The book begins with a quote from a popular musical by the American composer and songwriter of the early twentieth century Cole Porter (1891–1964), 'I've got you under my skin/I've got you deep in the heart of me', a song from which her autobiography takes its title. Porter's lines seem to have multiple connotations in the context of Lessing's extraordinary life – they may suggest the strong, inescapable influence of the two World Wars on the lives of the people living or born in the early twentieth century, including Doris and her family; or may indicate the indelible sway of the African culture, landscape and thinking on her life and psyche; they may also hint at her troubled relationship with her mother Emily Maude, a subject which has been discussed extensively by critics.

Under My Skin is a complex book. It begins with an introduction to the life of her parents, her birth in 1919 in Kermanshah, and moves on to trace the significant events and turning points in her life – social, physical, psychological, political and economic, as she grew from a defiant, independent child into a woman who still strongly possessed those traits. The book ends in 1949, at the midpoint of the twentieth century when Lessing moved to London from Salisbury. She published *Walking in the Shade: Volume Two of My Autobiography, 1949–1962* in 1997. The writer places an epigraph in the beginning of *Under My Skin* from *Caravan of Dreams* by the Sufi teacher Idries Shah. The lines suggest that individuals cannot catalyse any change in society until they themselves accept the dominating influence of the 'coercive institutions' around them. For an individual Shah states, 'No matter what his reason says, he will always relapse into obedience to the coercive agency while its pattern is within him' (2). The epigraph seems to comment on the overpowering influence of the different institutions in society which are difficult to surpass or to overthrow, one of which is racial discrimination, a policy which Lessing opposed in all her writings.

In the opening pages of her autobiography Lessing dwells on the problems a writer faces when attempting to write an autobiography – the difficulty in telling the complete truth, since people would be hurt if their names were revealed. She also discusses the problems created by 'shifting perspectives, for you see your life differently at different stages, like climbing a mountain while the landscape changes with every turn in the path' (12), a theme which has its echoes in a similar passage quoted earlier from *African Laughter*. The narrative would thus change with the passage of time, since a person writing at the age of thirty would see his/her life events differently than a person writing an autobiography at the age of eighty. Also, she states, that the mind starts creating facts: 'You can actually watch your mind doing it, taking a little fragment of fact and then spinning a tale out of it' (13). The writer believes that parents too are responsible for that, as they try to superimpose false images, or one-sided images of the past into the minds of young children. Yet Lessing is different, for she states, 'Clearly I had to fight to establish a reality of my own, against an insistence from the adults that I should accept theirs' (13). The process of writing an autobiography thus urges a conscientious writer to look back at the past, and look for meanings, motives and connections between different events and also look for the truth. Why one should write an autobiography, is a question that bothers many people. For Lessing – there is a clear reason – the need to understand her complex relationship with her mother. She states, 'I was in nervous flight from her ever since I can remember anything, and from the age of fourteen I set myself obdurately against her in a kind of inner emigration from everything she represented' (15). In *Under My Skin*, Lessing's mother appears as a strong force which the young girl attempts to escape or thwart in all the stages in her life.

The writer's profound relationship with Africa is revealed in the lines in *Under My Skin* where she describes the brick kilns where she and her brother Harry played with black children, stamping and dancing on the mud piles. Later, as the moulds were filled with mud, dried and placed in the kiln and lit with fire, Lessing was overwhelmed by the view of the flames in the kiln, and the warm glow of heat. She writes: 'I remember standing there by myself, my whole heart and soul going out and up into those flaming skies, knowing that was where I belonged, in all that splendour, which was so sad, so sorrowful'. The awareness of her not belonging strikes her painfully as she states: 'I was not here at all, or I wouldn't be for long, I would get away from here soon' (81).

Born in 1919, the writer calls herself a child of the war, when there was death and destruction all around the world. Lessing's was a forceps birth and her face remained scarred for several days. She states, 'Do I believe this difficult birth scarred me – that is to say, my nature? Who knows?' (8). But the devastating effects of the war did scar her childhood and her life with that of her parents as they struggled due to the dearth of money and bore mental agony and physical suffering throughout their lives in Southern Rhodesia. Lessing's life was strongly affected by the wars and she states, 'We are all of us made by war, twisted and warped by war, but we seem to forget it' (10). Marlene A. Briggs argues that in *Under My Skin*, Doris Lessing 'personifies the First World War as her birth parent, constituting herself as a collective subject subordinated to the protracted dynamics of historical strife' (3).

Deeply attached to her adopted country, Lessing was also troubled by the injustice practiced by the ruling whites against the native blacks. While the writer does not discuss this issue explicitly in *Under My Skin*, she mentions it briefly at certain points. At the age of fourteen, when she was getting into fights time and again with her mother, she writes: 'And now we were quarrelling about the Colour Bar, the Native Question'. Observing the political and social equations between the whites and the blacks around her, Lessing had 'a strong feeling there was something terribly wrong with the System'. This became a cause of dispute between Lessing and her parents, as she recollects her thoughts in *Under My Skin*: 'why were all these people working for so little money on our farm?' (179). Her question reflected her growing sensitivity towards human rights as she moved into adulthood.

Under My Skin captures the writer's gradual awakening towards self-understanding and towards the conscious distinction between right and wrong as she observed her parents and their relationship with the African people and the physical terrain. Her parents' helplessness and their financial predicament made an indelible impact on young Lessing's mind. She quotes an incident when she, as a little girl, watched them as they sat together, worrying about money. She found it intolerable to see their helplessness. Lessing recalls: 'I stand there, a fierce unforgiving adamant child, saying to myself: I won't … I am not going to be like them'. She takes a resolution: 'Remember this moment … Don't be like them' (120). This was her momentous decision to take control and not to yield. She states 'In other words, I was rejecting the human condition, which is to be trapped by circumstances'. The writer recalls such powerful moments of her childhood in *Under My Skin*.

Lessing through her autobiography also reveals that her mother's open dislike for her, the strict upbringing, the penury which curbed many opportunities and shrunk the possibilities of happiness, also scarred her life. She states in *Under My Skin*, 'I do not believe that even robust and sensitive children remain unaffected by the assault on their very existence. But I was born with skins too few. Or they were scrubbed off me by those robust and efficient hands' (30). In *Under My Skin*, the writer painstakingly pieces the events of the early part of her life, struggles to recall the stretches of time which remain marked as black holes in her memory, and develops a chronological and meaningful subjective narrative. Through her autobiographical writings, Lessing is able to come to terms with her past, its influences and its clearly directed course into a future which established her as a reputed writer and brought her incomparable fame and honour.

The last few lines of the book are sharp and striking, as she decides to migrate to England and live in London. She states, 'Behind me a door had slammed shut'. She had left her past behind 'meaning the tentacles of family … I was not going home to my family; I was fleeing away from it. The door had shut and that was that' (419). The lines indicate Lessing's breaking away from the past that was in Africa, her fleeing away from it to a different, a more promising life in London. They also reveal a desire to escape the clutches of her family – of her mother – who had always tried to dictate Lessing's choices. The phrase 'my family' may also relate to the writer's emotional connections with Africa, and her persistent attempts to become an insider in a land where she was always treated as an outsider due to her white lineage.

Both *African Laughter* and *Under My Skin* bring out Doris Lessing's nostalgia for her past spent in Southern Rhodesia, and her strong yearning to revive her bonds with her myth country. The narratives in both these autobiographical works evoke for the writer, as well as for the readers, images of a paradise that should have been preserved, but which, unfortunately has suffered at the hands of time and of man. While Lessing's four visits to Zimbabwe recollected in *African Laughter* give her an opportunity to return to the country close to her heart, the difficult, but satisfying task of writing the first part of her autobiography, *Under My Skin*, allows the writer to revisit her childhood as well as the land which had imbued her past with colours and her life with happy memories.

References

Briggs, Marlene A. 'Born in the Year 1919': Doris Lessing, the First World War, and the Children of Violence'. *Doris Lessing Studies* 27. pp. 1–2.

Leon, Carol E. *Movement and Belonging: Lines, Places and Spaces of Travel*. New York: Peter Lang, 2009.

Lessing, Doris. *African Laughter: Four Visits to Zimbabwe*. 1992. London: Flamingo, 1993.

——. 'Going Home'. *The Doris Lessing Reader*. New York: Knopf, 1988, pp. 593–603.

——. *Under My Skin: Volume One of My Autobiography, to 1949*. 1994. London: Flamingo, 1995.

Louw, Pat. 'Domestic Spaces: Huts and Houses in Doris Lessing's African Stories.' *Doris Lessing: Interrogating the Times*. Ed. Debrah Raschke, Phyllis Sternberg Perrakis and Sandra Singer. Columbus: The Ohio State UP, 2010, pp. 165–82.

Maslen, Elizabeth. *Doris Lessing*. Plymouth: Northcote House & British Council, 1994.

Scott, Lynda. 'Similarities between Virginia Woolf and Doris Lessing'. *Deep South* 3.2, 1997: n. Pag. Web. Source, Viewed on 26 December 2012.

Walder, Dennis. 'Alone in a Landscape': Lessing's African Stories Remembered'. *The Journal of Commonwealth Literature,* 43.2, pp. 99–115.

Walker, Melissa. 'An Eye Towards Recovery: Trauma, Nostalgia, and the Bush in *African Laughter*'. *Doris Lessing Studies,* 27. pp. 1–2. 2008: 29–33.

15 Travelling Subjectivities and Bridging Discourses in Ghosh's *The Glass Palace*

Urmil Talwar

> When you heave your final sigh and turn the last page of Amitav Ghosh's new novel, *The Glass Palace,* you feel as if you've travelled for hundred years on foot, through the most distant and lush lands on the globe. (Minna Proctor)

Amitav Ghosh is the most distinguishing Indian writer whose diverse oeuvre attempts to challenge the artificial boundaries that have been erected to separate nations from their neighbours, fact from fiction and academic disciplines from each other. He conflates different genres to achieve fictional recreation and travel constitutes an important aspect of his work. Meticulously researched his fiction is transnational, as his characters travel across countries, continents and oceans and refuse to stay contained in neat compartments. The accounts of his travel are significant documents of culture and anchor in the larger canvas of historical and socio-political reality. The two primary traits that have defined travel literature are construction of an autonomous travelling subject and movement across national boundaries. Both these traits find expression in Amitav Ghosh's novel *The Glass Palace* as he amalgamates his personal travels with those of his characters and gives detail insight into the geoscapes, its culture, tradition and ethos. Sprawling across three generations of the same family and moving from Burma and Malaya to India and the United States, this novel has a protagonist Rajkumar Raha, a shipwrecked sailor boy whose rags to riches story is counterpointed with that of the Burmese royal family. In this paper I propose to examine the disparate forms and intentions of travel and mobility that the characters experience and reconstruct, and how space has been re-territorialised in *The Glass Palace.* And also explore the connections in cultural diversities that create avenues to establish compatibility, enhance cross cultural understanding and respect for individual.

Travel has long been valued both in East and West because 'it annihilates the ego of the traveler, reduces patriotism, acquaints traveler with a common nature, fate and identity that persists beneath the diversity of cultural types' (Leed 219). The motivation for travel as well as the outcome of travel are various and unpredictable. Travel whether temporal or spatial, occasions comparisons between what is unfamiliar and familiar. Such journeys make one aware of the world and distance from home develops a critical perspective of one's commitments and attachments with home. In the context of globalisation the world has become smaller with rapid movement of peoples, ideas and information it entails. Today, travel both as a metaphor and as a practice of seeking knowledge is increasingly taken centre stage. Janet Wolff writes, 'notions of mobility, fluidity, provisionality and process have been preferable to alternative notions of statis and fixity' (228). Travel writing also has, become an attempt to introduce 'self' to the 'other' providing an opportunity to explore the other culture and record experiences in context of the cultural dialogue in the 'Contact Zone'.[1] Travel writers try to build bridges among human beings of different geographical areas through an understanding of diverse cultures. The literary writers have extolled this urge for exploration, since time immemorial, as in the stories of Ulysses and Herodotus, Iliad and Odyssey. The accounts of adventure and exploration constitute significant documents of culture and the writer especially the immigrant, diasporic writer presents his experience imaginatively and constructs or interprets reality from his own angle or vision. The accounts of travel are a record of the experiences and perceptions of the writer through a cultural dialogue. Today in the industrialised, modernised, global village cultural difference is not the problem. The subject of importance today is the hierarchical difference between a rational 'West' and a magical or exotic and seductive 'East'. Living together in a cosmopolitan world is not about erasing cultural differences but about being critical about the way difference is being represented. The condition of 'homelessness' that Said described as the state of postmodernity is replaced by a general sense of multiple homes in a globalised society. More and more people, in the contemporary world live away from their 'home' and different versions of 'culture' and 'homeland' are imagined rather than experienced. Even as the home culture gets translated, copied and imagined in the distance created between people and the place, the importance of cultural backgrounds for identifying the self does not dissolve in the crossing of borders.

'Location' and 'Culture' go together as anthropologists have conveniently represented it but with rapid means of transportation and communication their relationship is not undermined but it gets reoriented as 'deterritorialisation', 'reterritorialisation' or differently territorialised. In the cosmopolitan world the relationship between people and space has changed as people become attached to multiple spaces in complex ways. The anthropologist James Clifford in his essay 'Travelling Cultures' classified travellers travelling for social, political, economic or religious reasons as those who are materially privileged and others who are oppressed. These travellers produce knowledge, stories, music, books, diaries, traditions and other cultural expressions (108). While transcending cultural and historical boundaries, resonances and anxieties across language and time are evoked and travel writings become acts of translation practices. For Clifford travel is an invaluable term of translation because in the process of translation itself one can learn a lot about peoples, cultures, histories, different from one's own (105). In the contemporary world culture is in a state of flux and whatever is seen and heard are also in constant flux, even the categories of contrasts are not stable or fixed; each new encounter discloses different vectors of comparison for the traveller. Arjun Appadurai while discussing globalisation and transnationality argues that the global cultural flow has transformed our understanding of cultural and national 'identities'. The traditional postcolonial analysis of these global transformational forces is to identify their links into the hegemony of western cultural imperialism. The postcolonial argument posits that the West intrudes upon and changes cultural forms and practices of the East, while the latter passively submits itself to the hegemony. Abdul R. Jan Mohamed while defining, 'specular border intellectual'[2] has put together arguments and examples both of pain and privilege of homelessness –

> ... unhealable rift forced between a human being and a native place, between 'self' and its true home ... makes possible the privilege of having not just one set of eyes but half a dozen, each of them corresponding to the place you have been (1984: 49).

Edward Said's exposition of inequalities of power implicated in the imposition of Western language and his emphasis on the distortion of the 'Orient' does not hold today. His fixation with travel and knowledge about Europe and Orient reflects a narrowness of vision because today with multiple encounters and opportunities of multidirectional flow of knowledge the 'Other' is defined not just against the West but also by regional, racial, ethnic, linguistic, sexual and other differences somewhat closer home. The journey and the experience of difference suggest that the nature and locale of 'home' emerges out of, and is transformed by such voyages abroad. The movement of people across territorial boundaries, set forth by colonial disruption of relatively closed communal living in various parts of the world has problematised the definition of 'native'. James Clifford's (1992) notion of 'travelling culture' is a significant exposition of 'native' culture as a 'non-static entity', which is affected and transformed by the intrusion of imperialist culture and later in the age of globalisation the 'native' culture, is a culture that 'travels' and takes an active part in transforming both itself and the cultures it encounters. Chambers (1994) notes that the uprooted 'native' cultures in this transient electronic age are open to multiple possibilities and transmutations. Said (1979) has already discussed that transmutation and hybridisation of cultural identity, and the syncretic perspective that arises from it, can constitute a new space for the study of culture. Existing 'in a median state, neither completely at one with the new setting nor fully disencumbered of the old' (Said 1994: 36) the 'foreigner' is compelled to inhabit at least two identities, to speak at least two languages, and to negotiate and translate between them. Working with the postcolonial subject Said believes that the colonial subjects with precolonial identity develop a 'second nature' affected and unsettled by imperialism. However, neither of these two identities describe their true subjectivity and it becomes necessary 'to seek out, to map, to invent, or to discover a third nature' wherein resides the potential for better understanding the experiences of postcolonial subjects (Said 1993: 226). Bhabha (1994) too reacts against the polarisation and simplification of culture that contemporary critical theories dwell on in the binary opposition of self and other, centre and periphery, oppressor and oppressed. He defines 'a third space' to signify a new frame of reference and process of signification that occurs in between cultures as a result of contact and difference. For Bhabha, there is no simple definition of 'nation' in a globalised world. Those on the move are forever dwelling in the 'in-between-space' on the margins of nations. For Bhabha, hybridity is not an admixture of established cultures or identities, but an elusive condition where signs and meanings can be 'appropriated, translated, rehistoricised and read anew' (1994: 37). Bhabha, through his use of hybridity tries to examine the space of resistance and redefine it in colonial encounters where the colonial authority 'denies' knowledge of the colonised into the dominant discourse and estranges the basis of its authority. However for Bhabha the 'in-between' is a space of dynamic engagement and the identity of the postcolonial subject is not situated in the polarity of the native minority discourse or dominant colonial discourse but in the 'cutting edge of translation and negotiation', (1994: 38) where new subjectivity is formed. Bhabha theorises this liminal, interstitial border zone and focuses on texts where the anthropologists Lavie and Swedenberg (1996) focus on the lived experience. They have given the concept of 'a third timespace' through ethnographic examination. According to them, 'this is a terrain where opposition is not only responsive, but creative. It is guerrilla warfare of the interstices, where minorities rupture categories of race, gender, sexuality, class, nation and empire in the centre as well as on the margins' (1996: 165–6). The study of this third timespace is an attempt to displace the notion of the autonomy or boundedness of culture, and to map out some of the everyday practices that create historically grounded multiple subject positions.

In the last decade of the twentieth century there has been a new diasporic consciousness as this new community of Asian diaspora is able to negotiate the shifting dynamics of power and agency in order to produce alternative versions of modernity and postmodernity, new cosmopolitianism in response to the dominant narratives of globalisation. The easy accessibility of modes of travel for business and leisure, as opposed to forced migration and exile, too encouraged a radical rethinking of homeland, nation and culture. The new diaspora members have to be, simultaneously, of several overlapping 'imagined communities (Anderson 1989) and they have the capacity to live in and negotiate between and across several cultural worlds; they have the capacity to struggle with the burden of 'double consciousness' (Dubois (1904) 1989). On one hand they bear the traces of their own particular cultures, traditions, histories, languages and systems of belief. On the other hand, they must come to terms with and make sense of the new host culture and society they take residence in.

Michel de Certeau persuasively argues that, while translation 'presumes the hegemony of self over other', it does so dialogically in the quite specific sense that it is 'polysemic and multivocal rather than monological or unidirectional'. A model of translation that implies approximation rather than correspondence means that interpretative 'facts' must be represented as acts; partial recognitions are neither fully translatable nor fully comprehensible. Henry Giroux too espouses the need to 'construct a notion of border identity that challenges any essentialised notion of subjectivity while simultaneously demonstrating that the self as a historical and cultural formation is shaped in complex, related and multiple ways through its interaction with numerous and diverse communities' (38). It is in the 'border culture' that minorities resist subordination and try to incorporate themselves into the dominant structure, they create new alignments and solidarity with one another. In creating these transnational ties and cultural identification, immigrants engage in discourses which lead into an 'in-between space' that is used by the immigrant minority to subvert the dominant discourses of both their native and adopted countries. It is in the same 'border zone' that their subjectivity is formed in different social and cultural systems to forge new grounds for defining themselves in relation to both their host and home cultures. In creating this 'third space' in a transnational culture the writer draws on discourses both from his home and host cultures and nations. It is in this space zone that the writers and characters exercise agency in defining his subjectivity and reflecting on different social and cultural systems and ways of life around him. Multiple linguistic and cultural affiliations are formed and identity resists subordination to project a new subjective position through cross-cultural exchange and negotiation of difference.

Travel, migration and resettlement drastically affect and change the lives and culture of the immigrants and exile. Travel contributes an important aspect in Amitav Ghosh's fiction. A common element in Ghosh's entire corpus is that individuals do not feel the agony and pain in an alien land they travel to, neither there is nostalgia for the lost home nor the intense desire to return to their homeland and cultural roots. In *The Glass Palace* the deliberate mobility and the experience of dislocation of the characters redefines their subjectivity. Rajkumar's travelling subjectivity is negotiated at various levels from a young orphaned boy who works at Ma Cho's tea stall, moves in the service of Saya John, goes to east coast of India with Baburao to bring indentured labour for timber and rubber plantations, becomes a confident timber merchant. Later he leaves Burma as an Indian refugee. In fact his rise and fall is the story of Indian planters in Burma and also of the colonisation and independence of Burma after the Second World War. Ghosh's narrative *The Glass Palace* is a fictional exploration of the complexities of belonging and identity and the mobility of cross-cultural diasporas and its relocation. Migrancy or displacement here is enforced by colonial and postcolonial circumstances. Ghosh vividly depicts the consequences of migration in the life of ordinary people of the subcontinent who frequently cross borders either due to political, personal or economic reasons through fictional representation of migrant characters. Home, memory and marginalisation are problematised throughout his fiction. The political reasons being the second world war, and partition. Indentured labour, migration to the middle-east in 1970s and enrichment of life are the economic reasons. Ghosh is also extensively preoccupied with the issues of space, place and the idea of home. Departures, wanderings, homecomings are woven into this text as dominant preoccupation in relation to the exploration of identity and belonging. Most of Ghosh's fictional themes emerge from his transnational experience. Ghosh himself is a much travelled man and his travels have aided his understanding of the changes that take place in the life and culture of in individual to adjust in the alien land. His trip to Egypt for his research finds place in his novel *In an Antique Land*. *The Glass Palace* brings to limelight the neighbouring country Burma that he visited at a young age and his meeting with Aung Sung Su Kyi that inspired him to amalgamate his personal travels with those of his characters to give detail description of the place and an insight into the cultural tradition and ethos in Burma. His travelogue *Dancing in Cambodia* and *At Large in Burma* are based upon his travel experiences and his personal contacts with the native people and the interviews he had conducted. His fictional characters like Ghosh himself are always on the move. In the Author's Note to *The Glass Palace* Ghosh confesses that he has brought to life a fictional world except for King Thebaw, Queen Supayalata and his daughters, none of its characters bear any resemblance to real people, living or deceased (549). In the novel Ghosh portrays both exile and immigrant characters.

Travel for the exiled royal family is a compulsion whether they dislike or abhor travel. They were deported to Madras and then to Ratnagiri, a small hill town between Mumbai and Goa. They are forced into a different kind of life they had known in Burma. The physical and mental torture they experienced, the deprivation they suffered, the squalor and dirt they lived in and the agony and pain of an exile, is very vividly portrayed by the author. The king withdraws into silence and speaks only of the forecast events that he can foresee through his binoculars. The Queen meets the delegates and reveals her resentment at their captivity. Along with this, *The Glass Palace* is a story of hundred years of three generations of two families travelling across three nations – Burma, Malaya and India – interweaving Indian culture with Burmese and that of Malaya. Ghosh depicts the impact of cultural 'roots' and 'routes' upon the life of people of the subcontinent. Santosh Gupta writes, 'Ghosh is a writer of ongoing migrations and transnational cultural flows, who questions the validities of boundaries and borders imposed by some powerful race, country or community over others' (qtd Bhargava 242).

The historical characters, i.e. the Royal family and Dolly belong to the Burmese ethnic group who are deported to Ratnagiri, India. The King and the Queen bear hatred towards the colonisers and keep aloof from the culture of alien country, India. The four

Princesses and Dolly try to assimilate in the Indian culture and their subjectivity is not formed of resistance but of accommodation. They are inquisitive and wish to understand the Indian culture; interact with local people; learn their languages – Tamil, Hindi and Marathi; adopt their attire (saree) and rejoice in their festivities. Dolly's interaction with local inhabitants helps her to suggest solutions to various problems faced by the Royal family from time to time at Outram House. She becomes friendly with Uma, the wife of the collector Beni Prasad Dey, who initiates her into Indian culture and beseeches her into an intercultural marriage with Rajkumar Raha, an Indian timber merchant in Burma. The eldest princess is also married to the coach man Mohan Sawant. In fact the eldest princess and Dolly, the only attendant from Burma, begin to consider Ratnagiri – the Outram House – as their home. 'Twenty years and this is home to me now. In Burma, I would be a foreigner', says Dolly (112). Again when leaving for Burma with Rajkumar Raha, for her marriage, she says – 'This was home. She knew, she would never see it again. A cloth bundle, once again: only this time she wasn't carrying it on her head' (117). Rajkumar Raha, Uma Dey and Arjun belong to the Indian ethnic group and Saya John is from Malaya. Rajkumar Raha is an Indian immigrant form Chittagaon who rises to become a teak business tycoon in Burma. He and his mentor, in life and business, use the vast resources and potential of their settled country and adjust according to their business requirements. Saya John is a Chinese immigrant to Burma and later he moves to Malaya. He is described thus – 'His clothes were those of a European and he knew Hindustani – and yet the cast of his face was neither that of a white man nor an Indian. He was Chinese from Malaya' (8).

The valorisation of wandering and rootlessness has served to privilege a position of what Michael Walzer has called radical 'detachment' intellectual and emotional (29) which is portrayed in the character of Raj Kumar who does not have parents or a family to rely on, 'no fabric of small memories from which to cut a large cloth' (147). He has the freedom to choose his own attachments, his friends, family and wife'. His choice is not dictated by caste or class, race or nation. He chooses Dolly for his mate and Saya John for his mentor. From Saya John he learns about the teak industry, the logging and ferrying in the river, about elephants and their diseases. After becoming a successful timber merchant he travels to Ratnagiri to find Dolly, the queen's attendant and on Uma Dey's instigation marries her. Raj Kumar's family and friends are Uma's and Saya John's family. All these migrant characters Saya John, Rajkumar, Dolly, her children Neel and Dinu, Saya's son Matthew, Metthew's daughter Alison, Uma, her nephew Arjun, his friend Hardy have dual identities – by imbibing the moral codes, the dress, language and culture of the country to which they migrate and retaining their own native culture. To depict their dual identities Dolly and Raj Kumar's children are given double names. This also reflects the hybriditiy of two nations and two cultures. The elder son is Neeladhri Raha alias Neel has a Burmese name Sein Win and he looks more Indian than Burmese in built and colouring (202). The younger son Deenanath Raha or Deenu whose Burmese name is Tun Pe inherits his mother's delicate features as well as her ivory complexion and fine boned slimness of build (202). Their culture cannot be defined by national boundaries. Robert Dixon writes that Ghosh's characters 'do not occupy discrete cultures, but 'dwell-in-travel' in the cultural spaces that flow across borders' – 'the shadow lines' drawn around modern nation states' (10).

Rajkumar, Saya John and Arjun all imitate the life of colonial masters occupying a 'third space' (Hall 2003: 402), a 'third scenario', and their subjectivities are shaped by the colonial system of plantation and the army respectively. Arjun's experience at the battlefront breaks down his comforting illusion that the Indian commissioned officers are equal to their British counterparts. He discovered that he is merely a pawn to be used by the empire. After the death of Neel during the anti-Indian agitation in Burma Dolly, Rajkumar, Manju, her daughter Jaya travel to India as refugees. Rajkumar leads the rest of his life as a dependent in Uma's house. Dolly's life had been transformed after the illness of Deenu and she was drawn towards Buddhism. Leaving Jaya and Rajkumar with Uma, she goes for saging at the nunnery in Burma. Both Rajkumar and Dolly return to their homelands in the last days of their life. Raj Kumar's life is directly connected to the institution, and the rise and breakdown of plantation economy. It is only Deenu who survives the second world war. Living in Burma he now uses his Burmese name U Tun Pe and leads a solitary life in his studio 'The Glass Palace Studio' and later marries a Burmese writer.

The Glass Palace does not problematise the cultural difference as Edward Said does in *Orientalism,* i.e. a hierarchical difference between two cultures. Here it is living together in a world of actually existing cosmopolitans. It is not about erasing cultural differences but being critical about the way difference is being represented. In this novel the characters have a general sense of multiple homes. Dolly thinks Outram House to be her home. Manju, Neel's wife when reaches Mandalay feels she's home although she is going there for the first time. For an Indian woman believes that after marriage her husband's home is her actual home. There is attachment to multiple spaces in complex ways. In the 'contact zones' one finds complex and new ways of life and cultural categories formed by an intermingling of lifestyles among settlers and natives, trans-racial love story and marital alliances there by engaging discourses of identity, community, selfhood and otherness.

Notes

1. Contact Zone is 'space of colonial encounters, the space in which peoples geographically and historically separated come into contact with each other and establish ongoing relations, usually involving conditions of coercion, radical inequality and intractable conflict'. M.L. Pratt, *Imperial Eyes: Travel Writing and Transculturation.* London and New York: Routledge, 1992. p. 6.
2. Abdul R Jan Mohamed, 'Worldiness – Without-World, Homelessness-as-Home: Towards a Definition of the Specular Border Intellectual', in *Edward Said: A Critical Reader,* ed. Michael Sprinker (Cambridge, MA: Blackwell Pub. 1992, 96–120). defines specular Border Intellectual as.
3. 'The third scenario' is a non-binarist space of reflection and struggle in the politics of location … the space of demographic plurality … where diaspora identities are constantly producing and reproducing themselves anew, through transformation and difference. Hall 1993:402

References

Anderson, B. *Imagined Communities: Reflections on the Origin and Spread of Nations* London: Verso, 1991.

Appadurai, A. 'Disjuncture and Difference in the Global Cultural Economy'. *Public Culture* 2(2): 1–24, 1990.

——. *Modernity at Large: Cultural Dimensions of Globalization*. Public Worlds Minneapolis, University of Minnesota Press, 1996.

Bhabha, H. *The Location of Culture*, London: Routledge, 1994.

Bhargava, Rajul ed. *Indian Writing in English: The Last Decade*. New Delhi, Jaipur: Rawat Publications, 2002, pp. 242–252.

Chakraborty, D. *Provincializing Europe: Postcolonial Thought and Historical Difference*. Princeton, NJ: Princeton Univ. Press, 2000.

Chambers, I. *Migrancy, Culture, Identity*. New York: Routledge, 1994.

Clifford, J. *Routes: Travel and Translation in the Late Twentieth Century*. Cambridge, MA: Harvard Univ. Press, 1997.

Clifford, James. 'Travelling Cultures' in *Cultural Studies*. Eds. Lawrence Grossber, et al. New York, London: Routledge, 1992, pp. 96–116.

Daiya, K.. '"No Home but in Memory": Migrant Bodies and Belongings, Globalization and Nationalism in *The Circle of Reason* and *The Shadow Lines'*. *Amitav Ghosh: Critical Perspectives*. Ed. B. Bose Delhi: Pencraft International, 2003.

de Certeau, Michel. *The Practice of Everyday Life*. Berkeley and Los Angeles: University of California Press, 1988.

Dixon, Robert. 'Travelling in the West: The Writing of Amitav Ghosh'. *The Journal of Commonwealth Literature*. 31, 1. 1996, pp. 3–24.

Dubois, W.E.B. 'The Souls of Black Fold' in *The Independent*. 1904. Web Source. The official site of W.E.B. Dubois Bois.org

Ghosh. Amitav. 2000. *The Glass Palace*. New Delhi: Harper Collins Publishers, 2008.

Giroux, H.A. 'Living Dangerously: Identity Politics and the New Cultural Racism' in *Between Borders: Pedagogy and the Politics of Cultural Studies*, eds. H.A. Giroux and P. McLaren. New York: Routledge, 1994, pp. 29–56.

Gupta, Santosh, 'Looking into History: Amitav Ghosh's *The Glass Palace*,' in *Indian Writing in English: The Last Decade*. Ed. Rajul Bhargava. New Delhi, Jaipur: Rawat Publications, 2002.

Hall, Stuart, 'Cultural Identity and Diaspora' in *Identity: Community, Culture and Difference*. Ed. J Rutherford. London: Lawrence and Wishart, 1990.

Jan Mohamed, Abdul R. 'Worldiness – Without-World, Homelessness-as-Home: Towards a Definition of the Specular Border Intellectual', in *Edward Said: A Critical Reader*, ed. Michael Sprinker. Cambridge, MA: Blackwell Pub. 1992, pp. 96–120.

Lavie, S. and Swedenburg T. 'Between and Among Boundaries of Culture: Bridging Text and Lived Experience in the Third Timespace'. *Cultural Studies* 10 (1), 1996, pp. 154–179.

Leed, Eric. *The Mind of the Traveler: From Gilgamesh to Global Tourism.* Harper Collins, 1991.

Pratt, M.L. *Imperial Eyes: Travel Writing and Transculturation.* London and New York: Routledge, 1992.

Proctor, Minna. Rev. of *The Glass Palace.* Official site of Amitav Ghosh. Web source.

Said, E.W. *Orientalism.* New York: Vintage Books, 1979.

Said, E.W. 'The Mind of Winter: Reflections on Life in Exile', *Harper's*, Vol. 269 (September 1984).

Said, E.W. *Culture and Imperialism.* New York: Vintage Books, 1993.

Walzer, Michael. *The Company of Critics: Social Criticism and Political Commitment in the Twentieth Century.* London: Peter Malban, 1989.

Wolff, Janet. 'On the Road Again: Metaphors of Travel in Cultural Criticism', *Cultural Studies* 7, 1993.

16 Reviewing the Orient

Portrayals of China in the Novels of Kazuo Ishiguro and Kunal Basu

Santosh Gupta

Travel accounts have played an important role in creating interest in different, remote countries and cultures, and have been the initial openings for western empires. Travel routes opened up different areas of the world for the curious, the adventurer and the explorer. Eventually the races that conquered different regions of the world controlled them, sometimes directly and often the areas which were not conquered were dealt with indirectly such areas also experienced their power and control. Vast empires, however, were gradually dismantled, bringing about a process of reverse travels by the subjugated races, who began to create their own accounts of the metropolitan cultures and centres.

After colonisation, a reverse route of travelling began, where the formerly colonised or dominated indirectly visited the western metropolitan cities out of curiosity, wonder, and even awe, at the fabled grandeur, order and civilisations of these 'power wielders'. A 'meta-narrative journeying and return', and dislocation through diasporic settlement in the west has followed in the post-colonial period (Boehmer 190). Boehmer relates this tendency of travel (by the formerly dominated people) to the earlier travel accounts of the 'imperial expansion' and the tales that were 'voyage(s) into the mystery to the heart of darkness (192).

Such travellers have explored, among other things, the images of the colonised and exploited people that were constructed as part of the intellectual background to the conquest of these other countries and their people. Edward Said's well-researched and argued books *Orientalism* (1978) and *Culture and Imperialism* (1993) present the systematic manner in which the invading race built up images of the other races or communities that it was preparing to dominate, and the ground laid by such knowledge in the construction of power dominance.

Travellers' accounts from the formerly dominated and ruling classes/groups/races in some recent fiction use historical incidents and background to reconstruct the interface between the western and the eastern countries which were directly or indirectly subjugated and exploited. Post-colonial writers now living in the west but originally from eastern locations, juxtapose the races that were locked together in various relationships under colonial control. Two recent novels, Kazuo Ishiguro's *When We Were Orphans* (2000) and Kunal Basu's *The Yellow Emperor's Cure* (2012), are centred round travels to China by two European men; who come to China on important personal quests. These travels to China reexamine epistemological, moral and psychological issues related to the west's relations with China in the past five hundred years.

These two novels also reflect a renewal of interest in the strange relationship that has existed between the western countries and China, in the eighteenth and nineteenth centuries, after having gone through a 'cyclical pattern' which fluctuates between 'positive and negative representations' (Robinson 53).[1] The western representations of China began, as Robinson points out, the thirteenth century, when the early explorers experienced awe at its affluence, advanced knowledge systems and cultural developments; these stages of Chinese glory were acknowledged by the Jesuit Missionaries who began to travel to China after the fourteenth century. The next two stages involved a philosophical idealisation of Confucianism and finally, a disillusionment with Chinese changelessness' (Robinson 57). In all these representations the Chinese people and their culture were seen as the 'other pole of human existence', for the differences were far too many to be easily transcended. As a result, China became an object of myths, mysteries and was exoticised; even its degradation, brought about by internal and external factors, was turned into stories of strange, unbelievable tales of depravity, sordidness and cunning manipulativeness. In the twenty first century the emergence of China as an economically strong nation once again generates new 'othering' myths in the west, creating tales of exploited and submissive poor, ruled by power and money hungry, cruel and cold rulers, ignoring west's own similar exploitations of the poor and helpless citizens in different parts of the world.

The process of reviewing the exoticised China and examining it as a land of human struggles with its various forms of natural calamities, political disturbances and western assault upon its internal economy and policies is a postcolonial epistemiological effort to perceive China's histories of exploitation and uneven life that it shares with the other Asian countries, like India, and Burma. Such a reviewing tries to remove the veils of mystery and myths built around different cultural practices, political histories and communities that has persisted in west's relations with not only China but also other regions it has dominated. These novels question the assumptions underneath the western depiction of the eastern, African and other subjugated people which, as Cheryl McEwan writes, are mostly 'unacknowledged and unexamined' and are 'profoundly insensitive to the meanings, values and practices of other cultures' (25).

When We Were Orphans and *The Yellow Emperor's Cure* are among those fictional works that have appeared in the recent decades which look beyond the bamboo veil or the great wall of China, into its ravaged slums, poor shantytowns and question the diplomatic dealings and irresponsible human exploitation made by the several western countries that had forcibly entered and settled within China. There is another novel by Amitav Ghosh, *Sea of Poppies,* in which the depiction of the British traders forcing Indian opium into Chinese market and the people's lives also explores these historical moments. Ghosh shows the threats of war about trade dealings through which the European countries, led by the Britishers plan to destroy China's resistance to the forced inflow of opium. The British decide that 'John Chinaman's attempts to resist are indicative of an irrational, stubbornness, a backwardness in terms of international trade (250). Through a single Chinese character, Ah Fatt, Ghosh depicts the utter breakdown of a human being's physical and mental health, and his dehumanisation through his addiction to opium. The novel strongly suggests the wide spread damage to Chinese men and women who were being provided opium, to earn profit and, to ruin their physical and mental health (290–98).

Kunal Basu's *The Yellow Emperor's Cure* (2012) and Ishiguro's *When We Were Orphans* (2000) portray the conditions of ordinary Chinese city dwellers, rural peasantry and their experiences of the west's trade with their country. Rather than go into remote, ancient past, these novels are located in specifically mentioned historic moments in 1899–1900 when there was a popular uprising in China called the Boxer Revolution, and during 1933 to 1940s, when China was engaged in war with Japan. China's relations with the west had come full circle in the nineteenth century when the admiration for China's developed technology, industry, crafts and philosophy in the thirteenth century had changed into contempt, ridicule and mistrust. It was after forcing opium upon the Chinese people that England and the other Western countries had turned the Chinese and their rulers to helplessness, and dealt with them on their terms.

When Kunal Basu, an Indian living in England, and Kazuo Ishiguro, a Japanese living in England, write about China they do not repeat the stereotypical images constructed by the west. They move beyond the set images and prejudices governing the western mind, and one suspects that these authors' original location in the east perhaps helps them to discredit the prejudicial attitude. Placed in-between two locations, these writers can watch the relationships from a perspective different from that of any one location. They use this situation critically as they portray new perception and understanding. These novels present aspects of China that are part of its historical and political conditions between late nineteenth and mid-twentieth centuries, in more or less realistic mode. The impact of these socio-political and economic disturbances are seen upon the lives of ordinary people, for both these writers view the rural and urban poor Chinese more than the leaders of China.

Christopher Banks, the English hero of Ishiguro's *When We Were Orphans* visits China in October 1937 to pursue the most difficult and important case of his life that he has to solve. He is a professional detective, having solved some cases that have made him well known in England and other countries. The journey Banks makes in 1937 is the second important journey of his life. As an eight years old boy he had to leave Shanghai for England when he was left entirely alone after both has parents had disappeared, one after the other. He returns after about two decades, to look for the parents, who he believes were still being held captive somewhere in Shanghai. He had been led to believe, as a child, that the parents had been kidnapped, and the ambition to find them and free them had egged him on to take up this profession.

The hero of Kunal Basu's *The Yellow Emperor's Cure* (2012) Dr Antonio Henrique, Maria is a young Portugese surgeon skilled in western medical science. The novel opens in Lisbon's hospital but soon the scene shifts to the annual feast of St. Anthony, which is being celebrated like a carnival, with festivities, dances, drinking and open sexuality. The once rich and powerful empire is shown to have led to loose moral behaviour, now caught in a wide spread incidence of syphilus. Antonio learns with shock that his father too is suffering from the last stages of this incurable disease. He explores many medical sources only to be told that there was no known sure treatment. At the knowledge that China had very few patients of syphilis, Antonio plans to visit the country in search of the cure. The enquiries reveal that the disease spread as western travellers visited different Asian and other parts, taking along with them several other diseases as well.

Antonio's trip to China seems to be unwise and impractical from the outset. Perhaps this simplistic faith in finding the cure, the idea of travelling for knowledge earns him the name 'Candide' from Arees, the intelligent independent minded sister of Antonio's best friend, Ricardo. *Candide* – a novel of initiation by the French Enlightenment scholar, Voltaire, mocks its young hero's inexperience and heroic ideas of war, values and human relations which *Candide* learns to discard. The hero also learns to respect the knowledges and practices of the 'other' races that he meets during his travels. Basu uses this reference to *Candide* to highlight the respect that some Enlightenment philosophers had for diverse cultures and people despite their otherwise prejudiced opinion of the non-western. Basu's novel places his hero in a totally different world, that gradually acquaints him with a culture and country very different from his own. He begins the travel with the hope of finding a cure for the disease; what transpires in Peking bring him in the whirlwind of revolutionary activities, unrest caused mainly by the poor rural population living in the countryside, outside Peking.

Both Antonio and Christopher travel to China in quest of solutions to problems related to their parents. In their lives the absence of affective parental authority thrusts upon them significant challenges; as they face these tasks they learn truths that were hidden from them. The intellectual and emotional growth completes their journeys, even if they fail in their main objectives.

Memory plays an important role in Ishiguro's novel; the narrative shifts between the past and the present. Adult Christopher remembers some important events that had taken place in his childhood. He remembers the house in which he had lived; his parents and those who had been close to him – the old servant, his friend Akira (a Japanese) and the family friend Uncle Philip (an Englishman). These recollections are more or less reliable, but Banks seems to mis-remember his own behaviour in certain situations. The views of his school friends and of Colonel Chamberlain about his demeanour and general behaviour vary considerably from his; his earlier trip from Shanghai to England was made under the care of the Colonel, who does not think (now) that Christopher had remained very much undisturbed by the dislocation caused by his parents' disappearance (Ishiguro 55). Banks however insists that he had been controlled and cool in his dealing with the sudden changes in his life.

These minor points of discrepancies suggest Bank's keenness to emphasise his self-control and emotional maturity. The narration is made in the first person by Christopher and presents most of the incidents from his point of view. However the ironical differences between the different perceptions build the impression that Banks has constructed an image of himself which may not be entirely true. His emotional loneliness slowly surfaces as he revisits the scenes of childhood peace and security. Ishiguro builds up an undercurrent of ironic point of view towards Bank, as the efforts to suggest his self composure as a child are not shared by others. His inner loneliness, which reflects a ruined childhood and hollow sense of selfhood emerge from the narration.

Antonio, in Basu's novel is a more open and expressive person. His responses to various situations during his travel to China involve the stay at different European colonies in the East. He is amazed by the wealth, power and comforts they enjoyed, although remaining completely dismissive of the human beings they were exploiting. In Peking he finds the diplomatic missions of some eleven European nations. But in all of them he finds prevalent prejudices about the eastern people as immoral and unintelligent (80). When he reaches Peking political turmoil rages from the highest authority down to the lowest levels, as the power conflict between the Queen and her Nephew has created an instability all through the country.

In this situation Antonio begins his medical training through Dr Xu, the Royal Physician, who had agreed to tutor him, and teach the cure of syphilis, and Fumi, Xu's student. He gets to know his two attendants, Wang Shong and Jian, both eunuchs. Joachan Saldanha, the missionary, gives him information about the various European and Chinese characters, the underlying facts about the prevailing political turmoil, and the activities of the agitators of the Boxer Revolution of that time.

The anger and violent antagonism of the Chinese belonging to the lower sections of the society, including the rural population, surprises Antonio who had not expected such vehemence from them. The Boxers were, as he is told by the different European men and women, uneducated and indisciplined. The inability of the Europeans to perceive the actual problems and grievances of the poor people around them reflects their total self-absorption and selfish understanding. As they indulged continually in parties and good food, they became cold and insensitive to the suffering of these power less unemployed men and women.

The western missionaries had been as violent as the traders, for both had tried to interfere with their values and deeply held religious beliefs. The Christian rituals introduced by the nuns and priests led to grotesque hybridities which became finally unacceptable. Their reactions become so vehement that they form a revolution, beating or killing these outsiders who were tearing apart their cherished values and traditional sanctities.

The formation of unorganised peasant revolts in China that Basu presents in the novel recalls similar upsurges from the underground, the grassroots levels in other English and European colonies in Asia and Africa. Socially down-trodden sections were the victims of the destructive forces of the Europeans who lived in China (and in other countries) only to exploit them. Their resistance came more or less from their own anger and frustration for as they reached a point where they could not bear any further interference, they resorted to violence.

Antonio's stay in Peking acquaints him with the different social groups among the Chinese as well as the Europeans. He befriends his Chinese teacher Dr Xu, his (female) pupil, Fumi and tries to learn their medical knowledge. This openness of mind is unusual; for most Europeans the west alone possessed the most advanced medical knowledge. Antonio imagines his friend Ricardo say, 'Why China'? .... The grand libraries of Florence and Paris, London and Heidelberg, contain all that's known to mankind' (Basu 29). However personal urgency compels Antonio to suppress this Eurocentric approach to some extent and to explore Chinese knowledge. He finds their epistemological assumptions and purpose of treatment to be completely different from that of the west. He learns some of the initial principles, and begins to see the advantage of that approach.

Antonio moves between the various social groups in China, as he is lodged within the Royal Palace. He meets Dr Xu and Fumi, goes about the city and surrounding villages in sedan chairs. He observes at first hand the condition of the villagers and the turmoil in the other regions of Peking. The truth of Fanon's[2] analyses of the revolutionary potential of the common people living in the village and shanty towns is reflected here in the novel as several scenes depict the somewhat spontaneous, loosely organised people's uprising that Antonio witnesses. Their assault on the Legation does not lead to much damage to European lives or property for these agitators were poorly armed. But the Europeans painted these actions in most horrible images, turning the movement into some terrible disaster.

Antonio becomes disillusioned with the European characters further as he probes seriously into the killing of a Dutchman, Charles de Graff. Fumi's relations with the man were intimate as she lived with him. Charles' death in a fire in his press-cum-house, Fumi's desertion at the time of fire and her survival had given rise to scandal about her involvement in his death, supposed to have been caused by the anti-European agitators. It was Antorio's personal interest in Fumi that made him investigate the curious facts, leading to Charles' death.

The truth of the matter is revealed to Antonio through his discrete, but, persistent questioning of Chris Campbell, a British newspaper reporter, and Mr Pinchback, the local manager of Hong Kong Bank. They knew that Charles' business plans to import a number of printing machines to China, to print the translation of famed ancient Chinese texts for European markets scared the Europeans who were making huge profits from selling forged copies as genuine ancient books. Such businessmen, and Antonio meets one of them, could not allow Charles to disturb their flow of profits. Pinchback tells Antonio this truth, how 'Charles wanted to enlighten the world about our yellow brethrens and stop the sharks from forging old manuscripts for grand profits' (Basu 244).

It was the Europeans who had caused the cruel death of Charles, and also spread stories about the Chinese, including Fumi, being responsible for the situation. The cruel deaths of nuns, Joachim Saldanha (in the last part of the novel) does not allow the reader to view the Chinese as wholly innocent or non-violent. But what Antonio learns makes him conscious of the unscrupulous dealings, actions and policies of the western men in China, in their colonies that led to the magnificence, splendour and unbelievable wealth of the Europeans, where they had built empires, colonised others and 'traded' with them. He can see the greed, hypocrisy and unchristian conduct of most of the Christians.

Kunal Basu focuses on the grim and hard struggle that lowly placed Chinese made during the second half of the nineteenth century. Wang Shong, the senior eunuch attendant of Antonio, was responsible for the operation of his nephew to make him a eunuch so that at least the boy could be certain to have work and food throughout his life. Such maiming left deep emotional pain and scars (Basu 117–18); but grim sufferings caused by poverty faced large number of unemployed youth; the painful decision held within it the pains related to such struggles for survival. Their earlier frivolous and ludicrous mannerism had made Antonio curt and rude with them. As their hidden human warmth, their concerns about others, especially about Antonio and their past sufferings are revealed, the insight changes him. Eunuchs and prostitutes in China have affected to a large extent the western perceptions of Chinese society. The hidden human aspects of these practices is presented in their stories, bringing out accompanying suffering. The contexts of social and economic situations are used by Basu to reflect the untold sides of Chinese lives.

Antonio's interactions with the Chinese and Europeans in Peking develop his insight into the human weaknesses and realities within this space. Antonio acquires some insight into the problems of the common level of men and women in China. He begins to perceive their strengths, and qualities as individuals with specific lives of their own. He learns to become more sympathetic and tolerant as he becomes aware of all their past and present hardships. The European mind could not generally look at the real human person for it could not accept their different physical cultural religious characteristics. The Chinese had become an undecipherable Other, shut in an image that become impenetrable. Anthony learns that sympathy and patience, open mind and a willingness to 'look' at the other, the idea emphasised by Iris Murdoch in her essays, 'The Sublime and the Good Revisited'[3] could always remove these blinkers and allow for a meaningful perception. What Antonio learns about them in some months, Arees learns in a short while, after her arrival at Peking. She surmises at once that Fumi and Xu were themselves in need of help, and didn't possess any cure (Basu 296). Joachim Saldanha, who had spent a long time in China as a missionary had also told him that 'they weren't any different but just as weak as us' (Basu 297). A keen imaginative ability was needed to cut through the orientalist discourses to perceive the shared human emotions, needs and struggles against hardships.

Antonio's failure in procuring a cure for syphilis does not matter to him anymore since his father had died in the meantime. He has gained an education into the methods of empire building and affluence that the West had practiced. This awareness of the evil sources of the wealth, of the European nations makes him conscious of the modes of suffering the exploited had endured, their resistances and human aspects of their character. The geoscapes of his mind have expanded tremendously as Antonio returns to Lisbon with Arees, having learnt the necessity of being a good human being. The journey has been to a land that has seen upheavals, and continues to struggle for the freedom and well-being of its people, which in the nineteenth and early twentieth centuries was being fought against the British traders, and many other European countries' presence.

Both Basu and Ishiguro depict a China that is moving within a historical framework, as it struggles to gain its autonomy and freedom to define its own self. The internal turbulence and struggle with outside powers have put excessive strain on its people. The lives of ordinary citizens were the worst affected, as the western countries exploited them for their profits. Ishiguro's hero, Christopher Bank remembers his mother Diana's constant efforts against the opium trade carried on by the company in which Christopher's father worked. The novel shows the devastation caused by the efforts of this idealistic campaign upon the entire family, as the father left them, the mother was kidnapped by one of the Chinese warlords as an act of vengeance and the eight year old Christopher becomes an orphan. The truth is kept hidden from the young boy, who is sent to England to be brought up supposedly by an aunt.

Upon his return to Shanghai in October 1937, the second important journey Banks makes, he searches for the lost parents and at one point he enters the area which was being attacked by the Japanese. His personal sense of ruined life extends his imaginative insight into the pain borne by the large number of simple human beings, who have also suffered the effect of tussle for power between nations (Ishiguro 276–77). The Chinese Army and Police men offer some help, but after a point they leave him alone. He doggedly stumbles through the ruined area where people had been living so far. It looked like a 'vast ruined mansion' (Ishiguro 276), and he is moved by all the damage, making it the wasteland of modern world. Though a Britisher, an outsider in this conflict between two eastern countries, Christopher feels the pain of homes being ruined – just as his own had been by some unknown powerful persons. He reflects angrily upon the scene; he feels angry that all the western nations that had lived in China for so long had completely forsaken their moral responsibility towards these ordinary people, who lost their homes and families as the war took place. He says 'I thought again of those pompous man of the International Settlement, of all the prevarications they must have employed to evade their responsibilities down so many years ....' (Ishiguro 284). His extreme anger comes as an uncharacteristic overflow of emotion for so far Banks has built up the image of his being usually in control of his emotions. The contempt and anger at the western countries, lack of a sense of responsibility towards the communities they have oppressed and exploited through different stratagems raises serious historical, political and moral issues, which are part of the postcolonial questioning of their histories of colonial rule. Here Banks' sympathy is built upon his sense of the ruin in his own life, though the source of that damage may be very different.

This scene becomes an important point in the narrative – it suddenly turns the flow of Banks' quest into a larger political frame – bringing in the issue of the responsibility of a nation, race, community towards those it has dealt with. Just as the incidents of the desertion of Diana Bank by her husband, and subsequent betrayal by Philips, the friend trusted by the entire family, bring up the significant moral issues of individual's responsibility towards one's family and friends, Bank's anger here is directed towards the bonds between nations.

The opium trade that bound the fate of China with Britain and the other western nations plays an important role in the destiny of Bank's family. The mother's persistent arguments with her husband make him so uncomfortable that he walks out on his family and goes away with the mistress he had had, for a more easy life. Diana's humiliation under Wang Ku, the Chinese who keeps her as his concubine, along with the suffering of the large numbers whose addiction devastated their bodies, mind, and family lives raise questions about moral responsibility of the powerful towards the weak.

The novel's narrative repeats the theme of responsibility between individuals, nations and races, as there is recurrence of the betrayal of various nature in it – within family fold, between friends and lovers, and on a larger scale, between races. Diana raises an important moral issue when she objects to the English companies bringing opium within China. Christopher remembers some of the incidents when his mother expressed her views clearly on the subject. Christopher's father had worked for 'Morganbrook and Byatt' which was among the biggest British firms trading with China. Diana had several arguments with her husband and with the other employees of the company. On one occasion she spoke angrily in defence of the Chinese working within her household, when the Company's Health Inspector warned her against their opium intake. She tells him 'Are you not ashamed, Sir? As a Christian, as an Englishman, as a man with scruples?' Taking a clearly humanist stand she questions his own conscience, his own individual sense of moral responsibility in his view of the Chinese as human beings. She says pointedly 'Tell me, how is your conscience able to rest while you owe your existence to such ungodly wealth?' (Ishiguro 72). The importance of the means in attaining an end, specially gaining wealth is brought forth in Diana's criticism. She takes a critical view of her own country's policies in its dealings with other countries.

When We Were Orphans presents such moments of questioning of the ethical aspect of the economics of empires and colonial rule. The personal lives of the family members is ruined under the pressure of its immorality – and this is meant to represent the large number of English men and women who were in similar positions. The novel presents betrayal of lovers, friends and family relations, in a way indirectly connected with the deceit, betrayal and exploitation that existed between nations. Philips' betrayal of Diana to the warlord is yet another form of corruption, an expression of the snake lurking in his heart, that is recognised when he is given the name 'Yellow Snake' as he gets involved with Communists and Chiang Kai Shek's government, in the 1930s.

Christopher's vehement anger at the battle field, which destroyed homes and their cherished belongings, howsoever humble they might be, reflects his recognition of the ruins that attend the 'aftermath of empires ....' (Punter 55). These ruins within China, partly created by assaults from outside represent its downfall, which was part of its ongoing journey. The country and its people are seen through the windows of history and humane comparison, outside racist blinkers. The travellers, Christopher Banks and Antonio Henrique Maria, though Europeans try to become independent of the prejudiced European way of looking at the Chinese. They question the basic assumptions and misrepresentations that west has made of China, using their personal encounters and experiences of both, the west and east.

Notes

1. Derisive representation of the Chinese character, culture and way of life has become part of west's popular literature; later the Cinematic portrayal of the people as unreliable and devious, has perpetuated the nineteenth century mind set. See John Major's 'Stereotypes of Asians

in Western Literature'. Web Sources. www.solitares.net/racism/asiathru.htm, Kate Robinson. 'The other Pole of Human Existence': Western Representations of China between the 13th and 18th Centuries'.·*Cross-sections*, Vol. V, 2009, p. 57–65. She quotes several other texts that deal with the issue of representation of stereotypes of China as 'a mysterious and majestic dreamland' (p. 58). Web Sources. http.//Review.anu.edu.au/cross-sections/vol.5/pdf/05.pdf viewed on 17.08.2012.

2. Frantz Fanon. *The Wretched of the Earth*. Trans. Contance Farrington. new York: Grove, Weidenfeld, 1963. 109.
3. Iris Murdoch is among those novelists who argued about the moral aspects of human relationships, and treated the perception of the other to be itself an ethical act. To look should mean to see through the otherness, and become a means of building up strong connections.

References

Basu, Kunal. *The Yellow Emperor's Cure*. London: Picador, Macmillan, 2012.

Boehmer, Elleke. *Colonial and Postcolonial Literature. Migrant Metaphors*. New Delhi: Oxford University Press, 2005.

Fanon, Frantz: *The Wretched of the Earth*. Trans. Constance Farrington. New York: Grove, Weidenfeld, 1963.

Ishiguro, Kazuo. *When We Were Orphans*. London, Faber and Faber, 2000.

Ghosh, Amitav. *Sea of Poppies*. New Delhi: Penguin. Viking, India, 2008.

Major, John S. 'Stereotypes of Asians in Western Literature.' Web Source. www.solitares.net/racism/asiathru.htm. viewed on 5 September 2012.

McEwan, Cheryl, *Postcolonialism and Development*. London and New York: Routledge, 2009.

Murdoch, Iris. 'The Sublime and the Beautiful Revisited'. *Yale Review* 49, 195, pp. 247–271.

Punter, David. *Postcolonial Imaginings. Fictions For a New World Order*, New Delhi: Atlantic Publishers, 2000.

Robinson, Kate. "The Other Pole of Human Existence'. Western Representations of China between the 13th and 18th Centuries.' Web Source. http.//review.anu.edu.au//cross= sections//vol5/pdf/05.pdf. viewed on 17.08.2012.

17 Sojourns in the Geoscapes of the Mind

Interrogating Select Works of Diana Abu Jaber

Rama Hirawat

> Every voyage can be said to involve a re-siting of boundaries. The travelling self is here both the self that moves physically from one place to another, following 'public routes and beaten tracks' within a mapped movement, and the self that embarks on an undetermined journeying practice, having constantly to negotiate between home and abroad, native culture and adopted culture, or more creatively speaking, between a here, a there, and an elsewhere. (Trinh Ti Minha 10)

The self is a sojourning entity – it travels not only in the charted topographical places, but also in the realms of mind either in quest of an identity or in search of an imaginative stimulation which creates fantastical world within the mind. A layman definition of travel suggests movement from one place to another – between physical locations – but this minimal description can be expanded to look at the psychological and symbolic, purpose and interpretations of movements. The experience en route the journey impinges specific images on the mind which can be referred to as 'geoscapes'. The word geoscape is formed by combining the prefix 'geo-' meaning earth to the suffix 'scape' which means a picture or representation of a wide panoramic view. From this etymological orientation it can be derived that geoscapes of the mind means the etching of specific places on the canvas of the mind. These images are in direct tempo-spatial relation with a definite experience yet they are subject to transformations due to a constantly negotiable understanding of home and belonging. The paper will explore how the geoscapes of the mind can be mapped through memories and dreams and how the scapes of the architectural spaces like room and kitchen evolve in course of time, particularly in diasporic experience.

The journey, literally and metaphorically, emerges as a decisive factor in defining the experience of diaspora. The existential reality of diasporas can be understood by the 'hyphen' of their demographic designation as in Arab-American. The hyphen lends them new identity and simultaneously reflects the categorised demarcation in their lives. To move beyond the spatial confinement conferred on them by their relative position in the world, diasporas undertake voyages both physically and psychologically. This is aptly reflected in the diasporic literature. The journey of and by the diasporas is a crucial point of commencement in their narratives.

Arab-American literature is focused on the diasporic experience of the Arabs living in America who are configuring their sense of identity in face of constantly shifting and frequently clashing state of affairs between the Arab states and the United States of America. Owing to internal diversity of the Arab experience an increasing number of writers are narrating their individual journey through autobiographical writings. Author Diana Abu Jaber's stories deal with the losses and survival involved in the lives of Arab immigrants and their progeny and, simultaneously try to explode the myths regarding Arab culture. Diana's own diasporic voyage, which reflects in her works, is a glimpse of the universal experience of the diaspora wherein the individual transcends the precincts of race, gender, and nation. Like her personal odyssey, her fiction moves from dilemma and rejection in her first work to acceptance and assimilation in next and finally grows beyond narrow conception of ethnic and hyphenated identity in her fourth work. Journey as a metaphor resonates in her works. Abu Jaber's fiction explores the various geoscapes stored in the *tabula rasa* through dreams and memories which are rooted in the experiences of the self. Memories are what the self remembers about its past, while dreams are formulated by those experiences which leave a deep and mute mark of desire on the psyche. Together they are like the latitude and longitude of the mind's geoscape and their analysis helps in construction of a sense of identity. The narrative enclosure of dreams and memories makes the text emerge as a temporal travelogue, describing the inward journey along the timeline of the life span of the protagonist. On the application of temporal and spatial relationship in a text, writer Teresa Bridgeman observes:

> Narratives unfold in time, and the past, present, and future of a given event or action affects our interpretation of that action, while the characters who populate narrative texts move around, inhabit and experience different spaces and locations ... (52)

Characters may psychologically time travel to visit various spaces. A study of these spaces and mode of travelling leads to a deeper understanding of the characters and of the narrative itself. Memories are the medium to travel in the geoscapes of the mind in order to frame the contour and substance of identity. Memories are what the self reminisces about the past experiences and they depend on mind's ability to remember. This makes them subject to variations with the age. But when they are framed in some physical space it becomes easy to remember and conceptualise them. In *The Poetics of Space,* Gaston Bachelard writes about 'localisation of memories'. He believes that, 'memories are motionless, and the more securely they are fixed in space, the sounder they are' (9). When memories are associated with some space they become deeper. They are located in space and 'space contains compressed time', it holds time. Places are linked to time in different ways and may function as archives of personal or communal history. The relation between space and time is evident in the memories.

Through memories, Abu Jaber explores the locus of kitchen which emerges as a crucial and contested site in the gendered diasporic experience. Kitchen or *matbakh* as it is called in Arabic originated from the Albanian word *kuzhine*¨. Perhaps since its origin it has been seen as a symbol of subservience, as a stereotypical ideal zone for women. The physical space of kitchen is considered to be a women's place, a gendered space. Over the years it has been realised as not just an emblem of oppression and passivity but a precinct where the patriarchal norms can be modified and subverted. Kitchen is one of those places which, to borrow words from feminist bell hooks, 'can tell stories and unfold histories' and 'can be interpreted, appropriated and transformed through artistic and literary practices' (152). The territorial limitation of a kitchen holds uncharted horizons of imagination and creativity, resistance and authority, healing and solidarity. Writer Maria Andre says:

> Like a homeland without borders, the safe environment of a feminist kitchen provides a space where gender is no longer a given image defined by the masculine, but a means of exploration to a whole spectrum of sensual, sexual, and textual possibilities (17).

Though the kitchen is socially relegated to women yet it becomes a location where women try to construct the self beyond the frame laid down by the patriarchal society. Kitchen is a site of feminine knowledge and of collective memory of women. In this sense kitchen is important for Diana Abu Jaber. For her kitchen is, as historian Pierre Nora calls, 'site of memory' and in the etching of the kitchen's topography. She has used the objective place of kitchen to locate the memories in the genre of memoir. The process of writing a memoir is akin to travelling as to write it the memoirist needs to undertake journey to his/her past. A memoir is a retro-spective scrutiny of life, but it is different from an autobiography, in terms of chronology of events, and focus on personal growth. In words of Maureen Murdock:

> A memoir is the writer's particular memory of an actual, not imagined, incident that occurred in her life. It is her angle of perception on what happened, her emotional truth of the event. (Murdock, Writing)

As a form of quest, memoir has similarities with myth. Maureen says that both myth and memoir deals with the same set of questions like, who am I? Where am I going? And what is my tribe? She further adds, 'Memoirists are our contemporary myth makers helping us find meaning in our lives as they reveal the wisdom they have mined from their memories'. As myth reconciles human beings to the adversities of life by rooting them in pristine times, similarly by writing memoir the writer traces personal myths, gains insight into life and enriches the collective understanding of human life.

The memoir *The Language of Baklava* is Diana's journey through the archives of lived experiences in search of the roots of her hyphenated identity. It is ingrained in her experiences of growing up as an immigrant's daughter for whom her culture is laid bare through food. It is a food memoir which is the conflation of memories and food recipes in a narrative. *Routledge Encyclopedia of Narrative Theories* defines food memoir as:

> ... works of art which transgress genre boundaries by combining characteristics traits and elements of diverse literary and non-literary genres. (227)

The aim of hybrid genre is to distance itself from the single discourse of the conventional narratives. Abu Jaber has opted for a food memoir, a hybrid genre, perhaps to complement her own hybrid identity. The spatial restrictions and fluidity of a hybrid identity may be best summarised in a hybrid narrative. The title *The Language of Baklava* is metaphorical as it reflects the contents within. It's about language of food in two ways, first, the language of food in context of cuisine and secondly, in socio-cultural frame. As such the recipes are seen from the personal and cultural perspectives, according to the incidents related to them. In the beginning of the book, describing the relation between food and memories, Diana says, 'Memories give our lives their fullest shape, and eating together helps us to remember'. Relating cooking to memory Brinda Mehta writes that cooking affects all the senses and gets imprinted in our subconscious in such a way that even a slight scent of the specific food triggers all the moments attached to it. This makes food (or its absence) an essential element in an individual's journey taken to trace personal history which is embedded in communal history.

In the memoir Abu Jaber travels to the past by picking up sensory clues invoked by food. Her self adopts a tourist identity to understand relation with her father, the dynamics of being a hyphenated identity and the hardships pertaining to the second generation diaspora. As the background is of food and cooking,

Diana mentally travels back to the kitchen of her home (in America and in Jordan), and invokes all the happenings that shaped her perceptions. Her foremost memories of kitchen are of her father cooking Arab food in America. As she writes, 'Bud, my father, carries me slung over one shoulder when he cooks; he calls me his sack of potatoes' (4). Her father cooked Arab cuisine and at the kitchen table he filled his daughters with family histories and childhood stories. This made her associate kitchen with cultural heritage, as a locus of transmitting culture. In her childhood days she perceived kitchen as her father's zone but from the present time's perspective she links that place to her father's need to retain his homeland's culture and comfort himself with a sense of belonging in an alien land. Thus kitchen became a site to reclaim identity and a centre to propagate and pass on the culture. It was here that she learned to subvert the social norm of relegating kitchen to women. She experienced the kitchen as her father's private space and medium through which he channeled his emotions. Diana's quest for her twin identity takes her to the kitchen, where she learned about the Arab component of her identity while still residing in America. She understands the duality inherent in her identity, her being 'Arab at home and American in streets' (5).

The links that Abu Jaber made between the kitchen and culture is further strengthened when she mentally travels to the time spend in Jordan. To comprehend the constructs of her present self, Abu Jaber keeps journeying to the experienced past, crossing and negotiating borders, both physical (as she later travels to Jordan) and psychological. Abu Jaber reminiscences that how while in Jordan, within the spatial boundaries of the kitchen, she learned the basics of her identity, her hybridity and about cross-cultural bonding. In the Jordanian kitchen her mother prepares American pancakes with Arabic ingredients and the resultant dish though not up to mark is relished by their neighbours and is deeply satisfying to her. From the retrospective analysis of that incident she realises that the amalgamation of her Arab and American self is the core of her identity and the only contended elucidation for self.

As Abu Jaber moves up the memory lane in search for her gendered lessons, she once again arrives in the kitchen. This time it is inhabited by her Aunt Aya, who explains to her that how this space, which is specifically relegated to females to tie them to domesticity, can be treated as a seat of empowerment. It is in there, that the aunt teaches her that through the medium of cooking food she can win over others, as she does, e.g. by making baklava for Bud, she lures him against his own decision of sending Diana to Jordan. While teaching her the basics of food and cooking, aunt Aya teaches her a good deal about being human and about womanhood. She gave Diana interesting 'tutorials in womanliness', like 'high heels are good, but don't forget how to run' (189).

These reminiscences of Abu Jaber's past and of the wisdom learned in the space of kitchen is reflected in the character of Sirine in *Crescent* (2004). It is a tale of love situated in Los Angeles and revolves around the protagonists Sirine and Hanif, both Iraqi Americans. Their love story is crafted over the background of inter-twined thematic concerns like culture and hybridity, home and exile, women and cooking. The narrative has a sensory effect as the cultural praxis of cooking is used as a recurring motif. Sirine is a chef and kitchen is her realm to create, cherish and trace memories. In the novel the geoscape of the kitchen is sketched with hue and shades of Sirine's contemplative and creative cooking. Her cooking is a manifestation of her evolving understanding of the concept of home and identity, romance and estrangement, her dilemmas and decisions, her joys and sorrows. Owing to this symbolic aspect of cooking, in the novel, kitchen emerges as a locus of cultural and personal subjectivity. For Sirine kitchen is both: the point of departure and destination. The kitchen of the café sets her on a voyage of memories through which she reaches to her mother's kitchen. While performing the rituals of cooking Sirine often reminisces about her mother:

> The back kitchen is Sirine's retreat, her favourite place to sit at a table chopping carrots and thinking her thoughts. She can look out the window at the back courtyard and feel like she's a child again, working at her mother's table. (58)

The kitchen is the only place, to where she can trace fond memories of her parents especially mother. Along with the recipes of *knaffea* and *baklava* her mother shared secrets of love and life with her. In the novel, the generational sharing of knowledge within the spatial precincts of the kitchen is restricted only to the females, transforming this space of domesticity into a place one possessing infinite intellectual and spiritual possibilities.

Kitchen is presented as a vital space which energises Sirine by keeping her physically fit, 'She is used to the quick rhythms and physical demands of the kitchen and she likes to exert herself' (25). The exerting routine of cooking transforms kitchen into a fitness centre where women can concentrate on their body and through it express and assert themselves. Female body, Assia Djebar believes, is 'the fourth language' which seeks some less explored 'shore as destination for its message of love' (180). In *Crescent* this destination is kitchen and the message is imparted through cooking. Sirine's association with kitchen can be understood by subverting the patriarchal and masculine implications of womanhood. Through her female characters Abu Jaber has revealed that how the imposed spatial confinement of kitchen can ignite the imagination of the resident. Moreover, the mental image of a space like kitchen evolves and transforms with the time unveiling more profound meanings. The pictures of geo-locations does not necessarily fade but their significance often corresponds with the present scenario.

The geoscape of a kitchen becomes the destination for Abu Jaber's sojourns through memory lanes in order to frame her Arab-American identity. The spatial significances invoked by an architectural structure can also initiate a mental journey to the vestiges of memories. This is manifested in the places that serve food. Cafes and bakeries with their aroma are capable of arousing memories in various characters in Abu Jaber's fiction. These places as pictured in Diana's fiction are 'diaspora space' as defined by Avtar Brah in *Cartographies of Diaspora,* 'Diaspora space is the intersectionality of diaspora, border, and dislocation as a point of confluence of economic, political, cultural, and psychic processes' (208). At these joints the flavours of the food transport the immigrants, mentally to their homeland and satiate their nostalgic leanings. In Diana's fiction such places are Nadia's café (*Crescent*), Thanatoulas bakery (*Arabian Jazz*), Columbus bread bakery (*Origin*). These spaces are not only a joint where different cultures converge but are also a kind of intersecting point for memories, like a mid-port of travel.

Like memories another mode of mental time travel is dreams and in a text they disrupt the linear temporality of the narrative.

Dreams transpire in the psyche of a man and, as such don't take up any corporal space. They can be felt, and may be thought as occupying an abstract space (drawn from the abstract noun in grammar). This attribute makes the spatial comprehension of dreams a bit difficult. Foucault says that the space of dreams has 'an intrinsic quality' about them, as they occupy the space of mind, heart and consciousness. The clock time never stops, but sometimes one tends to become oblivious to the present, by drifting into an imaginary space of dreams and hopes and via dreams one may travel to the past, or to realms of fantasy. Psychologist Sigmund Freud in his book *The Interpretation of Dreams* held that dreams consists of elements from one's own personality and are mostly reflection of a dreamer's deep set fears, desires and wishes. Diana has created a web of dreams and memories in the thriller *Origin*. In this work of fiction, along with the investigation of SIDS cases, the protagonist Lena, a fingerprint expert, journeys through the puzzling memories of her past in order to find out the truth behind her existence. She leads a basically lonely life submerged in her memories and dreams of past. In the narrative dreams play an important role as they help in building the suspense and planting the clues that are necessary for the genre of thriller. Lena's sleep pattern are erratic and it is disturbed not just by dreams of her mother but also of demons and strangers. Her dreams of being taken away by invisible demons, of being lost, and of dissolving in snow, foretells the coming danger in her life. Lena's initial failure at capturing the murderer also reflects in her dream of seeing the back of a woman's head and when she turns the woman around it is again the back of her head (346). The dream suggests that she is reaching nowhere in her investigation to find the culprit.

Lena's dreams assist her in the quest in search of answers to the question, who am I and where do I come from. They are a comfort and solace to her, a way to connect to the past and through them she travels to the childhood days and to the place which she believes to be her true home. She fervently believes (supported by her foster mother) that she was brought up in a rain forest by an ape and this is her personal creation myth. This myth of her origin, memories of past invades her dreams constantly. Diana refers to her dreams as 'dream-memory' as she often dreams of the time that she had spent with her ape mother. Through her dreams she travels to the canopied rain forest where she thinks she has spent her childhood. Her dreams are a solace to her and at the same time instigate her to search for her existential reality. Eventually Lena figures out the truth behind her identity and realises how fallacious her memories have been. She was raised in an orphanage room which was decorated on forest theme, and she had a soft toy of monkey which she used to hold close. The reminiscence of the corporal space of room turned out to be deceptive. Her case reveals that memories which shape one's image of self and helps in construction of identity are fragile and susceptible to misconstruction. This raises the question of reliability of memories and simultaneously deals with the epistemological idea that how is knowledge formed and to what extent is it possible to completely know a person or a thing. Knowledge about identity is more or less dependent on set of variables, and some of them are created by memories and dreams which though help in the voyage for self-discovery, yet they can mislead. The novel suggests that geographical, cultural, social or familial criteria of identity are limiting rather in search of a coherent identity one should embark on a journey via collective memory of human beings. Lena's memories of being raised by apes is perhaps a reflection of this collective memory and in this way it's a kind of tribute to Darwinism, which largely proposes that all species has evolved from one single source, this spring of origin is the ultimate destination of all sojourns.

The narratives of Diana Abu Jaber which began as a journey in the search for a tangible implication of Arab-American identity, gradually move beyond the confines of both the Arab and the American, and aspire to understand the identity in context of the human origin. The geoscape of the mind is constructed by the various parameters of the dreams and memories framed by this knowledge and the need to explore identity leads one to sojourn in the domain of mind and reach unusual spaces.

References

Abu Jaber, Diana. *Origin.* New York: W.W. Norton and Company, 2007.

——. *The Language of Baklava.* New York: Anchor Books, 2006.

——. *Arabian Jazz.* New York: W.W. Norton and Company, 2003.

——. *Crescent.* New York: W.W. Norton and Company, 2004.

Andre, Maria Claudia. Ed. 'Culinary Fictions'. *Chicanas and Latin American Women Writers Exploring the realm of the kitchen as a self-empowering site*. New York: Edwin Mellen Press, 2001, pp. 1–45.

Avakian, Arlene Voski. ed. *Through the Kitchen Window: Women Writers explore the intimate meanings of food and cooking*. Boston: Beacon Press, 1997.

Bachelard, Gaston. *The Poetics of Space: the Classic Look at how we Experience Intimate Places*. Trans. Maria Jolas. Boston: Beacon Press, 1994.

Brah, Avtar. *Cartographies of Diaspora: Contesting Identities*. London: Routledge Press, 1996.

Bridgeman, Teresa. 'Time and Space'. *The Cambridge Companion to Narrative*. Ed. David Herman. Cambridge: Cambridge UP, 2007.

Djebar, Assia. *Fantasia: An Algerian Cavalcade*. Portsmouth, NH: Heinemann, 1993.

Foucault, Michel. 'Of Other Spaces'. Trans. By Jay Miskowiec. Web Source. 18 December 2012. <http://foucault.info/documents/heterotopias/Foucault.heteroTopia.en.html>

Freud, Sigmund. *The Interpretation of Dreams*. London: Hogarth Press, 1953.

Herman, David, Manfred Jahn and Marie-Laure Ryan, Ed. *Routledge Encyclopedia of Narrative Theory*. London: Routledge, 2005. Print

Mehta, Brinda. *Rituals of Memory in Contemporary Arab Women's Writing*. NY: Syracuse UP, 2007.

Minha, Trinh T. 'Other than Myself/My Other self.' *Traveller's Tales: Narratives of Home and Displacement*, ed. George Robertson, et al. London: Routledge, 1994.

Murdock, Maureen. 'Writing the Truth'. *Maureen Murdock*. Web Source. 5 August 2009.

Nora, Pierre. 'Between Memory and History: Les Lieux De Memoire'. *Representations*, 26 (1989): 7–24.

18 The Self in Transit

Tamim Ansary's *West of Kabul, East of New York*

Namita Singh

In the present era of transnational migration, the flow of people among different countries, convergence of different cultures, languages and hybridisation of identities have dismantled the concept of absolute territoriality. The journey of the people across different countries due to socio-political or cultural reasons shattered the concept of true home. Afghanistan is one of the countries of the world that has a third of its population displaced due to decades of war. Ethnical, geographical, religious, urban-rural and ideological contradictions all play a role in understanding the events that led to a mass displacement of Afghans. Afghans reside in different countries across the globe and most of them have found their way to the first world countries like US and Germany, and a few thousands were even born there. Money, goods and information circulate amongst them in these continents. These Afghans in their host land negotiated their sense of home and belonging which influenced their attitudes towards the land of their origin. During their journey from roots to the new destinations their self undergoes transformation. What is the connection between diaspora and their country of origin? How do they negotiate their sense of belonging and non-belonging to their 'homeland'? How do they relate to the issues of returning to homeland and how their dual identity leads to the transition of their self that emerges with a new identity? The paper seeks to explore these questions in Tamim Ansary's *West of Kabul, East of New York.*

The transition of the self results on account of two kinds of journeys the search for home and space of belonging – that take place simultaneously. The first is a physical one, across national borders, from Afghanistan to the host country and perhaps back to Afghanistan again. The other kind is a journey through questions of identity, history, cultures, ancestry and belonging. '...all changed on 11 September 2001 .... On 12 September, the abrupt notoriety of Afghanistan triggered a volcanic moment in my own small life ...' commences Tamim Ansary's memoir and goes on to describe the events of 11 September that led to the devastation and destruction of Afghans and became the reason for presenting his Afghan-American perspective to the world through his book. On September 11, 2001, the World Trade Park in New York was destroyed, the Pentagon in Washington heavily damaged and Afghanistan was re-discovered. Ever since the Soviet withdrawal from Afghanistan in 1989 the outside world had forgotten about this small state in South Central Asia, extremely poor with hardly any natural resources, inhabited by a vast array of different ethnic groups who more often than not use violence to solve their problems. Before terrorist attacks on the United States the outside world could not care less about what happened in Afghanistan. The United States and Western Europe left Afghans on their own resources and to their own mercies. The result was an extremely dark period in the history of Afghanistan. The terrible ethnic and tribal wars and the rise of Taliban resulted in the destruction of the country.

This journey by Tamim Ansary initiates the reconciliation between his religious Afghan Muslim identity and national American one. The introductory lines of the novel depict the dilemma of being straddled between the two cultures and reveals that Afghanistan, for most of the world, was only a concept but not a reality before the Soviet invasion '... when I introduced myself to people, they'd say 'Interesting name: Where are you from?' When I said Afghanistan, I could feel myself changing, not unpleasantly, into a curiosity ...' (1). Here 'name' is the marker of identity and difference. Immediately after the '9/11' events, Afghanistan was placed on the world map again as the breeding ground of terrorism. The 'War against Terrorism' that was launched by the United States and their allies brought a quick end to the Taliban era. The Afghan American-Muslim minority was deeply affected as the ramifications of the attacks of 11 September 2001 were felt throughout the United States. Since the attacks on the World Trade Center, Muslims, especially Afghans, residing in the United States experienced violations of economic and political liberties, as well as social discrimination. Media stereotypes and government legislation continually aggravated the human rights abuses and established institutional, social, and economic discrimination deeper in American society. At the heart of this discrimination were, clear misunderstandings about Islam and those who practiced the faith. This discrimination, destabilisation and military occupation of Afghanistan by the First world has triggered the hasty production of a large corpus of writings about the political and socio-cultural dynamics of the country by Euro-American academics, travellers, journalists, and development workers. In an effort to combat these challenges, diasporic Afghan writers and Islamic organisations are fighting to protect the community's civil liberties. Tamim Ansary through his novel *West of Kabul, East of New York* raises the question of legitimacy of the First World interventions in Afghanistan and their process of nation–building in the country. America's treatment of Afghan Muslim minorities has raised many questions. Ansary has depicted a cultural and political blossoming among the Afghan diaspora especially in the United States, revealing a vibrant, active, and intellectual Afghan American community.

Tamim Ansary's novel is in the form of a memoir which spans time, geography and political perspectives. The author writes about the journey that brought him from Afghanistan to New York and his journey to the Islamic countries. His experience of living in Afghanistan as a child and his later trip back to the Islamic world both involve a journey. This journey in a travelogue is a physical journey which occurs in order to map the geographical terrain while in a memoir it is an emotional and psychological journey that explores the inner terrain. Tamim Ansary's memoir includes both physical and psychological journeys. He says that the process of memory is a process of letting go because memory works by associations and it leads us to the psychological journey from one place to the other through associations. The writer further adds that a writer should not impose his mind on the structure of his memories so that he could get the authentic experience in order to write honestly which is necessary for a memoir or a travelogue. Tamim Ansary's novel combines the two genres of travelogue and memoir effectively to raise certain seminal issues related to the self that is balanced precariously between the two cultures. The experience of expatriation, alienation and transplantation has been shared in his memoir that includes a travelogue within. He explores the social memory of civilisation, his views about war in Afghanistan and discusses what being an American means to him. Born to an Afghan father and an American mother, Ansary grew up in the intimate world of Afghan family life and immigrated to San Francisco thinking that he had left Afghan culture behind forever. 'Was Afghanistan really my country? How can I be an adequate spokesman for Afghanistan or for Muslims?'(15). Through these questions he makes the reader aware of the difference between his attitude towards his homeland in Afghanistan and his home in the host country America.

The book has been divided into three parts. Part one entitled 'The Lost World' chronicles his childhood in Afghanistan and his move to the US as a teenager and his struggle to reconcile two facets of his identity as an adult. Part two 'Looking for Islam' is a travel narrative which details his journey to some Muslim countries like Morocco, Algeria, Tunisia and Turkey seeking to learn about Islam and his Muslim roots. Part three 'The Forgetting Afghanistan' analyses Afghanistan's past and present in the context of identity of a man divided between two cultures.

The first part is a psychological journey of Tamim Ansary to his childhood in Afghanistan. His sketches of the 'Lost World of Afghanistan' reveal the condition of his country before it came in contact with the west: the world of tightly knit clans living in large compounds surrounded by high walls in a large city with a densely interwoven fabric of village permeated by Islam. The memories of Tamim Ansary are selective recollections of an ideal childhood time spent in Afghanistan rooted in family bonding. The temporal and spatial distance from the native land makes the present perspective questionable. The writer is presenting a chimera space observed from geographical and historical distance. Tamim Ansary, while idealising his childhood is also conscious of the unease of being a hybrid. Because of his mixed parentage he was always treated as an outsider, both in Afghan community and in American community as well. Stories from a bi-cultural childhood illumine the difference between the worldview of Afghans and those of Americans. The diasporic dilemma related to the problematics of belonging gets enhanced due to the cultural hybridity of the writer. 'Growing up Bicultural is like straddling a crack in the earth. If the cultures are far apart – like those of Afghanistan and America – one feels an urge to get entirely over to one side or the other' (278).

Ansary discusses what it was like to grow up in Afghanistan, with one foot already in America. His experiences of being a product of two worlds makes him feel not quite at home in either and was always haunted by the question of identity. The state of being 'neither here nor there' is reminiscent of Uma Parmeswaran's concept of 'Trishanku' in relation to diasporic experience of Indians in Canada. His experience of racial prejudices impacted his life as he refers to his family as 'Americans with an asterisk' (67). *West of Kabul, East of New York* captures the confrontation between Islam and the West. A man's efforts to reconcile the anomalies of two cultures have been depicted in order to find some point of convergence through imagination. His story takes us to tiny *Lashkergah*, the headquarters of an American aid project in south western Afghanistan where Ansary and his siblings begin a dual life – Afghan by day and American by night. '... All my life, Rebecca and I had been the strange ones who wore the funny clothes, ate with forks, and always went home with their mommy and daddy at night ...' (66). The sense of diasporic solitude was deeply embedded in the psyche of the author. They were always treated differently from other Afghan children within their community. Strangers in their own community they felt happy when they got a chance to shift to the American aid project area. There they were expected to live with the fellow Americans and hoped for recognition as one of them. However even fellow American children refused to accept them because of their Afghan connection:

> ... 'Don't let those dirty Afghans in here!' I was shocked and confused -not just that he was calling Afghans dirty but that he was calling us Afghans. After all, among the Afghans, we were Americans; so if we weren't Americans, either, what were we? (67)

The refusal to be accepted by the American community depicts the problem of their unresolved bi-cultural identity which haunted the writer since his childhood. Through the psychological journey to his childhood Afghanistan, Tamin Ansary attempts to interrogate the questions that came to the mind of a child trying to reconcile his bicultural identity and the dilemma of where his home is. While describing his childhood in Afghanistan, he speaks in his American voice about not just his Afghan self but also the context that gave rise to that Afghan self. Although he considers himself an American, yet he expresses his concern about the lost homeland. Ansary ponders over the dissonance between the world he was living in and the world he left behind which is reflective of his diasporic sensibility. The dual identities within him are in conflict with each other. He asks himself 'Why won't my soul let go? It's not really comfortable to be bi-cultural ... among Afghans I've always felt allowances being made for my American side, as if it's a sort of disability. My American self makes me a little less Afghan' (285), finally he comes to the conclusion 'I am a kaleidoscope of parts now' (285). His identity emerges as a mosaic and the question of identity crisis remains unresolved.

Tamim Ansary makes a clear demarcation between the concept of homeland and home in the novel. His thoughts oscillate between homeland, Afghanistan that is left behind and home America, where he is presently residing. Although he compares his life in America with his childhood in Afghanistan yet he is unable to make a choice between his basement office in California and his childhood home. There is a sense of being out of tune with both the worlds due to his preoccupation with Islam and associated fundamentalism. He says he is conscious of '... the dissonance between the world I am living in now and the world I left behind, a world that is lost to me' (10).

'Looking for Islam' uses the motif of journey in order to explore Islam in the Muslim world in Asia. The writer uses travel narrative to give expression to the experiences related to the physical journey along with internal explorations. The reason for going on this journey was his brother Riaz who had adopted the orthodox aspect of Islam. Tamim Ansary's delicate little brother goes to Pakistan to 'live on his own' (117). After a few months he got the news that his brother had formally 'embraced Islam'. Ansary thought it to be just a phase because Riaz was: 'a long haired, intellectual college guy, serious about art, serious about environmental issue, serious about a lot of things and thoroughly rational in his approach to life' (117). On his return Riaz sported the appearance of a conservative Muslim. Ansary was shocked and surprised at the appearance of his brother and found that he had a fundamentalist approach towards religion. 'He had embraced an orthodox interpretation of Islam' (118). Both the brothers had an argument over Islam and could not convince each other. This discussion made Tamim Ansary undertake a journey to understand the views of Riaz on Islam.

Ansary came to Asia in order to explore Islam in the Muslim world. During this journey he made efforts to understand Islam and compared it with the Islamic ideologies of his brother. The road trips to Asia were seminal to his understanding of Islam. Islamic perceptions that he gained through his interaction with people were based on the extremist and fundamentalist rules and regulations, especially for women. He could not get satisfactory answers to the questions related to Islam, 'Everyone who talked to me about Islam fixated on alcohol, short skirts, the Sharia and believing in one God ...' (143). He says that segregation based on sex was the main reason of differences between the western ideology and Islam, 'on their issue of sex and the relationship between the sexes that Islam and the west have parted ways, and parting ways on this, have parted ways on everything' (92).

Tamim Ansary came across the rigid and dogmatic face of Islam which included severe punishments that were not in practice during his childhood. While describing his childhood he speaks in his adult American voice about not just his Afghan self but also the context that gives rise to that Afghan self. He explores the Islamic world in an attempt to discover its associations with the West. Along with the quest for his roots, Ansary affects a political and cultural analysis, both in real life as well as in the novel. This journey initiates the reconciliation between his religious Afghan Muslim identity and national American one. The writer problematises the issue of individual responses to diasporic experience. The difficulties he describes in growing up bicultural are resolved differently by each of the Ansary children. He muses about how he and his two siblings, all Afghan American, have become more or less Afghan or American. His younger brother Riaz embraced an orthodox interpretation of Islam and his elder sister Rebecca who had spent the longest time in Afghanistan settled into a wholly secular American life and seemed more easily to give up her Afghan self when in America. Out of his siblings, it was only he who had imbibed the Afghan culture and values that can be seen through some incidents in the novel as he says, 'It was as if some Afghan self inside me woke up and realised it didn't want to die' (223). In this statement he admits that his Afghan Identity can never be separated from his being and as a non-practicing Muslim he remains more firmly on the American western side. Growing up Islamic in Afghanistan, gave Ansary a vantage point for evaluating trends in the Muslim world. He finally left the faith, but he documents his struggles with accepting his younger brother's extremism.

This journey to the Islamic countries came to an end when Ansary got a satisfactory interpretation of 'Islamic Sharia' by a man named Qayum that was different from his brother's fundamentalist ideology. Qayum says:

> The *sharia* does indeed say cut of the hands of thieves, but the *sharia* is not a law directed at punishing an individual for his crimes; it is a guideline for the whole community. It is directed toward making the community function well. So when *sharia* is really in place, no hands are cut off, because there is no stealing! (215)

Qayum gave the meaning of Islam in a single phrase: 'Greet the guest and feed the stranger' (215). After listening to his views about Islam and its ideologies Tamim Ansary concluded that he was indeed an American and that discovering and pondering over the Muslim world was not his quest.

The last part of the novel *Forgetting Afghanistan* presents Ansary's experiences as an Afghan-American activist concerned about the problems prevailing there. He depicts a journey of self discovery and the conflicts inherent in multicultural sensibility. His struggle is to unite his divided self and to find a place in his imagination where his Afghan and American identities might meet. He watches uneasily as the Taliban philosophy spreads across national borders and even across oceans. He has taken up certain issues like his bi-cultural identity, the question of the differences, conflicts and possible reconciliation between these two cultures. He talks about the growing community of Afghan expatriates in the United States and the radical new ideology emerging from Islam and within his own family. He became progressively involved in the growing network of Afghans in America since 'it helped alleviate the guilt I felt over being safe and sound in America' (225). Ansary says that somewhere in his mind Afghanistan is alive forever and he is very emotional about writing this book as he was able to 'speak for Afghanistan' in his 'American voice' discussing the attack of 9/11 from his perspective as an Afghan American. At the end of the novel he highlights the rebuilding of Afghanistan by America. He says the lost world of his childhood that is destroyed can never be rebuilt. People of Afghanistan can never attain that peaceful life of extended communities that has been destroyed by war. A spiritual journey by the author in the third part of the novel led him towards an awakening that though he was an American yet a sense of belonging to Afghanistan remained alive within him. He is able to transcend and accept himself as a kaleidoscope. At the end of the novel he finds himself oscillating between his dual identities – Afghan and American – and feels a sense of responsibility towards both of them.

References

Ansary, Tamim. *West of Kabul, East of New York*. New York: Farrar, Straus and Giroux Publishers, 2002.

Cohen, Robin. *Global Diasporas: An Introduction*. London: UCL Press, 1997.

Parmeswaran, Uma. *Trishanku and Other Writings.*Vol.1of South Asian Canadian Literature Series: Prestige, 1998.

Rasheed, Ahmad. *Descent into Chaos*. England: The Penguin Group, 2008.

Sykes, Percy. *A History of Afghanistan*. New Delhi: Munshiram Manoharlal Publisher Pvt. Ltd., 2002.

19 Travel and Transformation of the Self

Gilbert's *Eat Pray Love*

Akansha Kaushik

We shall not cease from exploration
And the end of all our exploring
Will be to arrive where we started
And know the place for the first time.

(Eliot: *Four Quartets*)

To travel is to consciously learn about the self by going away intentionally from habitual and predictable environment. It is a way of self-discovery and transformation as it brings about an openness of heart and clarity of self. Susan Roberson in her book *Defining Travel: Diverse Vision* has stated that the ancient stories like that of Gilgamesh and Odysseus are plotted around the journey, where the heroic venture takes the protagonists out into a new world, something beyond imagination, to test the mental and physical prowess, to gain knowledge of the world, and to explore self-identity. These stories suggest that travel is a freeing and transformative experience from which a new man emerges with knowledge, confidence and power. Travel is traditionally considered as transformative for the individual and for the institutions because the traveller gains knowledge not only about the wider world but about the self, making the journey a double voyage of discovery. It enables us to re-examine our inner-self and by visiting or re-visiting places, our sensory experiences try to recreate the past and enable us to relate and re-identify. It also fuels the human psyche.

Elizabeth Gilbert's memoir *Eat Pray Love: One Woman's Search for Everything across Italy, India and Indonesia* (2006) chronicles her exploration of the cultures of the three countries: Italy, India and Indonesia after her separation from her husband. It is her spiritual and personal journey. Dissatisfied with her marriage, she often spends the nights weeping and sleeping on her bathroom floor and she decides to seek divorce from him. Struggling for a contentious divorce she decides, at the age of thirty two, to spend a year travelling to Italy, India and Indonesia. She is destined for personal transformation and revelation of life and purpose that is a transcendence of individual consciousness. The purpose of her journey is to find her original creative expressions of the self, self-integration and to find God. Her main focus is to increase awareness of the meaning of life and generate spiritual transformation within. During her travel she realises that movement from one place to the other acts as a therapy for adjusting personal priorities that is ultimately important in her life.

This paper aims at exploring how Gilbert reconciles in her life while moving from one culture to the other and imbibing precepts of three different cultures – Italian, Indian and Indonesian – which give meaning to her life. It includes the author's immersion in the beauty of the romantic Italian culture, Indian spirituality and adoption of Indonesian mindset that is maintenance of perfect equilibrium. It also aims at the transformation of a heart from gasping sobs to a wonderful smile. Gilbert's love for the Italian language and Italian food provides a natural framework to wade through the complex matrix of her sufferings. She is in love with the Italian language. She learns Italian from her friend, Giovanni and joins classes at the Leonardo da Vinci Academy of Language Studies to gain expertise in 'the most seductively beautiful language in the world' (44). She keeps Italian phrasebooks and dictionaries with her to get rid of her sufferings. Italian language, 'more beautiful than roses' (23), is the only thing that can bring pleasure to her during that period of loss. She loves each word of the language so much so that, 'every word was a singing sparrow, a magic trick, a truffle, for her' (24). She learns to change the philosophy of her life and move ahead.

Dr Leon James in his article 'Psychological and Physiological Aspects of Foreign Language Learning' states that the language of people is a living, growing, changing reflection of people's heart and mind. He also approves of the fact that when we learn a foreign language, we intermingle with the foreign people and culture also. So the contact with any language becomes inseparable from the contact with culture. Thus becoming bilingual entails becoming bicultural. The article by Leon supports the argument of Professor Wallace Lambert of McGill University in Canada that some may be anxious to learn another language as a means of being accepted in another cultural group because of dissatisfactions experienced in their own culture, whereas other individuals may be equally interested in both their native as well as the foreign culture (167–76). Gilbert's love for the Italian language testifies to Lambert's philosophy, as she writes:

> I would slosh home through the rain after class, draw a hot bath, and lie there in the bubbles reading the Italian dictionary aloud to myself, taking my mind off my divorce pressure and my heartache. (24)

Gilbert reveals that Sicily for centuries suffered poverty, wars and traumas, and Mafia was the only successful business there. Palermo, the Italian city once possessed 'an impossible-to-describe beauty' (113), developed only after World War II. The town has been systematically 'uglified beyond description' by the Mafia. She continues, 'But it does make the concrete stronger to be reinforced with all those bones and teeth' (114). Italy has a history of corruption by local leaders and politicians and of exploitation by the foreign dominators that is why they do not trust anybody in this world. They trust only what they themselves experience believing that in a world of fraud and corruption only beauty can be trusted. Only artistic excellence is incorruptible.

> That is why, Bargini says, Italians will tolerate hideously incompetent generals, presidents, tyrants, professors, bureaucrats, journalists and captains of industry, but will never tolerate incompetent opera singers, conductors, ballerinas, courtesans, actors, film directors, ... (114)

Gilbert compares her destiny to the history of Sicily. She shares that Sicilians are facing that trauma because of others but her tragedies are self created. She suffers a crisis of identity but she has the financial, artistic and emotional resources with which she could try to work out her life just as all Sicilians have. This comparison helps her to maintain her identity. She learns that the appreciation of pleasure alone can hold humanity together. The place inspired her to find pleasure in everything and she learnt the art of living from the Italians. Unlike Gilbert, Charles Dickens in his *Pictures From Italy* tries to bridge the gap between psychological and physical appearances of the places. Dickens observed that the city is decrepit, yet its people enjoy a vibrancy of life and customs. It shocked and tantalised Dickens who was much impressed by the vivacious street carnivals, the festivals, the costumes and effusive personality of the ordinary Italian (69–77).

Gilbert goes to Naples, a city 'that gives the world pizza and ice-cream' (78) where she felt that it was the easy to understand Neapolitans in Italy. In Naples she gets rid of the 'Depression' and 'Loneliness' and enjoys pizzas only. Benjamin Taylor in *Naples Declared: A Walk around the Bay* asserts that Naples is a city of seemingly irreconcilable opposites simultaneously glorious and ghastly. He further adds that Naples is a very fine blend of realism and romanticism. It is more ancient, less well-off and less clean but a more skeptical city. In Taylor's enriching and enchanting description of Naples, he informs that it is known for its crime and poverty and is derogatorily called a sinkhole of superstition. Henry James also asserts that Naples is a wild, weird and sinister city. Taylor attests that all of these clichés are rooted in facts, to a certain extent, but he also celebrates Naples as the great open-air theatre of Europe. There is co-existence of these two myths. His travelogue has been an effort to enrich himself with the knowledge of Naples.

During the time of her journey, the struggle for power was raging amongst European countries. They were competing with each other and striving hard to emerge as the great twenty first century European metropolis but Rome did not join the power struggle. Gilbert is inspired by the 'regal self-assurance' (72) of Rome. She would like to be like Rome when she is an old lady and longs to imbibe the self-assurance, endurance and happiness of the Romans. Overwhelmed by the grace of Queen Christina of Sweden, she feels happy on seeing baby Jesus of Rome and experiences the quietness and transcendence of the Tiber Island which helped her heal her sorrows. The history of the drastic deformation of Augusteum, warns her 'not to get attached to any obsolete ideas about who I am, what I represent, whom I belong to, or what function I may once have intended to serve' (75). She discovers, 'Even in the eternal city, says the silent Augusteum, one must always be prepared for riotous and endless waves of transformation' (75). Gilbert observes that Italians never make plans for the future not even for a week. They believe that everything is in God's hands and nobody can plan their future. She learns a lot from the places as well as from the people. Dickens in his book *Pictures from Italy* gives an account of a journey describing the social life and customs of Italy wherein he lays a constant emphasis on the contrast that exists in Italian life. He finds the beautiful houses and poverty-stricken streets of Venice as imaginary and dramatic as dreams and is of the opinion that the contrasts affect us most. He points out the coexistence of the beautiful and the ugly insisting that we should not fall into the habit of viewing things from a distance. Presenting a new way of seeing things he suggests that the beauty of Venice is superficial (172–73). For Johann Wolfgang Von Goethe Italy was the place where the classical past was still alive, though in ruins. He appreciates Italian art and style of living in *Italian Journey* which is a report of his travel to Italy from 1786–1788. The journey helped him to come out of the psychological crisis and also inspired him to write the great works of his career. During his stay there Art played a vital role in his transformation.

After a four month long journey of pleasure, Gilbert finally reaches India. India, known for its spirituality and rich culture, has always drawn people from all over the world. The quest for spirituality grows more with the increase in the materialistic approach of people. The traditional Indian way of life has helped in the evolution and growth of spiritualism. Numerous cultures and religions have thrived and flourished together for ages and resulted in a unique Indian way of life. Numerous spiritual gurus and saints have delivered the message of peace, self-realisation, happiness and coexistence that is well rooted in the Indian culture. Through the ages, various *ashrams* and centres of excellence have helped in spreading the message of peace, care and positive living. Gilbert wants to find God, explore spirituality in India under her guru's guidance, at the *ashram*. She chants the mantra *'Om Namah Shivaya'* and gets to know the significance and meaning of the mantra which means, 'I honor the divinity that resides within me' (120). She conveys here that the mantra has the power to transport oneself to a state of transcendence. When this mantra is chanted properly each syllable activates certain energy within our bodies as we meditate upon the energy of Lord Shiva. Shiva is often considered the greatest of the yogis, the lord of meditation and the lord of all that is mystic and mysterious in Hindu practices. This mantra invokes Lord Shiva and all his energies to bless us and lead us to the highest state of peace.

Being a few thousand miles away from Italy, Gilbert practices meditation and yoga. She becomes a part of Indian culture and bids farewell to the pleasure of Italy and begins a new journey to spirituality and finds herself fully engrossed in the chanting and practice of meditation and yoga. She learns the real meaning of the word 'yoga' which has originated from the Sanskrit root 'yuj' which means 'to yoke' or 'union'. She further explores the word yoga which means 'to attach yourself to a task at hand with ox-like discipline. And the task at hand in yoga is to find union – between mind and body, between the individual and her god, between our thoughts and the source of our thoughts ...' (121). Gilbert realises that yoga is a medium 'to find god through meditation, through scholarly study, through the practice of silence, through devotional service or through mantra – the repetition of sacred words in Sanskrit' (121).

Reeling from a volatile divorce and a bout of depression, she finds peace in yoga. For her yoga is a means of self mastery, a better way to keep herself away from her endless brooding over the past and her nonstop worrying about the future. According to the Yoga Sutra of *Patanjali*[1] the ultimate aim of yoga is to reach *Kaivalya* (emancipation or ultimate freedom). *Kaivalya* is the attainment of absolute knowledge of the difference between the spiritual which is a state of peace and tranquility and the material which is not. The authority of *Bhagwat Gita*[2] reveals that there are three paths which directly lead to establishing a relationship with God. These paths have been designated as the yoga of perfect action, the yoga of perfect devotion and the yoga of perfect knowledge. Krishna says that yoga is the communion with the ultimate truth that is god. It is the science of individual consciousness. She realises that a teacher is considered essential for learning yoga. In India at the *ashram* she gets to learn that the guru has a divine power to transform a heart in darkness to a delighted one. In the word *guru, 'gu'* means 'darkness' and *'ru'* means 'light'. *Gurugita* which is an excerpt from the *Skanda Purana* also delineates the importance of guru in one's life. In the *Skanda Purana*[3] there is a dialogue between Lord Shiva and Goddess Parvati in which Lord Shiva tells her that *guru* is more important than Shiva. The *Bhagavad Gita* is a dialogue between Lord Krishna and his friend Arjun, who accepts Krishna as his *guru*. Krishna speaks to Arjun of the importance of a *guru* that *guru* is one's spiritual guide on earth and he imparts the transcendental knowledge to his disciple. A guru can awaken dormant spiritual knowledge within the devotee.

Shiva was worshipped in the ancient times in various parts of not only the Indian subcontinent but elsewhere also. Some believe that there is a great affinity between Shiva and the Greek God, Dionysus. Some aspects of Shiva are also ascribed to the Buddha in the *Vajrayana* sects of Buddhism. The *Pashupati* seal, discovered from *Mohanjodaro,* gives us ample reason to believe that the seated yogi depicted in the seal might have been Shiva. There is also a deep connection between Shiva and the ancient tradition of yoga. He is also described as the source of art and music. Gilbert explores another spiritual state of mind – the 'turia' – 'the elusive fourth level of human consciousness' (196). Human beings move between three different levels of consciousness – walking, dreaming or deep dreamless sleep, but there is one more level which is the 'integral awareness that links all three levels together' (196). This is pure consciousness, an intelligent awareness, a vigilance that brings you back to your memory in the morning when you wake up and when we are asleep, someone is there who is watching over us. All this brought about some surreal, physical and emotional changes in her. At the end of her stay in India she felt as if her old abysmal mysteries had forever disappeared and positive rays of thought had come into her life and she has accomplished the goal of her spiritual journey to India.

From India she went to Indonesia, a place where one can see men chanting in a temple and running barefoot across a fire. Many believe that there are magnetic grids on the planet and Bali is on a magnetic intersection that generates an extraordinary amount of energy and knowledge. There is a feeling of magic in the air. Gilbert feels a mission-accomplished sensation during her stay at Bali. The motive behind her journey to Indonesia was to find a balance between worldly pleasure and spirituality. She finds peace and love in her innermost heart and enjoys her daily routine that is swinging between her devotional practices and the pleasures of the beautiful landscape, friends and food. Her prayers become the expression of sheer gratitude for the brimming contentment that she attained during her journey. In Indonesia she learns the *mantra* of happiness from her guru that 'happiness is the consequence of personal effort' (260). Martin E.P. Seligman, an American psychologist, believes that the good life consists in deriving happiness by using your signature strengths (such as humanity, temperance and persistence) in everyday life. Meaningful life adds one more component using these same strengths to forward knowledge, power or goodness. A life that does this is pregnant with meaning, and if good comes at the end, such a life is sacred.

She tries to explore the concept of *Karmic* philosophy that heaven and hell exist on earth itself. If one repeats mistakes it means that some adverse circumstances are being created like hell. And if one's deeds are good then it brings good circumstances as one is in heaven. One does not really go to hell or heaven at the end of one's life, in fact one gets 'recycled back to the earth again in another form, in order to resolve whatever relationships or mistakes (you) left incomplete last time. When (you) finally achieve perfection, (you) graduate out of the cycle entirely and melt into the void' (262). As a consequence she falls in love unexpectedly with a Brazilian man, Felip. Unlike Gilbert, Adam Potkey in his book *The Passion for Happiness: Samuel Johnson and David Hume* makes a strong assertion that Johnson and Hume unanimously argue that happiness is intrinsically social. He is of the opinion that if we respect ourselves then only we shall be esteemed by the others. Hume declares that perfect solitude is a very severe punishment that we can suffer. Hume and Johnson both agree that cities afford the greatest happiness through a multiplicity of agreeable consciousness. 'Depression' and 'Loneliness' that 'came upon me all silent and menacing like Pinkerton detectives .... Depression on my left, Loneliness on my right. They don't need to show me their badges. I know these guys very well. We have been playing a cat and mouse game for years now' (47) have now departed as she has now changed her philosophy of life. Gilbert gains back her strength and health. Ellen Sussman in her novel *The Paradise Guest House* also depicts the same kind of transformation of an American adventure guide, Jamie Hyde, who survives a tragic nightclub bombing in Bali in 2002. One year later Jamie returns to Bali in search of peace, closure, love and answers to unspoken questions. She hopes to find Gabe who helped her in the wake of the explosions. Sussman brings out elements of the Island's culture and sense of community. Gilbert gains knowledge about how to 'cross over' in Italy, scrubbing clean the temple of her heart, polishing her soul and purifying the self in India and maintaining a perfect equilibrium between worldly pleasures and spirituality and finds true love in Indonesia. She learns and adheres to the philosophy of the different places, '*Attraversiamo* – let's cross over' (72) for Italy, '*Antevasin* – one who lives at the border' (203) for India.

Gilbert's prose is lively, conversational, personal and colloquial. It is full of vivid details and entertaining anecdotes. She relates even her most profound spiritual experiences with enough self-deprecation and unpretentiousness. The novel is built on the notion of a woman trying to heal the self from a severe emotional crisis. At the end of the journey there is a clear demarcation between her old pessimism and her new optimistic understanding. She finally becomes the woman who is liberated from the farce of pretending to be other than her true self.

Notes

1. The yoga sutras of *Patanjali* are 196 Indian sutras that constitute the fundamental text of *Raja Yoga*. The opinion of most scholars is that *Patanjali* was not the creator of yoga but merely a great expounder.
2. *Bhagwad Gita* is referred to as a 700 verse *Hindu* Scripture that is part of the ancient epic *Mahabharata.* It contains a conversation between *Pandava* prince, Arjun and guide, Krishna on a variety of philosophical issues.
3. *Skanda Purana* is a Hindu religious text dedicated to Shiva.

References

Auden, W.H. and Mayer, Elizabeth (trans.). *Italian Journey*. New York: Penguin Classics, 1982.

Dickens, Charles. *Pictures From Italy*. New York: Penguin Classics, 1998.

Gilbert, Elizabeth. *Eat Pray Love: One Woman's Search for Everything Across Italy, India and Indonesia.* New York: Penguin Press, 2006.

History and Antiquity of Shiva and Shaivism, www.allsaivism.com. Web Source. Viewed 28 May 12.

James, Leon. *Psychological and Physiological Aspects of Foreign Language Learnings*, www.soc.hawaii.edu. Web Source. Viewed: 26.05.12.

Sussman, Ellen. *The Paradise Guest*. London: Ballantine Books, 2013.

Seligman, Martin E.P. 'The Pursuit of Happiness', www.pursuit-of-happiness.org. Web Source. Viewed 03 June 2012.

Seligman, Martin E.P. 'Authentic Happiness Using the New Positive Psychology to Realize Your Potential for Lasting Fulfillment' *New York* New York: Free Press, pp. 263–65.

Sivananda, Sri Swami. *Bhagwad Gita.* Garhwal: The Divine Life Society, 2000.

Taylor, Benjamin. *Naples Declared: A Walk Around the Bay*. Putham: A Marian Wood Book, 2012.

Contributors

Akansha Kaushik teaches English at Rajasthan School of Art, Jaipur.

Bandana Chakrabarty has taught English in various Government colleges of Rajasthan and is presently Principal, Rajasthan School of Art, Jaipur.

Divya Joshi is Associate Professor in English at Government Dungar College, Bikaner.

Eunice de Souza is a contemporary Indian English poet, literary critic and writes column in *Mirror* Bombay.

Jasbir Jain is Director, Institute for Research in Interdisciplinary Studies (IRIS). Formerly Head, Department of English, University of Rajasthan, Jaipur she has worked in various capacities including the directorship of Academic Staff College.

Karen Swenson is a widely travelled American poet and journalist. She has also edited several story collections and anthologies.

Manju Nemad is a Research Scholar, Department of Humanities and Social Sciences at Malaviya National Institute of Technology, Jaipur.

Namita Singh is Assistant Professor in English at Subodh PG College, Jaipur

Pooja Joshi is Assistant Professor in English at Khandelwal Girls College, Jaipur.

Preeti Bhatt is Assistant Professor, Department of Humanities and Social Sciences at Malviya National Institute of Technology, Jaipur.

Prerna Vanjani is Associate Professor in English at Anand International College of Engineering, Jaipur.

Rama Hirawat Assistant Professor in English at Subodh PG College, Jaipur.

Ranjana Jaitly formerly Head, Department of History at Kanoria College, Jaipur.

Rimika Singhvi is Head, Department of English at the IIS University, Jaipur.

S. Asha is Head, Department of English at Government PG College, Tonk.

Samina Khan is Associate Professor, Department of English at Aligarh Muslim University, Aligarh.

Sangeeta Handa Professor and Head, Department of English at Government College, Patiala.

Santosh Gupta formerly Head, Department of English, University of Rajasthan, Jaipur has worked in many capacities including Dean of Humanities.

Shahla Ghauri is Associate Professor, Department of English at Aligarh Muslim University, Aligarh.

Urmil Talwar is Head, Department of English at Government Girls College, Shahpura, Jaipur.

Index